NORMATIVITY AND POWER

Normativity and Power

Analyzing Social Orders of Justification

RAINER FORST

Translated by
Ciaran Cronin

OXFORD
UNIVERSITY PRESS

OXFORD
UNIVERSITY PRESS

Great Clarendon Street, Oxford, OX2 6DP,
United Kingdom

Oxford University Press is a department of the University of Oxford.
It furthers the University's objective of excellence in research, scholarship,
and education by publishing worldwide. Oxford is a registered trade mark of
Oxford University Press in the UK and in certain other countries

First published in Germany in 2015 with the title
Normativität und Macht—Zur Analyse sozialer Rechtfertigungsordnungen

First Edition published in 2017

Impression: 1

Published in the United States of America by Oxford University Press
198 Madison Avenue, New York, NY 10016, United States of America

British Library Cataloguing in Publication Data
Data available

Library of Congress Control Number: 2017947321

ISBN 978–0–19–879887–3

Printed and bound by
CPI Group (UK) Ltd, Croydon, CR0 4YY

Preface

We tend to assume that the terms "normativity" and "power" have opposite meanings: the former is characterized by justifying reasons for our thought and action, the latter by the absence of justifications and the rule of pure facticity—or so it seems, at any rate. On closer consideration, however, normativity must also develop power if it is to be able to move us, and if social power is to be effective it must permeate the normativity of social life, of our thought and action, even when it is not well founded. This book attempts to analyze these relationships with the help of the concepts of justification and of orders of justification, the guiding idea being that justification must be viewed both normatively and descriptively. This approach makes it possible to connect the perspective of philosophy with those of social science and history without succumbing to reductionism. However, the main focus of the individual studies is on philosophical analyses.

The texts in this volume owe their existence to a number of scientific contexts that inspire and shape my thought in a variety of ways. First of all, there is the Frankfurt Cluster of Excellence "The Formation of Normative Orders," which repeatedly requires me to take account of the perspectives of disciplines besides philosophy. Any meaningful discourse concerning normative orders is predicated on such interdisciplinarity. Here, I would like to express my thanks, as representative for many others, to Klaus Günther, with whom it is always a pleasure to reflect on these questions, even if this is sometimes connected with writing research proposals. Furthermore, the Centre for Advanced Studies "Justitia Amplificata," which is primarily situated at the Institute for Advanced Studies in the Humanities in Bad Homburg, has greatly enriched my work. For this I am particularly grateful to Stefan Gosepath with whom I direct the Centre, also across the distance separating Frankfurt and Berlin. Finally, the award of the Gottfried Wilhelm Leibniz Prize in 2012 placed me in the comfortable position of being able to form a research group on issues of transnational justice whose goal is to integrate a wide range of perspectives on these problems. For all of these funding relationships, I owe a major debt of gratitude to the German Research Foundation.

In addition, I am indebted to my Tuesday Research Colloquium, which I offer together with Darrel Moellendorf, for a multitude of suggestions and criticisms that benefit my work. The contributions of the guests and participants are invaluable for engaging with the plurality of approaches in current political philosophy. A fellowship at the Jean Monnet Center of New York University Law School in 2013 was also highly productive, for which I would like to thank Mattias Kumm and Joseph Weiler in particular.

Besides those mentioned, I am indebted for valuable suggestions to colleagues, too numerous to list here, who wrote reviews, provided replies and comments, and invited me to give lectures or attended talks that I gave. I have tried to mention them at the relevant places in the individual texts. But here I would like to express my gratitude specifically to the academic staff members with whom I have collaborated in recent years at my university, in the Cluster, in the Centre for Advanced Studies, and in the Leibniz group: Nathan Adams, Ayelet Banai, Mahmoud Bassiouni, Thomas Biebricher, Eva Buddeberg, Julian Culp, Dimitrios Efthymiou, Dorothea Gädeke, Malte Ibsen, Mattias Iser, Tamara Jugov, Anja Karnein, Heike List, Jekaterina Markow, Esther Neuhann, Miriam Ronzoni, Martin Saar, Christian Schemmel, Antoinette Scherz, Regina Schidel, and Johannes Schulz.

Sonja Sickert was, as always, of great help in preparing the manuscript; in addition, Marius Piwonka and Quincy Stemmler provided invaluable help with the revisions. I am most grateful to Ciaran Cronin for his excellent translations and to Jamie Berezin and Alex Flach from Oxford University Press for seeing this translation through to publication. Those chapters (2, 9, and 10) that had previously been published in English have been slightly modified for this volume, and the original Chapter 10 on transnational justice has been replaced by a more recent text on the same topic.

To Mechthild, Sophie, and Jonathan I owe more than I can possibly say here.

Rainer Forst

Contents

Introduction

Orders of Justification: On the Relationship between Philosophy, Social Theory, and Criticism

The aim of the texts collected in this volume is to realize a comprehensive program of critical analysis of social orders of justification informed by philosophy and social science. Of course, given the sheer diversity of the relevant research perspectives and methods, they cannot hope to realize such a program in its entirety any more than can any single work or any single author.[1] Therefore, the individual chapters will be confined to specific, important aspects of such an undertaking, with a particular emphasis on philosophical questions. As a counterweight, this introduction will present some general remarks on the design of such a theory with references to the relevant chapters. I will concentrate on the question of what it means to regard such a theory as "critical."

1. Critical Theory

By critical theory we mean a connection between reflection in philosophy and in social science informed by an interest in emancipation. It inquires into the rational form of a social order that is both historically possible and normatively justified in general terms. At the same time it asks why the existing power relations within (and beyond) a society prevent the emergence of such an order. This is consistent with Horkheimer's original understanding of critical theory as "a theory guided at every turn by a concern for reasonable conditions of life."[2]

As the history of this theoretical program demonstrates, these definitions pose a multitude of questions: How should the "interest in emancipation" be defined? What kinds of cooperation between social theory and philosophy does it call for?

[1] Here I can only refer in a summary way to the past and current research of the Frankfurt research center "The Formation of Normative Orders." On its guiding principles see Rainer Forst and Klaus Günther, "Die Herausbildung normativer Ordnungen: Zur Idee eines interdisziplinären Forschungsprogramms," in Rainer Forst and Klaus Günther (eds.), *Die Herausbildung normativer Ordnungen* (Campus 2011) 11–30.

[2] Max Horkheimer, "Traditional and Critical Theory," in Max Horkheimer, *Critical Theory: Selected Essays*, trans. Matthew J. O'Connell (Continuum 2002) 188–243, at 199 (translation amended).

Is such a comprehensive social theory still even possible now that confidence in the explanatory power of a unified materialistic theory has dwindled? And, finally, what is meant here by "historically possible" and "normatively justified?" Which concept of reason should be used when what is at issue is a "rational" form of social order? How should we conceive of modes of justification that mediate between the claim to rational justification and lived social practice? What kind of theory of power and ideology enables us to understand the existing order of justification as one which prevents emancipation—also especially in the light of transnational power relations?

In my studies presented here and elsewhere,[3] the concept of justification serves to establish an immanent connection between philosophy, social theory, and social criticism. Central to my approach is the idea that a critical theory turns the question of justification into a theoretical *and* a practical one and seeks to analyze and transform existing *orders* and *relations of justification*. It offers a twofold analysis of such normative orders: first, it treats justifications that legitimize and constitute norms, institutions, and social relations as "raw material" or social facts for a critical examination of their emergence (for example, in the context of *justification narratives*), stability, and complexity; and, second, it takes a critical stance on these justifications by scrutinizing their normative constitution, how they came about, and the structures they justify. "Justifications" and corresponding "orders," therefore, are the object, on the one hand, of a descriptive and critical analysis and, on the other, of normative reflection that lends the question of justification a practical turn. This is ultimately a question for those who are subjected to a normative order *themselves* and not one to be decided elsewhere, whether in the justification complexes that have evolved in societies discursively (in Foucault's sense, among others) or in expert or proxy discourses, such as those Habermas criticizes in his discourse theory. When we speak of "justifications," therefore, we are not only thinking of "good justifications" but also of ones which are socially effective, even if (and perhaps because) they have an ideological character. When the concept of justification is used critically, by contrast, it refers to a practice of discursive justification among the norm addressees who are supposed to become authors of norms. In a critical theory, everything turns on correctly distinguishing and combining these dimensions. This is the key to the relationship between philosophy, social theory, and criticism.

In order to achieve progress in this regard, it is indispensable to de-reify conventional philosophical definitions of concepts that suppress their practical, political character. This is where critical and, if you will, "traditional" theories part company. The latter was Horkheimer's term for theories that do not reflect sufficiently on the

[3] See Rainer Forst, *Justification and Critique: Towards a Critical Theory of Politics*, trans. Ciaran Cronin (Polity 2014) and "Justifying Justification: Reply to My Critics" in Rainer Forst, *Justice, Democracy and the Right to Justification: Rainer Forst in Dialogue* (Bloomsbury 2014) 169–216, in which I answer a range of criticisms. See also my two replies to further objections: "A Critical Theory of Politics: Grounds, Method and Aims. Reply to Simone Chambers, Stephen White and Lea Ypi," in *Philosophy and Social Criticism* 41/3 (2015): 225–34; and "The Right to Justification: Moral and Political, Transcendental and Historical. Reply to Seyla Benhabib, Jeffrey Flynn and Matthias Fritsch," in *Political Theory* 43/6 (2015): 822–37.

social dynamics of which they themselves are a part—in both descriptive and normative senses.

In the first place, the concept of *reason* must be understood practically—following, but going beyond, Habermas—in terms of a theory of discourse or justification.[4] Reason is the faculty of being guided by reasons or justifications; and to employ this faculty in the best way possible is to know which justifications should be examined and in what way. Thus, a generally valid principle of reason or justification is that those norms are rationally justified whose validity claim can be redeemed in a way that is implicit in this claim—for example, that reciprocal and general binding power must be redeemed through reciprocal-general justification.

Here it must be observed that a theory cannot claim to be "critical" unless it seeks explicit reassurance about its concept of reason and subjects it to criticism.[5] For no matter how much critical theory opposes the "pathologies of reason" in modernity, it nevertheless always subjects, as Axel Honneth emphasizes, "universality—which should, at the same time, be both embodied by and realized through social cooperation—to the standards of rational justification."[6] Hence, no other concepts—for example, concepts of the "good"—can take the place of the imperative and the criteria of rational justification. Contrary to such attempts to lend critical theory an ethical character, we must insist that all candidates for the "good," if they are to count as generally and reciprocally valid, must withstand the discursive test of reciprocal and general justification and not, on the contrary, claim intrinsic validity (appealing, for example, to anthropological considerations). This is what sets certain theories that appeal directly to ethical concepts (such as that of "resonance")[7] apart from those that try to evaluate ethical forms of life, but in doing so look for ethically parsimonious, formal criteria of the relevant problem-solving rationality.[8]

The conception of reason outlined not only enables us to understand what counts in social discourses in a descriptive sense as "reasonable" (and hence as justified), even though on critical examination it is not so. It also shows that the question of whether the principle of reason has a transcendent (in fact, transcendental), an abstract, or, on the contrary, a historical, context-specific character, is wrongly posed. The question of justification always arises in concrete contexts and equally points beyond them. It sets in train a dynamic that specifically calls into question "ethically reasonable"

[4] See Rainer Forst, *The Right to Justification*, trans. Jeffrey Flynn (Columbia University Press 2012) Pt. I, and "Critique of Justifying Reason: Explaining Practical Normativity," ch. 1 in this volume. Generally speaking, my conception of reason is more normative than Habermas's, especially in the context of morality and justice.

[5] On this see in general Jürgen Habermas, *The Theory of Communicative Action*, trans. Thomas McCarthy, 2 vols. (Beacon Press 1984, 1987).

[6] Axel Honneth, *Pathologies of Reason: On the Legacy of Critical Theory*, trans. James Ingram (Columbia University Press 2009) 28.

[7] Hartmut Rosa, *Weltbeziehungen im Zeitalter der Beschleunigung: Umrisse einer neuen Gesellschaftskritik* (Suhrkamp 2012) 9: "Successful world relationships are ones in which the world appears to acting subjects as a responsive, breathing, supportive, and at certain moments even a benevolent, forthcoming, or 'benign' 'resonance system.'" It is doubtful whether this kind of social criticism is compatible with the tradition of a critical theory, as Rosa seems to think. The problem is that if "resonance" is not filtered through reasonable justification among free and equal persons, it can be produced in ways that have scant emancipatory potential.

[8] Rahel Jaeggi, *Kritik von Lebensformen* (Suhrkamp 2014).

standards of justification in an intensified reflective process that concerns not only the immanence of a context of justification, but is also able to subject the latter to general critical scrutiny. One can, of course, try to offer the best possible answer to a normative question within the context of established norms and institutions. But one can equally place these established norms and institutions in question in principle, whether immanently (do they fulfill their purpose?) or radically (what is their purpose and is it an appropriate purpose that is justified in general terms?). Although all of these questions begin as immanent ones, the demand for reciprocal and general justification cannot be restricted by appealing to "prior ethical life." Reason is at once the most immanent and the most transcendent faculty that human beings possess, and hence it is neither exclusively immanent nor exclusively transcendent. It always appeals contextually and recursively to what counts as justified and what may be valid (the formal criteria of justification having a transcendental character). In between lies the space of criticism, which can also be opened up toward utopian conceptions.[9]

Therefore, a historical a priori is not possible which could claim priority for the purposes of a theory of validity over the imperative of reciprocal and general justification, such that it could determine what counts as genuine progress and what does not. The kind of "normative reconstruction" of the "promise of freedom"[10] of modern societies undertaken by Honneth presupposes that the "moral rationality"[11] that is supposed to become effective in realizing individual freedom points beyond the established institutions from the viewpoint of a theory of validity. Therefore, the notion of reason must have a "free-standing" character. But then the reflexive and justificatory pressure exerted by individuals and groups on social institutions is not bound to a "pre-given" ethical life or promise and the critique of injustice is not only able to look, as Honneth claims following Hegel, "just beyond the horizon of existing ethical life."[12] On the contrary, it can see as far as reciprocal-general justification permits or demands. Normatively speaking, therefore, it is not true that "social and historical conditions [are] needed to determine what can count as 'justified' in each case."[13] This cannot be stipulated by any person or institution, but must instead be determined in a collective discursive practice. The conditions that make social learning processes possible cannot set limits to these processes when it comes to a theory of validity.[14] That would be to stand the relation between genesis and validity on its head and *facilitating freedom* would become inverted into *limiting freedom*, which would amount to a dialectic of (un-)freedom.[15] The normative possibility of freedom has a higher status than its normative reality.

[9] See my discussion of utopia in Forst, *Justification and Critique* (n. 3) ch. 9, and my rejoinder to Lea Ypi, "Two Pictures of Nowhere", *Philosophy and Social Criticism* 41/3 (2015): 219–23, in Forst, "A Critical Theory of Politics: Grounds, Method and Aims" (n. 3).

[10] Axel Honneth, *Freedom's Right: The Social Foundations of Democratic Life*, trans. Joseph Ganahl (Columbia University Press 2014) viii.

[11] ibid 2.

[12] ibid 8. (In German: "knapp über den Horizont der existierenden Sittlichkeit.")

[13] ibid 337, n. 6.

[14] Although this is what Honneth asserts in *Freedom's Right* (n. 10) 63 ff.

[15] Where this is avoided in Honneth's reconstruction a reflexive form of freedom is at work that forces established institutions to go beyond themselves by demanding reciprocity and generality. An example is when "old role fixations" must succumb to a "permanent pressure [to justify]" (*Freedom's Right* (n. 10) 164), when the economic system is measured by whether it lives "up to moral norms to

The only form of critique that merits the name is one oriented to rational standards because it confronts the test of discursive justification. That it is always "immanent" in the sense that it takes the status quo as its starting point is trivial; what is not obvious, however, is the demand that it should orient itself to "settled," "pre-given," "accepted," or "inherent" norms.[16] There are forms of criticism of which this is true because they reveal the explicit or implicit contradictions within an order of justification in an immanent way, and with good reasons. But that the reasons in question are good does not follow from the fact that one appeals to accepted or inherent norms. For example, libertarians who criticize capitalism for not adhering consistently enough to the market principle and thus becoming mired in contradictions also argue in an immanent way that appeals to systemic features of capitalism. But they cannot justify their criticism toward those who, qua free and equal persons, should be the authorities who determine which economic system can be politically justified, insofar as market processes undermine this very authority (as must be shown in a justice-based analysis).[17] Hence, the fact that a critique is immanent is neither a reason for nor a hallmark of its legitimacy. A radical critique that rejects an entire historically developed understanding of the market, by contrast, may have much more going for it. And a critique that seeks to transform a liberal understanding of the market into a socialist one will hardly be able to justify this in a purely "immanent" way—nor will it have to.

Besides, who would want to suggest to a critic of the Indian caste system who rejects this system in toto that she should please proceed in an "immanent" way? Or remind a critic of patriarchy in a given society in which this was hardly ever challenged that she should not speak a "foreign language"? Would that not amount to ostracizing such critics from social discourses?[18] Those who understand criticism as an autonomous practice of challenging existing orders of justification will not formulate an artificial opposition between internal or immanent criticism, on the one hand, and external criticism, on the other. Rather, they will orient themselves exclusively to the quality of the social analysis and the demand for reciprocity and generality, even where this is "unheard of" and goes far beyond the firmly established understandings of justifiability or ethical life. Radical criticism may be immanent *or* transcending so that it is no longer clear where the one form of criticism ends and the other begins—as, for example, when Luther described the Pope as the true "Antichrist," the Levellers declared the king to be the servant of the people "by the grace of God," or Marx saw bourgeois society as the locus of modern slavery. Settled

which everybody could consent in principle" (184), and correspondingly the "heart" of the political order for Honneth is not Hegel's state but "public deliberation and will-formation" (253).

[16] The two latter provisions can be found in Jaeggi, *Kritik von Lebensformen* (n. 8) 297, 288.

[17] See Forst, *The Right to Justification* (n. 4) ch. 8.

[18] On this see Uma Narayan, "Contesting Cultures: 'Westernization', Respect for Cultures and Third-World-Feminists," in Uma Narayan, *Dislocating Cultures: Identities, Traditions, and Third World Feminism* (Routledge 1997) 1–40. This is also the point at which certain forms of "postcolonial" criticism become inverted into their opposite—that is, into essentialistic and culturalistic homogenizations of non-Western cultures or societies. This can be observed in Amy Allen, *The End of Progress: Decolonizing the Normative Foundations of Critical Theory* (Columbia University Press 2016).

ethical life is the *object* of criticism, not its *ground* or *limit*. Critical theory cannot dispense with the transcending power of reason, which may venture into regions that were previously unthinkable. To recall the words of Adorno: "The limit of immanent critique is that the law of the immanent context is ultimately one with the delusion that has to be overcome."[19]

These remarks bear on a further problem, namely, that of the historicity of the normative foundations of criticism. Again, the fact that the latter assume a historical form is trivial. What is not trivial, by contrast, is whether the criteria of reason or normativity should be regarded as "historically contingent," as Seyla Benhabib, for example, argues when she describes the right to justification as "a contingent legacy of struggles against slavery, oppression, inequality, degradation, and humiliation over centuries," and accordingly as a historical "achievement."[20] As I tried to show in my historical analysis of the development of the practice of toleration in its many different forms and justifications, we do in fact have to understand such concepts against the background of concrete historical processes of which we ourselves are part. This enables us to see how the demand for reciprocal and general justifications gave rise, and continues to give rise, to a historical dynamic that forces existing conceptions and justifications to go beyond themselves—always in a dialectical process involving new attempts to bring this dynamic to a close.[21]

If we want to distinguish in a historically situated way between emancipatory and non-emancipatory struggles and to view certain developments as "achievements" or "learning processes," we cannot assume that they are merely "contingent." We cannot claim that they are "necessary" either, however, for want of an equivalent of Hegel's absolute. Finite reason does not have access to a "worldless" standpoint from which it can regard its own norms as "merely contingent" or to a divine standpoint from which it could recognize historical necessity. From a finite rational perspective that understands itself as practical, the principle of justification is *the* principle of reason and the right to justification is its moral implication—no more, but no less either. There is no perspective from which its contingency or necessity could be transcended in a further step; but we have no need of such a perspective either. The only perspective to which we have access is that of a participant, not one of a trans-historical observer. We take stances as part of this history, therefore, and when we speak of moral achievements we mean that they are in fact moral achievements and

[19] Theodor W. Adorno, *Negative Dialectics*, trans. E. B. Ashton (Continuum, 1973) 182.

[20] Seyla Benhabib, "The Uses and Abuses of Kantian Rigorism: On Rainer Forst's Moral and Political Philosophy," *Political Theory* 43/6 (2015): 777–92, at 13. In what follows, I draw on my reply in "The Right to Justification: Moral and Political, Transcendental and Historical" (n. 3). These questions concerning justification are also the focus of my discussion with Stephen White, "Does Critical Theory Need Strong Foundations?" in *Philosophy & Social Criticism* 41/3 (2015): 207–11, and my reply "A Critical Theory of Politics: Grounds, Method and Aims" (n. 3). See also Amy Allen, "The Power of Justification," in Forst, *Justice, Democracy and the Right to Justification* (n. 3) 65–86, Andrea Sangiovanni, "Scottish Constructivism and the Right to Justification," in Forst, *Justice, Democracy and the Right to Justification* (n. 3) 29–64, and Tony Laden "The Practice of Equality," in Forst, *Justice, Democracy and the Right to Justification* (n. 3) 103–26, and my reply "Justifying Justification: Reply to My Critics" (n. 3).

[21] Rainer Forst, *Toleration in Conflict: Past and Present*, trans. Ciaran Cronin (Cambridge University Press 2013).

we relate to them accordingly with reasons—and of course we know that further learning processes could prove us wrong.

Consistency demands that we recognize that the pioneers of emancipation developed their positions, described above as "unheard of," in societies in which they were regarded as immoral or crazy—for example, the aforementioned radical Levellers or Pierre Bayle who defended the thesis, which was frowned upon at the time, that even atheists are capable of being moral.[22] Should we follow the historicist in saying that what first made these positions true was that they won out over time, and hence that they were neither true *nor justified* when these radical thinkers were alive? Should we join with those who condemned Bayle and others in crying "heresy" because this corresponded to the order of justification valid at the time? Could we ever understand and valorize emancipatory and radical criticism on this basis—the criticism of those who in their own day spoke a language in which they called slavery a crime and not a form of benevolence, in which they called tyranny by its name and not divine right, and in which intolerance no longer counted as service to God but instead as brutal violence? If we view these languages as achievements, then we cannot regard them either as contingent or as necessary, but only as *moral progress*, as progress in our moral self-understanding through *morally justified* innovation, but not through historical "success." The latter would represent a form of moral Darwinism in which the winners decide what constitutes moral truth. But that would have nothing to do with a critical theory.[23] "Prevailing" historically cannot determine the criteria for what counts as success in evaluative terms; only critical reason can. But reason does not elevate itself to a super-historical power in this regard either. It only scrutinizes here and now what counted and what may count as reasonable. The twofold analysis of orders of justification as historically occurring social facts and as orders with a claim to justification that opens them up to criticism enables us to say that, even though certain criticisms were considered to be unjustified in their time, they were nevertheless justified from a normative point of view because they brought the principle of justification itself to bear.[24] As an aside, the assertion that the history of certain societies was shaped by the historical success of emancipatory movements is frequently overoptimistic and overlooks the many ways in which forms of domination are reproduced in contemporary societies.

The perspective outlined enables us to define a conception of *progress* that cannot be suspected of disguising ethnocentrisms behind the claim to justification.[25] Only those processes can count as progress that break open orders of justification in ways

[22] On this see Rainer Forst, "Religion and Toleration from the Enlightenment to the Post-Secular Era: Bayle, Kant, and Habermas," ch. 5 in this volume.

[23] On this see Rainer Forst, "The Concept of Progress," ch. 4 in this volume. I elaborate on this further in my essay "The Justification of Progress and the Progress of Justification," forthcoming in Amy Allen and Eduardo Mendieta (eds.), *Justification and Emancipation: The Political Philosophy of Rainer Forst* (Penn State Press).

[24] On this see my interpretation of Bayle in "Religion and Toleration from the Enlightenment to the Post-Secular Era" (n. 22).

[25] For a differentiated account see Thomas McCarthy, *Race, Empire, and the Idea of Human Development* (Cambridge University Press 2009). Allen, by contrast, formulates a radical critique of progress in *The End of Progress* (n. 18).

that make new forms of reciprocal and general justification possible, so that those affected *themselves* can determine in which direction their society should develop. Only in this way can the alleged "increase in autonomy" be prevented from becoming an instrument through which social and political autonomy is lost—for example, by other economically or politically powerful societies or institutions dictating to a society how it should develop. Genuine progress occurs where new levels of justification are made accessible or are achieved through struggles that make subjects into justificatory authorities in the first place. Comprehensive progress involves more than just the existence of better justified social relations (for example, ones involving a higher standard of living). It occurs when the justification conditions within a society are such that a basic structure of justification either exists or is being aimed at. Discursive autonomy is realized only in internal processes and procedures, not in conditions imposed from the outside. A critical theory cannot dispense with such a concept of progress.[26]

A whole series of basic concepts of practical philosophy must be de-reified or re-politicized in the light of these orientations in the theory of reason.[27] Or, to put it differently, they must be interpreted in a "dialectical" way that understands them as having the character of social processes.

This is especially true of the concept of *justice*, which is equally essential for critical theory. As I have emphasized in a number of places,[28] the question of justice should not be answered in an apolitical way in terms of a false picture that looks at packages of goods, minimum standards of material provision, and other units of welfare. For these could just as well be conferred on "those in need" by a benevolent dictator, a correctly programmed distribution machine, or a welfare institution. Rather, political and social justice is an autonomous collective process of producing social and political conditions that are not only susceptible of justification in reciprocal and general terms, but can themselves be established via justification and aim to realize a basic structure of justification. Thus, the question of power, qua social and political power that shapes collective processes, is central to justice. Reified, unpolitical conceptions of justice, by contrast, detach justice from political autonomy in accordance with ideas of recipients and goods, resulting in deficient conceptions of justice. Horkheimer, on the other hand, advocates an unabridged notion that points to the reflexivity of the concept: "That is the universal content of the concept of justice; according to this concept, the social inequality prevailing at any given time requires a rational justification. It ceases to be considered as a good, and becomes something that should be overcome."[29]

In this context, I would like to make an observation about the much used and repeatedly misunderstood concept of the "ethical neutrality" of a reflexive conception of justice. Among the learning processes of modernity is that societies with a

[26] On this see Forst, "The Concept of Progress" (n. 23).

[27] Here I can only mention a couple of additional concepts. On the concepts of freedom and equality, to which this also applies see Forst, *The Right to Justification* (n. 4) Pt. 2.

[28] On this see chs. 7–10 in this volume.

[29] Max Horkheimer, "Materialism and Morality," in Max Horkheimer, *Between Philosophy and Social Science: Selected Early Writings*, trans. G. Friedrich Hunter *et al.* (MIT Press 1995) 15–48, at 40.

plurality of religious or cultural communities have to find a way to justify universally binding norms of justice that does not absolutize the particular values of one community and thereby dominate the others. The only viable candidate for this role is the discursive mode of justification. It seeks to identify norms that cannot be reciprocally and generally rejected and considers the foundation of fundamental justice, of a basic structure of justification among free and equal persons, to be indispensable for this purpose.[30]

How relevant this idea of "neutrality of justification" is in social reality is shown by the numerous debates over discrimination against forms of life, as reflected, for example, in occupational bans on women who wear headscarves for religious reasons.[31] This by no means implies, as Rahel Jaeggi conjectures, that forms of life are or should be immune to criticism.[32] For, as was always pointed out in the neutrality debate,[33] the foundations of this neutrality of justification are themselves substantive, and the corresponding conception of justice is critical of all forms of life that are not compatible with it. Something like "neutrality of effects" was never intended. Forms of life are undoubtedly part of the social relations that are open to criticism: economic conditions and institutions, social educational institutions, and the patriarchal family and recent medical technologies, to name just a few of those Jaeggi has in mind.[34] But the fact that ethical forms of life are objects of criticism does not mean that the criticism must have an ethical basis. There is a difference between finding an educational practice morally reprehensible (for example, because it involves the use of force) or ethically wrong (for example, on religious grounds). Both forms of criticism are possible. But when it comes to the reasons and possible consequences (for example, legal intervention), it is highly relevant which criticism is put forward. Eroding the boundaries, which indeed are not always easy to draw and are subject to historical change,[35] is problematic in this context, because to have one's basic rights protected against ethical condemnations by others (especially majorities) represents an important increase in freedom, if one thinks, for example, of homosexual lifestyles. Of course, ethical forms of criticism, whether they are based on values or are rationally grounded (as in Jaeggi), remain unaffected by this. The theories that demand reciprocal and general justifications for conceptions of justice, and only for these, by no means regard ethical discussions and criticisms as irrational; already the concept of "reasonable disagreement" (Rawls) speaks against this.[36] Finally, whether the general

[30] For a detailed account see Forst, *Toleration in Conflict* (n. 21) and "Religion and Toleration from the Enlightenment to the Post-Secular Era" (n. 22).

[31] On this see my discussions of the rulings of the German Federal Constitutional Court in "One Court and Many Cultures: Jurisprudence in Conflict," ch. 6 in this volume.

[32] See Jaeggi, *Kritik von Lebensformen* (n. 8).

[33] On this see the seven meanings of neutrality in Rainer Forst, *Contexts of Justice*, trans. John M. M. Farrell (University of California Press 2002) 45–8.

[34] Theories that are blind to the fact that the market is not a "neutral" institution are indeed "ideological" (see Jaeggi, *Kritik von Lebensformen* (n. 8) 40). However, the theories of Rawls and Habermas discussed by Jaeggi do not fall into this category.

[35] Thus Jaeggi, *Kritik von Lebensformen* (n. 8) 41–7.

[36] The "irrationalization" of ethics bemoaned by Jaeggi (*Kritik von Lebensformen* (n. 8) 50) is not to be found in Habermas either; see e.g. Habermas's discussion "Was macht eine Lebensform rational?," in Jürgen Habermas, *Erläuterungen zur Diskursethik* (Suhrkamp 1991) 31–48.

conception of forms of life as "experiments"[37] does justice to the nature of religious forms of life, for example, remains to be seen. At any rate, this ethical view, which advocates a form of "experimental pluralism of forms of life,"[38] is closely related to John Stuart Mill's plea for a plurality of "different experiments of living" and thus closer to Liberalism than Jaeggi thinks.[39]

Recent discussions that seek to place social philosophy on an ethical footing[40] largely ignore one of the fundamental concepts of critical theory, namely, *power*. But a concept of power is indispensable to a critical theory. Like the concept of justice, however, the concept of power also needs to be de-reified. Power should be understood in processual terms as the ability to determine, or if necessary even to close off (or also to open up), the space of reasons for others, whether based on a good argument, an ideological justification, or a threat. Social power does not have its "seat" in certain means, institutions, or structures, but instead in the *noumenal* space in which struggles over hegemony take place.[41] Thus the concept of power is neither positively nor negatively charged, but is instead neutral;[42] only its modes of exercise, ranging from "empowerment" to domination and oppression, whether interpersonal or structural, must be differentiated and evaluated. Power is always "discursive" in nature, therefore, but it is not always "communicative" in Habermas's sense or exclusively part of subject-constituting, disciplining "epistemes," as Foucault argues. This shows once again the advantages of varying our use of the concept of justification between descriptive and normative understandings. Oftentimes social power can be explained only by reconstructing the *justification narratives*[43] that shape and in part constitute a normative order. Here a genealogy in the Foucauldian sense creates an important normative distance.[44] But this does not exhaust the critical task. First, it must be shown whether this narrative contains (epistemically or normatively) false or contradictory justifications. In this way, as suggested above, one can also develop an understanding of *ideology* that does not operate with problematic constructions of "genuine interests," but instead proceeds on the basis of a right to justification that is falsely portrayed by ideologies either as nonexistent or as already satisfied.

Another essential concept that must be de-reified is that of *democracy*. Democracy does not designate a static institutional model. Rather, it must be understood as a process of criticism and justification, both within and outside of institutions, in which those who are subjected to rule become the co-authors of their political order.

[37] As Jaeggi argues in *Kritik von Lebensformen* (n. 8) 451. [38] ibid.

[39] John Stuart Mill, *On Liberty* (Penguin 1974) 120. On this see my critique of Mill in *Toleration in Conflict* (n. 21) §24.

[40] A further interesting variant that tries to establish an ethical connection between immanence and transcendence is Maeve Cooke, *Re-Presenting the Good Society* (MIT Press 2006).

[41] On this see Rainer Forst, "Noumenal Power," ch. 2 in this volume.

[42] On this see Wolfgang Detel, *Foucault and Classical Antiquity: Power, Ethics and Knowledge*, trans. David Wigg-Wolf (Cambridge University Press 2005) in contrast to Axel Honneth, *The Critique of Power: Reflective Stages in a Critical Social Theory*, trans. Kenneth Baynes (MIT Press 1991).

[43] On this see Rainer Forst, "On the Concept of a Justification Narrative," ch. 3 in this volume. See also in general Andreas Fahrmeir (ed.), *Rechtfertigungsnarrative: Zur Begründung normativer Ordnung durch Erzählungen* (Campus 2013).

[44] On this see Martin Saar, *Genealogie als Kritik: Geschichte und Theorie des Subjekts nach Nietzsche und Foucault* (Campus 2007).

Democracy on this conception is *the* political form of justice.[45] Within a political normative order, no mode of "problem-solving" can count as legitimate unless it assumes a democratic form or is democratically legitimized. In this way, the concept of democracy does not remain wedded to "ethical" preunderstandings or national framings either, but extends to transnational relations. This is important, in particular, where a realistic picture of existing relations of rule and domination is necessary to determine the locus of democratic justice within, between, and beyond states.[46] In this regard collaboration with social science is indispensable.

From here further concepts in need of re-politicization also become accessible. *Human rights*, for example, are not a means of satisfying the pleas for help of needy beings, but are instead rights to be involved in all aspects of the design of the social and political order to which one is subjected, which means that one must know the nature of the orders to which one belongs.[47] The primary locus of human rights is and remains the normative legal order of which one is a member, because this is where the political self-determination that is central to the idea of human rights begins. However, self-determination includes not only active democratic participation but also the elaboration of all of the rights that assure persons the status of free and equal legal and political authorities. And it does not end at the borders of nation-states either.

Against this background, it becomes possible to formulate a political concept of *alienation* such as the one sketched by Horkheimer (and is central to Marx[48]):

> The collaboration of men in society is the mode of existence which reason urges upon them, and so they do apply their powers and thus confirm their own rationality. But at the same time their work and its results are alienated from them, and the whole process with all its waste of work-power and human life, and with its wars and all its senseless wretchedness, seems to be an unchangeable force of nature, a fate beyond man's control.[49]

The goal of a critical theory concerned with recovering political autonomy is to overcome this alienation—that is, alienation from social reality and from the possibility of political intervention as a form of collective action. True alienation consists in failing to see oneself and others as socially, morally, and politically autonomous subjects of justification or as authorities within a normative order. This reflection is more Kantian than Aristotelian and is close to Marx, without itself presupposing a theory of the good or authentic life.[50] Alienation is a violation of the dignity of

[45] On this see Forst, "Legitimacy, Democracy, and Justice: On the Reflexivity of Normative Orders," ch. 8 in this volume.

[46] On this see Forst, "Realisms in International Political Theory," ch. 9, and "Transnational Justice and Non-Domination: A Discourse-Theoretical Approach," ch. 10 in this volume.

[47] See Forst, *Justification and Critique* (n. 3) ch. 2, and Rainer Forst, "The Point and Ground of Human Rights: A Kantian Constructivist View," in David Held and Pietro Maffettone (eds.), *Global Political Theory* (Polity 2016) 22–39.

[48] On this see Rainer Forst, "Justice after Marx," ch. 7 in this volume. I elaborate this further in my essay "Noumenal Alienation: Rousseau, Kant and Marx on the Dialectics of Self-Determination," in *Kantian Review* (forthcoming).

[49] See Horkheimer, "Traditional and Critical Theory" (n. 2) 204.

[50] For Adorno's critique of an ethical concept of alienation see *Negative Dialectics* (n. 19) 278.

subjects of justification. It may also prevent them from living the "good life," but that is another story.

The key difference from other forms of political theory and social philosophy, therefore, is that the critical approach, on the one hand, accords central theoretical importance to the question of justification as a *political* and *practical* question, and thereby lends the aforementioned concepts dialectical resonance: and, on the other hand, it starts from an analysis of the *real* relations of subjugation in order to develop a "grounded" conception of critical justice. By contrast, someone who thinks up an "ideal" theory unconnected with these relations can still make a productive contribution to a normative discussion; but if this ideal theory is conceived in such a way that it must be "applied" by a *deus ex machina*, then it is mistaken: it fails to understand the need to conceive of the process of realizing justice as a politically autonomous procedure. Anyone who fails to see this inverts the theory of justice into a technocratic program. There are better addressees of such a criticism than Rawls—for example, approaches that focus on equalizing happiness.[51]

Theories of justice that are blind to the structural injustices characteristic of our postcolonial global capitalist era are especially deserving of criticism. They either paint a positive picture of "cooperation" at the international level[52] or are content to strengthen "capabilities," whereas the key issue should actually be to put an end to structural exploitation. The problem appears most clearly when it is proposed to compensate the effects of such injustice through benevolent conduct by individuals. Then a political issue is converted into a question of individual morality.[53]

A critical theory of justice, as we have seen, is in need of a social scientific theory of structural dependence and asymmetry, ideally one embedded in a comprehensive social theory. This is an ambitious goal, especially as the analysis of transnational relations would have to be integral to such a theory. But the imperative to develop a theory of in-justice that is at once critical and realistic means that we have no alternative.

2. A Sociology of Justification

Within critical social theory, Jürgen Habermas's *Theory of Communicative Action* remains the most comprehensive attempt to provide a general sociological theory with an immanent connection to the normative perspective. Competing theories have to be measured against its explanatory power.

The concept of an order of justification has the potential to take important steps toward a more developed theory which—very much along Habermas's lines—retains the twofold perspective of a normative and a descriptive understanding of

[51] See Forst, *Justification and Critique* (n. 3) ch. 1. Unlike Raymond Geuss in *Philosophy and Real Politics* (Princeton University Press 2008), therefore, I do not think that Kantian approaches typically lean toward a moral ideal theory that is far removed from contexts of action and power.

[52] On this see my critique of "practice positivism" in "Transnational Justice and Non-Domination" (n. 46).

[53] See Forst, *The Right to Justification* (n. 4) ch. 11.

justification and makes this central to its approach. A key difference from Habermas, however, is that it also specifically captures "systemic" contexts of the economy and the state in their quality as contexts of justification and explores the narratives and justifications on which they and their power effects are based. The systems in question, therefore, are far from "norm-free."[54] Here we should reemphasize that the terms "norm" and "justification" are not being used in the sense of a well-founded norm or a reciprocal and general justification; ideological justifications are also socially effective justifications that must be analyzed when examining orders of justification.

In the landscape of sociological theories of recent decades an approach has developed that has a striking affinity with these reflections, namely, the "sociology of critique" that has been developed in particular by Luc Boltanski and Laurent Thévenot. In contrast to a "critical sociology" that follows Bourdieu in viewing societies as being pervaded by asymmetrical power relations that are not transparent for individuals, the pragmatic "sociology of criticism" starts from the everyday perspectives of social actors and tries to understand the normative grammar of social rules and institutions as a grammar of *justification*.[55] In so doing, Boltanski and Thévenot concentrate on the different conceptions of justice that can be found in a society and play a central role in social conflicts. They distinguish six (or, in an extended version, seven) languages or structures of justification, called "*cités*" in the original, a term variously translated as "polis," "polity" or "order of justification."[56] These languages of justice all observe a social "imperative to justify,"[57] which requires that they contain a general interpretation of the common good and evaluate the achievements and contributions of individuals to the common good—and thus their "value" or their "worth" (*grandeur*)—in a transparent way. Accordingly, consistency would require a distinction between two understandings of "order of justification": the order as a whole within which the *cités* compete, and the individual *cités*. According to Boltanski and Thévenot, the former incorporates for all conceptions a morally egalitarian "principle of common humanity"[58] that is characteristic of modern societies and may not be placed in question by the different interpretations of values. The "common dignity"[59] of persons is regarded as an "axiom."

Against this background, there are wide variations among the individual conceptions of justification.[60] In the religiously defined order of "inspiration," the worth of individuals and their contributions is measured by their faith and their mindsets,

[54] See Jürgen Habermas, *The Theory of Communicative Action* (n. 5) Vol. 2, 173. On this see the criticisms in Axel Honneth and Hans Joas (eds.), *Communicative Action: Essays on Jürgen Habermas's The Theory of Communicative Action* (MIT Press 1991).

[55] On this see the detailed account in Luc Boltanski, *On Critique: A Sociology of Emancipation*, trans. Gregory Elliott (Polity 2011) chs. 1 and 2, as well as the essay collection Rainer Diaz-Bone (ed.), *Soziologie der Konventionen: Grundlagen einer pragmatischen Anthropologie* (Campus 2011).

[56] The latter term [*Rechtfertigungsordnung*] is used in the German translation of Luc Boltanski and Laurent Thévenot, *On Justification: Economies of Worth*, trans. Catherine Porter (Princeton University Press 2006); *Über die Rechtfertigung: Eine Soziologie der kritischen Urteilskraft*, trans. Andreas Pfeuffer (Hamburger Edition 2007).

[57] ibid 37 ff. [58] ibid 74. [59] ibid 75.

[60] See in general Boltanski and Thévenot, *On Justification* (n. 56) Ps. 2 and 3.

whereas in the polis of the "house" personal relationships and dependencies, as defined, for example, by a hereditary monarchy, are decisive. In contrast to such a paternalistic conception of order, in the political community of "opinion" the worth of individuals depends on their public reputation. Things are different in the "civic" order in which the decisive issue is to follow the "general will" (Rousseau) beyond particularistic self-interest and to realize it through collective action. The "industrial" polity, on the other hand, measures individual worth according to economic productivity; in the order of the "market," by contrast, relations of exchange and variable prices regulate individual worth in accordance with profit-seeking, so that economic success is the key factor. Building on this, Boltanski and Ève Chiapello have developed a corresponding analysis of the "new spirit" of contemporary capitalism as a further, seventh "polis," which they call the "project-based polis."[61] Here what count as criteria of worth are individual commitment, flexibility, mobility, and networking.

Even though such a reading may suggest itself, the individual systems of values should not be correlated with specific social spheres, as Michael Walzer does, for example, in *Spheres of Justice*. Rather, they compete over the definition of the social order *as a whole*. Correspondingly, critical discourses arise where different logics and principles or "tests" of worth clash,[62] and between them there is no overriding language or authority of justification that could evaluate this dispute in accordance with a general notion of justice. At best, compromises can be reached in accordance with the common good.[63]

From this vantage point, we can identify the important similarities between this approach and the conception of orders of justification as I use it, as well as the differences between them.[64] A common feature is that both try to take seriously and develop the normative character of the social participant perspective and, in so doing, to understand social justifications as both social facts and normative claims—and in this sense to mediate between facticity and validity. Social orders are understood as orders of justification in which there is an imperative to justify that "compels" social agents to speak in terms of justice. However, Boltanski and Thévenot's approach does not trace this imperative back to a basic norm of social life corresponding to a *duty* or a *right to justification*.[65] Rather, their theory can make normativity accessible only descriptively and thus fails to provide a philosophical account of the criteria for *legitimate justifications*. My approach goes further in this respect, because it reconstructs the normative grammar of the demand for and claim

[61] Luc Boltanski and Ève Chiapello, *The New Spirit of Capitalism*, trans. Gregory Elliott (Verso 2005) 103 ff.

[62] See Boltanski and Thévenot, *On Justification* (n. 56) 237 ff.

[63] ibid 277ff.

[64] Klaus Günther and I were able to discuss some of the differences with Laurent Thévenot on a panel at the Frankfurt sociology conference in October 2010, an opportunity for which I am grateful to them both. Two years earlier, Luc Boltanski's Adorno Lectures (published in translation as *On Critique: A Sociology of Emancipation* (n. 55)) provided an occasion to discuss his approach.

[65] Thus also the critique of Martin Hartmann, "Rechtfertigungsordnungen und Anerkennungsordnungen: Zum Vergleich zweier Theoriemodelle," in *WestEnd. Neue Zeitschrift für Sozialforschung* 5/2 (2008): 104–19, at 111.

to justice itself as a moral and a morally justified one, including the criteria of reciprocity and generality. This alone leads to a non-reductionist unity of philosophy and sociology, something that Boltanski and Thévenot also aim at,[66] although they cannot realize it based on their sociological paradigm. They do not have access to an independent normative perspective that could appeal to recursive concepts of practical reason, morality, and justice. For them the world of norms remains one that must be described in sociological terms and not one that could be made philosophically accessible using normative concepts in such a way that the imperative to justify, and the corresponding conception of dignity (as a justification authority on a par with others, as I would put it), would themselves be *justified*.[67] The reason is that this imperative is not located and effective in the social world as a contingent matter, but follows a normative logic of its own, namely, the logic of justification that implants the critical claim of reason in social practices. Here the issue is again to recognize that social immanence and transcendence understood in terms of a theory of validity form a unity; to put it almost in Hegelian terms, one could say that true immanence consists in transcendence.

It is important in this context to recognize that the approach of orders of justification defended here is not only able to encompass the normative bases of justification and criticism that correspond to the participant perspective of those who demand justice. In addition, this insight forces us to redefine the sociological conception of an order of justification. For a concomitant of the fundamental claim to justification and dignity is that societies develop spaces in which these claims are expressed, fought for and institutionalized, so that the political sphere—from the informal public sphere to political institutions—forms forums in which the right to justification, as a challenge to the dominant discourses and justifications, is exercised in a way that goes beyond the individual languages of the *cités*. The "civic" order, therefore, is an overarching order insofar as—liberated from a narrower Rousseauean understanding of collective unanimity—it encompasses the other orders and includes a higher-order *political* level of justification (whose elaboration is a permanent task). Then societies must be evaluated not least according to whether they open up such spaces of justification and ensure a fair distribution of discursive power among the subjects. That is the central imperative of discursive justice, and this has implications for political and sociological analysis of an order of justification. In the conception of Boltanski and Thévenot, by contrast, the locus of "the political" remains underdetermined, as it were.

Another implication of my approach in terms of a theory of justification is that the languages of social criticism do not remain captive to the individual languages of the *cités*, for the criteria of reciprocity and general are context-transcending in nature: they can be used *within, between*, and *beyond* the *cités* to criticize social norms, justifications and institutions. This remains a matter for the judgment and creativity

[66] See Boltanski and Thévenot, *On Justification* (n. 56) 14.
[67] See Forst, *Justification and Critique* (n. 3) ch. 4.

of individuals and social groups. In this way, the social conventionalism implicit in the approach of Boltanski and Thévenot can be overcome. Boltanski likewise aspires to do this in his discussion of "radical" criticism, but he uses a concept of "totality" for this purpose that remains too closely wedded to the dichotomy between the "internal" and the "external" perspective, where the latter is inconsistent with the premises of pragmatic sociology.[68] Thus, in spite of the productivity of the analysis when it comes to detecting contradictions in social orders of justification, the route to a form of criticism that takes its orientation from independent rational standards but is nevertheless socially situated remains blocked. This is also shown by the fact that, beyond the "tests" within the established orders, Boltanski ultimately attributes a radical, innovative character primarily to an "existential" critique from a subjective perspective.[69]

The theory of justification advocated here shares with the sociology of criticism the intention to describe power relations as relations of justification. This makes possible a nuanced understanding of power, rule, and repression, depending on the level of justification or the degree of (overt or covert) denial of justification. But Thévenot and Boltanski ultimately defend a negative conception of power,[70] whereas it is generally more instructive to analyze power in terms of justification. On such an analysis, it is not conceptually predetermined from the outset whether the respective space of justifications and of social relations is effectively legitimized, and whether it is a space of democratically generated justifications or one of ideologically veiled or dictatorially restricted justifications.[71]

Finally, the theory of orders of justification based on historically evolved justification narratives allows a more pluralistic, dynamic, and open definition of these orders than the notion of *cités*, which are indebted to particular paradigms in political philosophy from Augustine to Adam Smith.[72] For the corresponding narratives and complexes of justification can be very general in nature (for example, certain paradigmatic narratives of political philosophy). But, as a general rule, they are also associated with specific experiences, traditions, history, and images, whose specific nature must also be disclosed.[73] The plurality of social languages of justification cannot be restricted in principle and, notwithstanding all "path dependencies" that may exist, these languages remain mutable and open. This is true of the general level of justification of a whole order, as well as below this level with regard to parts or "subsystems" of the order, for example, the market in certain social contexts.[74] In their specificity, the latter also resists excessively general categorizations that impede

[68] See Boltanski, *On Critique* (n. 55) 33 ff. [69] ibid 103.

[70] See Boltanski and Thévenot, *On Justification* (n. 56) 354; Boltanski, *On Critique* (n. 55) 124 ff.

[71] On this see Forst, "Noumenal Power" (n. 41).

[72] This schematic prior orientation is also criticized by Axel Honneth, "Dissolutions of the Social: On the Social Theory of Luc Boltanski and Laurent Thévenot," *Constellations* 17/3 (2010): 376–89.

[73] On this see Forst, "On the Concept of a Justification Narrative" (n. 43) (in general and with reference to the USA); "One Court and Many Cultures" (n. 31), likewise contains a context-specific analysis of justification narratives that are relevant in German legal conflicts.

[74] See Jens Beckert, "The Social Order of Markets," *Theory and Society* 38/3 (2009): 245–69.

access to specific contradictions of such orders. And, not least in times of globalized political and economic orders, the national interpretive framework, which is dominant in Boltanski and Thévenot, must be overcome if we want to analyze the formation of transnational normative orders.[75]

The significance of these remarks for a critical theory, which I cannot elaborate on here, is that it must be configured as a *critique of relations of justification*.[76] This has five key aspects that I would like to mention briefly here.

First, it calls for a critical social scientific analysis of social and political relations of domination that includes cultural and, not least, economic structures and relationships. It uncovers structures and relationships that are not reciprocally and generally justifiable, and those which render a practice of justification impossible as a political practice. This corresponds to the two dimensions of domination: subjugation to unjustifiable norms and institutions, and subjugation to conditions that prevent practices of justification—and hence criticism and construction.[77]

Secondly, this critical analysis must be connected with a discourse-theoretical, genealogical critique of the justifications and justification narratives that confer legitimacy on unjustifiable relations. The task here is to reconstruct how these justifications arose and what forces of inertia they are based on.[78]

Thirdly, we must use a historical-sociological study to inquire into the root causes for the lack of institutions and practices of democratic justification. Which path dependencies exist here and which structural alternatives were suppressed or failed? In particular, what are the effects of the interplay between economic and political power relations? What role do religious beliefs play?[79]

Fourthly, we must pose the constructive question of how a "basic structure of justification" can be conceived as a requirement of fundamental justice and be realized in social practice—not as an ideal or a model to be imposed on societies, but as a normative order to be developed autonomously. In all of this, we must observe the principle that such a structure must be proportional to the existing power relations, also in the transnational context.[80]

Finally, such a critical theory not only has to be able to justify its own standards normatively but also to regard them in a way that takes account of the risk of concepts and normative criteria becoming reified, and thus applies the principle of self-criticism to itself. This ties every normative "certainty" back to discursive criticism and redefinition by those who are subject to the norms, so that nothing is "fixed" except the principle of the need for justification. In other words, that theory can be

[75] See Peter Niesen (ed.), *Transnationale Gerechtigkeit und Demokratie* (Campus 2012).

[76] On the following see Forst, *Justification and Critique* (n. 3) 7 ff.

[77] Compare the concept of domination in Forst, "Noumenal Power" (n. 29).

[78] See in particular Forst, "On the Concept of a Justification Narrative" (n. 43) and "One Court and Many Cultures" (n. 31).

[79] See in particular Forst, "Religion and Toleration from the Enlightenment to the Post-Secular Era," ch. 5, and "Justice after Marx," ch. 7 in this volume.

[80] On this see Forst, "Realisms in International Political Theory" (n. 46) and "Transnational Justice and Non-Domination" (n. 46).

called *critical* which is based on the *principle of criticism itself*. Its medium is justifying reason understood as critical, public reason.[81] This principle can be described with equal legitimacy as a transcendental principle and as a socially immanent and historical one; progress in the spirit of emancipation occurs where this principle becomes established and social spaces of justification are opened up.[82]

[81] See in particular Forst, "Critique of Justifying Reason" (n. 4) ch. 1, and "Legitimacy, Democracy, and Justice" (n. 45).

[82] See in particular Forst, "The Concept of Progress" (n. 23).

PART I

REASON, NORMATIVITY, AND POWER

1

Critique of Justifying Reason

Explaining Practical Normativity

1. In philosophy, a great deal depends on which definition of the human being is made central to the investigation, and this role can be played by very different interpretations of that being—for example, as a being endowed with reason, as a social, evaluating, cultural or historical being, as a communicating being, a free or a bound being, an autonomous or a finite, limited being, to mention just a few.[1] I think that these interpretations can be connected in a way that incorporates what is most important in each of them. In order to do so, human beings must be viewed as *justifying beings*. Reason is understood accordingly as the ability to take one's orientation in the world from good, justifying reasons, whether they are used in a theoretical or a practical way. "*Ratio, raison, reason*," as Ernst Tugendhat emphasizes, "can mean both 'ground' (*Grund*) and 'reason' (*Vernunft*). The capacity of reason is the faculty of being able to answer for one's beliefs and actions (Latin: *rationem reddere*; Greek: *logon didonai*)."[2] Taking this as our starting point, the other determinations also fall into place: this way of justifying oneself is a social practice of evaluating, cultural, historical, and communicating beings who, on the one hand, are free to choose and examine their reasons but, on the other, are constrained by the reasons available to them that count as good or justifying. The finitude of reason means that nobody can reinvent the space of reasons from scratch, and certainly not on their own, but that everyone must find their bearings within it independently. This is at the root of the autonomy that is possible for human beings who take responsibility for themselves.

If we want to answer the question of normativity, therefore, we must engage in a *critique of justifying reason* and liberate ourselves from the false alternative that we have to start either from abstract principles or from concrete contexts. Human beings must be situated within all of the cultural and social contexts and practices of justification in which they exist and in which they have to find answers to theoretical and practical

[1] This chapter originated in a lecture delivered as part of the lecture series "Normativität: Frankfurter Perspektiven," which I co-organized with Klaus Günther in the Winter Semester 2011–12 in the Cluster of Excellence "Normative Orders" and to which we conducted an accompanying seminar. I am grateful to the colleagues and students who participated in these events and from whom I learned a great deal. Later versions were presented at a conference on normativity in Frankfurt and at the New School for Social Research in New York. I am indebted to Ulrike Heuer for a detailed commentary.

[2] Ernst Tugendhat, *Traditional and Analytical Philosophy: Lectures on the Philosophy of Language*, trans. P. A. Gorner (Cambridge University Press 1982) 76.

questions. Intrinsic to these *practices* are *principles* that determine what constitutes a good, justifying reason. Anyone who fully understands a practice also understands its rules, its point, and hence—in a more Kantian vein—its principles. Therefore, let us set aside right from the beginning what is merely an apparent contradiction between social practice and principles of reason. To be part of a practice means to understand its rules and principles in a practical way and to follow them, as Wittgenstein says in his argument against private rules.[3] Someone who knows what a practice is, is aware of its specific justificatory features and logics and what they demand. This knowledge belongs to reason.

Practices of justification are the contexts in which normativity has its place for us. Particular standards of justification apply to the respective contexts and these standards are normative in nature: the standards of theoretical reason are binding because they have truth as their goal; the standards of practical reason are binding because they aim at the good or the right. Our task is to throw light on this connection; but here already it should be noted that we must seek normativity in the faculty of reason and nowhere else. For reason alone is the ability to take one's orientation from this normativity and, more importantly, to generate it. Reason is itself normative and helps us to distinguish the *supposed* good or right from the *examined*—that is, justified—good or right. Reason is the faculty of justification and the faculty of justification is what makes us normative beings. Reason, in other words, is the ability and the power that normatively binds us—it *connects* us with others in the light of principles and values that it examines with a view to their justification.

By contrast, other explanations of normativity come too late or remain too superficial. Someone who thinks that normativity can be traced back to *sanctions*[4] fails to understand that a sanction is itself in need of justification and presupposes the norm that was supposed to be observed. Therefore, it cannot justify the normativity of practical obligations. Also, in the very specific contexts in which instrumental norms are followed in order to achieve one's goals and avoid sanctions, the actual normativity resides in the goals, not in the sanctions. Those who think that normativity is grounded in moral *feelings* overlook the fact that, in order to be described as moral, these feelings must contain valuations and convictions connected with reasons—and whose validity must be tested with reasons. Viewed in this way, it is impossible to follow one's feelings "blindly" because feelings already enable us to see something, albeit often in a one-sided and incorrect way. Feelings are expressions of our beliefs and evaluations, not their opposite; someone who did not have any moral feelings would not really be a participant in social, evaluating practices. Finally, someone who thinks—following Hume, for example—that normative obligations can be traced back to subjective *desires* fails to recognize that desires have a normative aspect only if they are directed and only if they are justified for a person and thus involve reasons.[5] In general, we must

[3] Ludwig Wittgenstein, *Philosophical Investigations*, trans. G. E. M. Anscombe (Blackwell 1978) § 202.

[4] Thus Peter Stemmer, *Normativität: Eine ontologische Untersuchung* (de Gruyter 2008). For a critical response see Rainer Forst, "Die Reise nach Phantasia," review essay on Peter Stemmer, *Normativität: Eine ontologische Untersuchung*, in *Deutsche Zeitschrift für Philosophie* 58/1 (2010): 157–61.

[5] See Thomas Nagel, *The Possibility of Altruism* (Princeton University Press 1970); Thomas M. Scanlon, *Being Realistic about Reasons* (Oxford University Press 2014); and Rainer Forst, *The Right to Justification: Elements of a Constructivist Theory of Justice*, trans. Jeffrey Flynn (Columbia University Press 2012) ch. 1.

liberate ourselves from the notion that offering, demanding, and employing reasons is a purely abstract—because cognitive—affair. It is the most mundane thing imaginable, a basic mode of being-in-the-world, to use Heideggerian language. Moreover, reasons assume the most diverse, more or less reflected forms. An *animal rationale* is still an *animal* of flesh and blood, although one which moves in the space of reasons.

Because of the immanent relation between reason, justification, and normativity, only a critique of justifying reason can throw light on the phenomenon of normativity. I do not pretend to be able to carry out such a program here and if I so much as venture to invoke Kant, it is because a critique of reason as the "faculty of principles"[6] remains our most important philosophical task, even if I choose an approach that is more immanent to practice. The reconstruction of the contextual logic of justification is the reconstruction of the use of reason, and here reason counts as something essentially normative, not as a pure instrument. It binds us.

2. At this point we must consider a finding that is decisive for any philosophical theory of normativity and is ignored at the expense of a great deal of incongruity in this field. It concerns the question of whether a theory of normativity should itself be *normative* and, if so, in what sense. On the one hand, the answer to the first question seems to be clearly "yes" because we are aiming at a theory that allows us to understand reason as a faculty of good, examined justification. Here, however, we face a problem and a danger. For we could misjudge the facticity of our normative relations to the world if we confined ourselves to the normativity that is tested and reflected. For don't we normally encounter norms as something familiar and untested[7] and, more importantly, from a critical perspective, as something merely conventional that often fails to withstand reflexive examination—indeed, at the extreme, as something ideological and false that "normalizes" us and our relations to the world?[8] In the context of a critique of justifying reason, don't we have to subject the factual normative relations, which not only "train" [*abrichten*] us (to adopt Wittgensteinian language) to a second nature but also "shape" and "finish" [*zurichten*] us (in Adorno's terms), to critical analysis? Must the theory of normativity not also take the form of a *critical theory*?

Indeed it must. And this means that we must assume a *threefold normativity*: the *normalizing normativity* of the established, often unexamined justifications, some of which may be so reified that they are insulated against further problematization; but, in addition, the rational *normativity of principles of reason* that allow, and perhaps even require, us to question these forms of normativity; and, finally, the world of *reflected norms* that can count as justified, whether factually, because they have been generated through suitably discursive procedures, or counterfactually, because they appear to us on the most careful examination to be the best justified.

[6] Immanuel Kant, *Critique of Pure Reason*, ed. and trans. Paul Guyer and Allen W. Wood (Cambridge University Press 1998), 387 (A 299/B 356).

[7] See Marcus Willaschek, "Bedingtes Vertrauen: Auf dem Weg zu einer pragmatistischen Transformation der Metaphysik," in Martin Hartmann, Jasper Liptow, and Marcus Willaschek (eds.), *Die Gegenwart des Pragmatismus* (Suhrkamp 2013) 97–120.

[8] On the latter see Michel Foucault, *Power*, ed. James Faubion, trans. Robert Hurley (New Press 2000).

In what follows, I will defend the thesis that a critique of justifying reason must always keep these levels in mind simultaneously—and, in addition, that only someone who is able to question the reified forms of normativity of established ethical life in a well-founded way was properly socialized into the space of reasons. If you will, to the second nature of conventional ethical life I add the *third nature* of the reflected ethical life and claim that only this completes the picture of the practice of normativity. If we take the first person perspective seriously, as we should if we are posing the question of the world of the normative "for me," then we must divide up the latter into *three worlds*: the world of what holds as a matter of fact, the world of what holds counterfactually, and the world of critique that lies between them. Only in this way can we avoid a one-sided theory that either clings to the given in a conventionalist manner or idealizes our life and accepts as normative only what can claim to be valid in a reflexive sense. The world of justifications, to put it in still different terms, must always be viewed simultaneously as a world of *power*—as a world of the "noumenal" power of existing justifications that can be either good or bad, and hence can either liberate or dominate us.[9]

This leads to a complication, although an unavoidable one, for the program of a critique of justifying reason. For not only must the various contexts of justification be reconstructed but the justifications proper to each of them must also be regarded as conventional or "normal" or as examined and reflected. Both are phenomena of being-in-the-world, but of very different—one could almost say, again using Heidegger: inauthentic and authentic—kinds. Thus, the title of a "critique" of reason reflects a twofold intention: on the one hand, it is a philosophical reconstruction of the logic of justification that is immanent in practice while simultaneously transcending it; but, on the other, it is also a self-critique, less of its speculative excesses (as in Kant) than of its own reification and ossification or atrophying in closed and inaccessible spaces of justification. However, no one can perform the task of criticizing reason except reason itself.[10]

3. Practices of justification should be analyzed according to the contexts in which different claims to validity are raised. Habermas once proposed a distinction between three types of validity claims—namely, to truth, to rightness, and to truthfulness.[11] This analysis needs to be differentiated further, because one can specify a series of additional contexts of justification that Habermas has explored himself, although without readjusting the basic concepts of his formal pragmatic framework: in the domain of truth claims, the conditions of justification of religious claims need to be

[9] On this see Rainer Forst, "Noumenal Power," ch. 2 in this volume.

[10] On this see Amy Allen, Rainer Forst, and Mark Haugaard, "Power and Reason, Justice and Domination: A Conversation," in *Journal of Political Power* 7 (2014): 7–33. In addition see Stephen White, "Does Critical Theory Need Strong Foundations?," in *Philosophy & Social Criticism* 41/3 (2015): 207–11, and my reply "A Critical Theory of Politics: Grounds, Method and Aims. Reply to Simone Chambers, Stephen White and Lea Ypi," in *Philosophy and Social Criticism* 41/3 (2015): 225–34.

[11] Jürgen Habermas, "What is Universal Pragmatics?" in Jürgen Habermas, *On the Pragmatics of Communication*, ed. Maeve Cooke (MIT Press 1998), 21–104, at 81, and Jürgen Habermas, "Some Further Clarifications of the Concept of Communicative Rationality," in *On the Pragmatics of Communication*, 307–42.

clarified, for example, and in the practical domain the reference to expressive truthfulness is insufficient for analyzing ethical claims to validity if we are to do justice to their cognitive content.[12]

In the following, I cannot offer such an analysis across all contexts. But we should take note of a principle that overarches and transcends all of these contexts—namely, the general *principle of reason*, which states that claims to validity must be justified in precisely the way in which they hold in their respective contexts. The general principle of reason is therefore a principle of justification that is differentiated according to contexts. At the same time, however, we must recognize that it is a reflexive principle. It must not only refer to how a contextual dispute is to be resolved—for example, a conflict in which one side regards religious reasons as appropriate and another scientific reasons (think of the debate over "creationism"). What is more, the principle of reason deserves this name only if it is self-referential, thus only if it also examines every practice of justification to determine whether it envisages the correct criteria and applies these criteria correctly. Kant has this radicality in mind when he ties reason already in its purely epistemic use to a right of justification and critique:

> Reason must submit itself to critique in all its undertakings, and cannot restrict the freedom of critique through any prohibition without damaging itself and drawing upon itself a disadvantageous suspicion. Now there is nothing so important because of its utility, nothing so holy, that it may be exempted from this searching review and inspection, which knows no respect for persons. The very existence of reason depends upon this freedom, which has no dictatorial authority, but whose claim is never anything more than the agreement of free citizens, each of whom must be able to express his reservations, indeed even his *veto*, without holding back.[13]

As I read it, this states that reason does not allow itself to be pigeonholed in a reifying way. Rather, the higher-order principle of justification always allows us to ask whether an assertion is really justified and whether it was justified in the right way—even if only a single individual raises this question. Thus, to cite an example, at a certain point in history the claim to rule by divine right was problematized on both epistemic and normative grounds, something which also points to the interconnections between the individual contexts of justification. However, an unshakable foundation remains—namely, the reason-based right of individuals to problematize given justifications at any time. At this point, this should not yet be understood as a moral right.[14]

4. In the following analysis, I will concentrate on the justification of practical assertions or norms, hence on answers to the question of what I should do or of what should hold for me or for us in our actions and social relations. In *ethical* contexts, what is at stake is the question of the good life *for me*. An ethically autonomous and reflecting person—one who is searching for justification—must *answer* this

[12] See Forst, *The Right to Justification* (n. 5) ch. 3.

[13] Kant, *Critique of Pure Reason* (n. 6) 643 (A 738 f./B 766 f.).

[14] This constitutes an essential difference from the transcendental pragmatics of Karl-Otto Apel, who interprets the entire practice of reason, including the theoretical, as having a strong normative, moral content. On the contrary, only in moral contexts do I assume that there is a moral right to justification.

question for herself together with others, but she must *take responsibility* for it alone. Here, a complex space of justification opens up, a normative web that must be differentiated. Although the mode of validity of ethical justification ultimately refers to "me" because it concerns my life, others are part of this justification in a variety of ways: as concrete "significant others"[15] who are important and indispensable for me, as others in the sense of social valuations and expectations, hence in a more general sense, but also as generalized others who make moral claims, for example. The answer to an ethical question for a person may also have a religious dimension that points to strong validity claims. When analyzing ethical justification, therefore, we must guard against subjectivist and conventionalist, but also against objectivist, simplifications, because what is at stake is the *good* life in a *community-related*, although ultimately *individual*, form that strives for truthfulness.

We must understand the normativity of ethical justification in terms of a network of relations shaped by individual life decisions, but also by "volitional necessities" in Harry Frankfurt's sense[16]—hence, by ethical valuations and relations that simply constitute me as the person I am. Furthermore, apart from concrete ties to others, social valuations also count, although they may be connected with further—for example, religious—beliefs. And, finally, moral beliefs can play a limiting role. All of these strands come together to form what I would like to call a *knot of normativity*. And ethical reflection can be conceived as a matter of consciously tying this knot, where it is left up to this form of reflection to bring all of these components together into "reflective equilibrium." The mode of validity "good for me" does not specify how this occurs in terms of a single principle.

In this connection, we must avoid a number of misconceptions. In the first place, this analysis does not imply that ethical autonomy has anything to do with "radical self-choice"; it can just as well accept the components which belong to me, and which I have not chosen or even "made," as my own—but ethical autonomy can also mean combating them. Furthermore, there is no implication that ethically autonomous reflection is a *necessary* condition for the good life, as liberal theories often assert.[17] The ethical use of reason asks about the good—but it remains moot whether the good can be achieved only in an autonomous way and not also in a less reflexive form of life. It is also presumptuous to think that only a liberal form of life could lead to the good.

Finally, it should also be emphasized that moral considerations play an important role in the context of ethical justification; however, I do not see any reason for the thesis, often defended since Plato, that only the moral life can be a good life.[18] One can claim that someone who shuns morality and respects and shows consideration

[15] Thus Charles Taylor, "The Politics of Recognition," in Amy Gutman (ed.), *Multiculturalism: Examining the Politics of Recognition* (Princeton University Press 1992) 25–73, at 32–7.

[16] Harry Frankfurt, *Necessity, Volition, and Love* (Cambridge University Press 1999).

[17] Ronald Dworkin, *Justice for Hedgehogs* (Harvard University Press, 2011); Will Kymlicka, *Multicultural Citizenship: A Liberal Theory of Minority Rights* (Oxford University Press 1995); Martin Seel, *Versuch über die Form des Glücks* (Suhrkamp 1995).

[18] Thus, in particular, Seel, *Versuch über die Form des Glücks* (n. 17). For a critical response see Forst, *The Right to Justification* (n. 5) ch. 3.

only for members of a limited community is squandering his life; but that strikes me as just one ethical hypothesis among others over which people can reasonably differ. Rather, I agree with Kant that ethical happiness is "not an ideal of reason"[19] and that, although ethical questions can be answered with the aid of reason, they do not have to be answered in accordance with a principle of moral justification. This does not turn the ethical either into a subjective or "private" matter or into something entirely arbitrary, but only liberates it from an excessive moral claim to validity. The good life is one thing, moral action another—they are connected in a variety of ways but are not necessarily bound up with each other, either in one direction or the other. We cannot define away the tensions within our practical life. A variety of moral-ethical conflicts exist between the good and the right for the simple reason that the good life is also conceivable and livable without strict morality.

It is important, by contrast, to conceive of ethical reflection from the above-mentioned twofold perspective *of conventional* or "normal" as opposed to *reflected* normativity. For a person can ask herself not only whether she is conducting her life in a good way and is pursuing the values that she thinks important; she can also ask whether the social valuations which count as ethical are really worth pursuing. Do they conceal, for example, stereotypes, biases, even repressive or disciplining elements that restrict autonomy? This opens up a critical, reflexive space in which social criticism proceeds from ethical considerations, although it must be asked further whether this critique speaks in the name of an ethical ideal, and hence is itself only ethical in nature, or whether it raises a general morally relevant problem of restrictions on autonomy. These components often overlap in theories of the alienated, reified life.[20]

It follows that ethical normativity develops in the normal mode of the self-evaluating life; but, based on a radicalization of the question of what is really good for me, it allows not only a more intensive form of self-interrogation but also an interrogation of social modes of valuation. In the normal case we trust the social normativity in the light of which we evaluate our life choices; in the other mode we problematize this normativity. This ability, even allowing for the different ways in which it may have developed in particular historical contexts, also belongs to socialization and individualization. George Herbert Mead expresses this in the figure of a dialectical relation between the "Me" of social conventions and the "I" that transcends these conventions and also adopts a critical stance on them.[21]

The normal and normalizing normativity is also one of justifications—of what counts in a society or community for certain reasons as good, right, or opportune. The more complex a society becomes the more complex this context of justification also becomes. It is the lifeworld context in which we trust first and foremost. But this can also develop into a hard carapace of reified constructions of identity and

[19] Immanuel Kant, *Groundwork of the Metaphysics of Morals*, ed. and trans. Mary Gregor (Cambridge University Press, 1998) 38 (4:429 ff.).

[20] See Rahel Jaeggi, *Kritik von Lebensformen* (Suhrkamp 2014).

[21] George Herbert Mead, *Mind, Self, and Society*, ed. Charles W. Morris, annotated by Daniel B. Huebner and Hans Joas (Chicago University Press 2015 [1934]) pt. 3.

"subjectivizations,"[22] into a disciplining and alienating form of life—one need only think of the forms of racism or sexism that all too often occupy the social space of justification. In that case the existing order of justification must be transcended and, once this reflection begins, this transcending has already occurred. Then discourses arise which problematize the dominant discourse. And here one can already see that, given this twofold normativity, it makes no sense to ask whether the concept "discourse" should be understood in Foucauldian or Habermasian terms. We need to be able to do both—to view justifications as reifying facticity and as a medium of critique and new justification.

We should note that every time the normative knot between me, concrete others, social expectations, and general considerations is tied in a reflexive way, the ethical mode of validity emphasizes in particular the *individual responsibility* of the person for her life with and toward others; it is ultimately the individual who pays the price for a false answer to the ethical question, because it is her life that goes wrong as a result. Here the subjective index is more decisive than in any other practical context. Ethical normativity cannot ultimately be explained abstractly in terms of all of the components of the knot, but must be explained instead in terms of the specificity of the one who binds it. In tying this knot, the self binds and forms itself as a normative being who relates to itself and others in the mode of ethical justification.

5. Autonomous individual responsibility is also central *in the moral context*, although in a different way. For, in contrast to ethical values, the validity claim of moral norms is not "that is good for me" but instead "that is what is morally required as something valid for every person in a reciprocal and general way." Here, self-responsibility and decentering must be conceived as belonging together: although the subject is not an absolute sovereign when it comes to answering ethical questions, she is nevertheless the final court of appeal; in the case of moral justifications, by contrast, the mode of justification is strictly intersubjective from the outset and is tied to a specific principle of justification. Understanding this requires *recursive* reflection: in the moral context, norms raise a categorical, unconditional, reciprocal, and general claim to validity—*nobody* is allowed to violate a moral norm and everyone can expect everyone else to observe the norm. If we trace this validity claim back to its conditions of validity, then every moral norm must rest on a justification that corresponds to the criteria of reciprocity and generality. This means that no one may raise claims that she refuses to grant to others (reciprocity of contents) and that no one may simply assume that others share her own evaluative conceptions and interests so that she could claim to speak in their name or in the name of higher values (reciprocity of reasons). Finally, nobody may be excluded from the community of justification either (generality). Thus, in moral contexts the principle of reciprocal and general justification holds as a principle of practical reason.

Adapting Thomas Scanlon's formulation ("not reasonable to reject"),[23] I believe that moral justification requires that norms must rest on reasons that are *not*

[22] Apart from the work of Foucault, here that of Judith Butler is especially important: for example Judith Butler, *The Psychic Life of Power: Theories in Subjection* (Stanford University Press 1997).

[23] Thomas M. Scanlon, *What We Owe to Each Other* (Harvard University Press 1988) ch. 5.

reciprocally and generally rejectable. This means that claims that one may reject can very well also be accepted in a supererogatory spirit; moreover, this negative formulation provides criteria for how moral judgements can be justified also in cases of disagreement. Thus, here we are not dealing with a consensus theory based on a theory of discourse, because the criteria permit a judgment of which claims or arguments can or cannot be reciprocally and generally rejected in a specific conflict—as a general rule, at any rate. In order to stress the counterfactual normativity of justification, therefore, here it would be better to speak in terms of "shareable" rather than of "shared" reasons. Again the difference between factual and reflected validity takes effect; in the light of shareable reasons, shared reasons may prove to be one-sided.

Nevertheless, the constructivism implied by this is a discourse-theoretical form of constructivism—*constructivism* because here norms are constructed in accordance with a principle of reasonable justification, *discourse-theoretical* constructivism because the emphasis is on the voice of every single moral person as a free and equal justificatory authority. According to the principle of justification, in moral contexts every person has an equal *right to justification* of all of those norms that claim to be morally binding on her. Her moral autonomy or "dignity" resides in her counting as an "end in herself" insofar as she is a justificatory authority of moral norms with equal rights to others and has a basic moral right to count as such. To be sure, here—to cut short another long discussion—we are not dealing with a form of metaphysical constructivism according to which the justification would "give rise to" a world of norms[24] but of *practical constructivism* according to which only the principle of reciprocal-general justification can ground moral validity. Whether this *opens* up access to a Platonic world of reasons or, instead, *creates* a world of reasons can be left undecided. Finite reason is aware of the limits of its speculative power.[25]

Moral justification should likewise be situated within a normative knot tied by reflection, only this time it is tied in a different way. It is tied by the acting and reflecting moral person who must answer to concrete others who are affected morally by her actions (which may be controversial and hence itself be a subject of discourse), but in such a way that she must present reasons that can transcend this relationship and be universalized: the others are at once concrete and generalized others,[26] at once irreplaceable individuals and members of an all-inclusive human community.[27] The success of this reflection is contingent on paying adequate heed to the principle of reciprocal-general justification; for this alone creates the right distance from one's own interests and from those of concrete others. In normal reflection, one may fall back on conventional interpretations of norms; however, the moment it becomes apparent that reciprocity and generality are being violated as a result,

[24] Thus Jürgen Habermas, "Rightness versus Truth: On the Sense of Normative Validity in Moral Judgements and Norms," in Jürgen Habermas, *Truth and Justification*, trans. Barbara Fultner (MIT Press 2003) 237–76, at 268.

[25] For a defense of a different, moral realist conception in this context see Charles Larmore, *Vernunft und Subjektivität: Frankfurter Vorlesungen* (Suhrkamp 2012).

[26] Seyla Benhabib, *Situating the Self: Gender, Community, and Postmodernism in Contemporary Ethics* (Routledge 1992) ch. 5.

[27] Lutz Wingert, *Gemeinsinn und Moral* (Suhrkamp 1993).

whether by privileging defined groups or by showing insufficient consideration for concrete individuals, the knot must be retied and, if necessary, tied more tightly in order to be able to justify an action or a norm.

The normativity of moral justifications, finally, can be explained by the fact that this process has followed its correct course; and justifications that were generated in this way simultaneously *motivate* moral action insofar as the correct insight corresponds to them and other reasons do not interfere. For moral action must always occur for the right reasons and, if the effectiveness of moral insights depended on their being linked with ethical considerations, this would not be the case. Therefore, those philosophers who take their orientation from Hume are the true "externalists," because they explain moral action in terms of desires that do not rest on moral insight. But there is no reason why a moral insight—that is, an insight into the justification of an action based on moral respect—should not be sufficient to motivate action. Moreover, the externalist view turns morality on its head, because moral norms are supposed to obligate categorically and to be based on insight without any need of ethical or religious support. Anyone who thinks that a moral norm needs not only insight into its justification in order to motivate but must also refer to the fact that one's own well-being is promoted as a result either relativizes moral validity and turns it into a merely hypothetical validity or has too strong a moral idea of his own well-being. Both conceptions should be avoided because they do justice neither to ethics nor to morality. Paraphrasing Bernard Williams (and contrary to his intention), I would say that those who connect moral insights with further ethical motives in order to explain their practical effectiveness use "one thought too many."[28]

In the moral context, a special point of the practice of justification must be borne in mind. For the above is sufficient to explain only the normativity of the norms that have undergone the procedure of justification, but not the *normativity of the principle of justification* itself—in Kantian terms, the moral law—which is valid here simultaneously as a principle of reason *and* as a moral principle and which, according to Kant, "has no need of justifying grounds."[29] This is a central aspect of the approach I advocate, for in this way practical reason is traced back not only to the insight into the *how* but also into the *that* of justification; as Kant explains in the *Critique of Practical Reason*, the "fact of reason" consists in the fact that reason itself is morally binding and imperative; it contains the *duty* to justify.[30]

How is that possible? This question is justified but it points to the reductive character of the modern understanding of reason in many of its variants. That reason itself cannot motivate is asserted especially by those who think that human beings can be moved only by the mechanism of desires. As I observed at the beginning, however, to be part of a social practice means understanding its rules and hence its point; and to see the point of the practice of moral justification means *accepting* the principle that I owe this justification to every moral person equally, *independently* of

[28] See Forst, *The Right to Justification* (n. 5) ch. 1.

[29] Immanuel Kant, *Critique of Practical Reason*, ed. and trans. Mary Gregor (Cambridge University Press 1997) 42 (5:47).

[30] For a more detailed discussion see Forst, *The Right to Justification* (n. 5) ch. 2.

any prior performance on their part and independently of my ethical preferences. It is far-fetched to assume that someone understands what moral duties are but needs additional arguments in order to acknowledge them not only epistemically but also practically. Rather, someone who has been socialized in the right way into the moral practice of tying normative knots knows and recognizes that morality is required for the sake of others—without privileged reference to my good and only insofar as it is required by their and my status as free and equal persons. Morality is not an instrument of self-abnegation and enslavement but an expression of mutual respect among morally autonomous persons. They recognize in the "countenance" (Lévinas) of the other a moral authority; but, contrary to Lévinas, in so doing, they also recognize in the same moment their own, equal authority. Anyone who understands the practice of morality knows that morality must be practiced "without any further why" and "gratis"[31]; but the individual also knows that she can demand this of any other person at any time. That is the supreme form of respect: recognition of the fact that one always already owes respect, but reciprocally and generally, with reference to the principle of justification, which is therefore an irreducible part of this practice. Without practical reason, we lack the cord to tie the morally binding knot. Viewed in this light, practical reason is what binds us as moral persons to others with ties of responsibility, because in this way we answer them and take responsibility for that answer. It is not an abstract faculty but is in this sense a concrete moral capacity that connects us with others.

It is, once again, a reference to Mead that is of help here. For just as the "I" challenges the conventional "Me" in ethical contexts to be and become a self, so, too, it can morally transcend the "Me" of ethical life. Then it establishes a "higher sort of community":[32]

> A man rises up and defends himself for what he does; he has his "day in court"; he can present his views. He can perhaps change the attitude of the community toward himself. The process of conversation is one in which the individual has not only the right but the duty of talking to the community of which he is a part, and bringing about those changes which take place through the interaction of individuals. This is the way, of course, in which society gets ahead namely, by just such interactions as those in which some person thinks a thing out.[33]

Following Peirce, Mead conceives of this more inclusive community as the community "of all rational beings"[34] and, for us, this means that the space of examined justifications is always a space that refers to, but also transcends, a given society. That is the principle of a critical morality: every reciprocal-general justification is a social justification; but the principle of justification is inexhaustibly creative. It is immanent in and transcends practice and that is precisely what constitutes the practice of morality. We can call it second or third nature; what is important is that we understand this transcendence that we ourselves are, as it were.

[31] To quote Luther's words on moral motivation—although for Luther it is out of love for God and hence is not unconditional in the moral sense; on this see Rainer Forst, *Toleration in Conflict: Past and Present*, trans. Ciaran Cronin (Cambridge University Press 2013) 117.

[32] Mead, *Mind, Self, and Society* (n. 21) 167–8. [33] ibid 168. [34] ibid 200.

It follows that every moral person has an unconditional, categorical *right* to the justification of moral norms—and an exactly correlative *duty*. For recognition of this right and this duty is immanent in the practice of morality; being part of it does not presuppose any proof of membership or a particular ethical self-understanding or a God. It is an autonomous human practice. The only ladder leading to this practice is a moral one. Thus, Prichard was right when he criticized modern moral philosophy for looking for a false, because non-moral, reason as an answer to the question "Why be moral?"[35] For this reason can only be a *moral* one and understanding this is a question of practical reason. Here, again, a moral realist interpretation of this connection must be rejected: moral respect is a moral achievement, not an epistemic one; cognition of one's duty is primarily a matter of moral recognition.

What, then, is the source of moral normativity? On a first level of reflection, it resides in the justification procedure of reciprocity and generality, which strikes the correct balance between me, concrete others, and all others. At a deeper level, it is grounded in reflection on me as a justifying being who needs and employs reasons, in such a way that I recognize and acknowledge that I am inherently obligated in a particular way to justify. Being a subject of justification is a normative status involving rights and duties; and understanding my original accountability toward and with others reveals the basic, fundamental normativity.[36] Moral normativity is created by tying the knot of self-responsibility in the right way—but only with the help of the principle of justification, which binds and connects me, you, and us as morally autonomous beings. Herein resides the truth of the connection between self-constitution and morality—but only with reference to the moral self, not to selfhood in general.[37] An amoral or immoral person can also be conceived as an independent subject who follows reasons and has a practical identity.

6. Following these general reflections on morality, I would like to turn in conclusion to more concrete contexts of political and social *justice*. They are situated at the intersection between ethics, morality, law, and politics—specifically, where the right to justification becomes the right not to be subjected to norms or institutions that are an expression of arbitrariness or domination, and hence cannot be justified among free and equal persons.[38] If the principle of justification in moral contexts conforms to the "all affected principle," in contexts of justice it conforms to the "all subjected principle," where "subjected" is understood in a broader sense that includes, besides

[35] H. A. Prichard, "Does Moral Philosophy Rest on a Mistake?," in Wilfrid Sellars and John Hospers (eds.), *Readings in Ethical Theory*, 2nd edn. (Prentice Hall 1970) 86–96.

[36] This implies that every moral person has the right to justification, even if, because of their age or illness, they are not able to formulate their claims.

[37] The more sweeping hypothesis is defended by Dieter Henrich, "Der Begriff der sittlichen Einsicht und Kants Lehre vom Faktum der Vernunft," in Gerold Prauss (ed.), *Kant: Zur Deutung seiner Theorie vom Erkennen und Handeln* (Kiepenheuer & Witsch 1973) 223–54, and Christine Korsgaard, *Self-Constitution: Agency, Identity, and Integrity* (Oxford University Press 2009).

[38] See Rainer Forst, *Contexts of Justice: Political Philosophy beyond Liberalism and Communitarianism*, trans. John M. M. Farrell (University of California Press 2002) and *The Right to Justification* (n. 5) pts. 2 and 3, and Rainer Forst, *Justification and Critique: Towards a Critical Theory of Politics*, trans. Ciaran Cronin (Polity 2014).

legal and political relations, also informal (e.g., economic) relations of subjection and negative ones—that is, ones that involve neither cooperation nor reciprocity.[39] The goddess of justice comes into the world in order to rectify relations between human beings; however, she does not do this for them but instead ensures that the subjects, as individuals who are subjected, first become autonomous authorities over their relations who are endowed with equal rights. Herein resides the political point of justice: contexts of justice are contexts of political, legal, or, in the broader sense, social rule or domination and the basic claim of justice in such contexts is to be free from domination and to be an autonomous subject of justification. With this emphasis on the right of justification, I contrast my position with Philip Pettit's neorepublican version of freedom as non-domination, which accords a negative dimension of freedom priority over the active dimension of justification.[40]

Again it should be emphasized that justice must be situated in practical contexts. And here we need a differentiated theory that distinguishes between national, international and transnational contexts and one which contrasts contexts of legitimate rule with those of illegitimate, or insufficiently legitimate, rule (i.e. domination). Here everything depends on reciprocal-general justification becoming practical, which means that there must be legally institutionalized forms of political justification where until now arbitrariness ruled and that arbitrariness must be banished within such institutions. Such a theory is practice-oriented but, in contrast to some theories described as *practice-dependent*, it does not focus exclusively on positively constituted relations of cooperation as contexts of justice.[41] Against such a twofold form of practice positivism, it must be emphasized within the framework of a realist theory that justice as a practical project must take injustice as its starting point, be it within formal-positive legal and political contexts or within informal social contexts. Analysis must begin with the real relations, which are relations of rule or of domination.[42]

In this context, the political impetus of justice must be emphasized and we must reject a truncated conception that understands "social" or "distributive" justice as a matter of the distribution of basic goods, resources, or even capabilities and is primarily focused on who gets how much or "enough" of what.[43] In such goods- or recipient-fixated theories, complex distributive arrangements are worked out, as if it were a matter of programming a huge distribution machine capable of producing

[39] See Rainer Forst, "Transnational Justice and Non-Domination: A Discourse-Theoretical Approach," ch. 10 in this volume. See also Eva Erman, "The Boundary Problem and the Right to Justification," in Rainer Forst, *Justice, Democracy and the Right to Justification: Rainer Forst in Dialogue* (Bloomsbury 2014) 127–46; Simon Caney, "Justice and the Basic Right to Justification," in Forst, *Justice, Democracy and the Right to Justification* (n. 5) 147–66, and my reply "Justifying Justification: Reply to My Critics," in Forst, *Justice, Democracy and the Right to Justification*, 205–15.

[40] For a more detailed account see Rainer Forst, "A Kantian Republican Conception of Justice as Nondomination," in Andreas Niederberger and Philipp Schink (eds.), *Republican Democracy* (Edinburgh University Press 2013) 154–68, and "Transnational Justice and Non-Domination: A Discourse-Theoretical Approach" (n. 39).

[41] See Forst, "Transnational Justice and Non-Domination" (n. 39).

[42] See Rainer Forst, "Legitimacy, Democracy, and Justice: On the Reflexivity of Normative Orders," ch. 8 in this volume.

[43] On this see Forst, *Justification and Critique* (n. 5) ch. 1.

justice. But justice is a strictly relational and structural matter. Its primary focus is not on results but on the social relations in which goods are produced and acquired in the first place and in which it is decided what is produced and distributed and how. This is the "primal scene" of justice and justice must aim at this—at the *relations of justification* in political and social space, understood as institutional and discursive relations. Democracy is therefore the basic form of political and social justice and it relates to all socially relevant domains of exercising rule, including economic relations,[44] both national and transnational.

Once again, the advantage of a dialectical analysis of normativity with a twofold perspective becomes apparent. For the existing relations of justification must be analyzed in the first instance as power relations: here it is decided who is able to influence the political space of reasons, to use it, occupy it or even seal it off, possibly with an ideology. Therefore, power must be understood as essentially a mental phenomenon, as the capacity to bring others to think and do things that they would not otherwise have thought or done.[45] That can be the result of a good argument or of a threat, and the art of analyzing power is to understand how this occurs in concrete cases. Thus, neither the concept of power nor that of rule is negatively charged; the concept of domination, by contrast, is. A critical theory as a critique of relations of justification concentrates not only on the social relations that cannot be justified but also on the justifications that nevertheless legitimate them and on what it would mean to establish a basic structure of justification in which those involved could acquire sufficient justificatory power to problematize structures that appear to be cemented and to create others. The normativity of justice is a critical and also a constructive normativity of the shared practice of justification. It is in this practice that the normative knot of justice is tied; this practice itself *is* justice, reflexively speaking.

The principle of justification underlying this conception of discursive justice is as immanent in social practice as it transcends the latter. Every social order must be conceived as an *order of justification*.[46] It consists of a complex web of different justifications, some of which have congealed into justification narratives,[47] that exercise hegemonic power—and provoke counter-narratives, such as those put forward in the seventeenth century by the Levellers or by Locke against Filmer's defense of absolute monarchy as the exercise of paternal power. However self-enclosed such an order of justification may be, it always presents points of attack for critique through its claim to legitimacy. Whether this critique is a radical or a hermeneutic one is not always easily discernable, for replacing the discourse of the divine right of kings with a discourse of divinely endowed natural rights to self-determination is both revolutionary and an internal claim to a "better" Christianity. Whatever concrete form the demands assume, one *basic claim* is fundamental here—namely, the claim not to be subjected to any form of rule that cannot be adequately legitimized toward

[44] Compare Rainer Forst, "Justice after Marx," ch. 7 in this volume.

[45] See Forst, "Noumenal Power" (n. 9).

[46] On this see Rainer Forst und Klaus Günther, "Die Herausbildung normativer Ordnungen: Zur Idee eines interdisziplinären Forschungsprogramms," in Rainer Forst and Klaus Günther (eds.), *Die Herausbildung normativer Ordnungen* (Campus 2011) 11–30.

[47] See Rainer Forst, "On the Concept of a Justification Narrative," ch. 3 in this volume.

those who are subjected to it. This is the basic principle of a just social order and it always allows new, radicalized demands for justification. It forces existing orders to go beyond themselves and thus makes social progress possible—but also regression, for instance in the form of new closures of the space of justification or new techniques of power.[48] But in the struggles of those affected, the call for the right no longer to count as a social nullity but instead to have rights to co-determination and self-determination is at once the moving force and the norm proper to political practice, while nevertheless placing it in question.

A critical theory of normativity keeps its eye on the three worlds of existing justifications, reciprocal-general justifications, and the in-between world, the world of critique, and sees bringing them into relation to each other as a question of autonomy and of reason. In a nutshell, it makes the principle of critique itself into the foundation of the theory. And this principle is that of the reason of justifying beings like ourselves.

[48] I analyze this dynamic in the context of social conflicts over toleration in Forst, *Toleration in Conflict* (n. 31).

2

Noumenal Power

1. In political and social philosophy, we speak about power all the time.[1] Yet the meaning of this important concept is rarely made explicit, especially in the context of normative discussions.[2] But, as with many other concepts, once one examines it more closely, fundamental questions arise, such as whether a power relation is necessarily a relation of subordination and domination, a view that makes it difficult to identify legitimate forms of the exercise of power. To contribute to conceptual as well as normative clarification, in what follows I suggest a novel way to conceive of power. I argue that we only understand what power is and how it is exercised once we understand its essentially *noumenal* nature. On that basis, I defend a normatively neutral notion of power that enables us to distinguish more particular forms of power, such as rule, coercion, and domination. The analysis aims to prepare the way for a critical theory of power.

[1] A first version of this chapter was prepared as a paper for a panel on power organized by Casiano Hacker-Cordón at the annual meeting of the American Political Science Association in Washington in September 2010. I am grateful to C. Hacker-Cordón and Frank Lovett for their comments on that occasion. I also presented versions of the paper at the New School for Social Research in New York, the Humboldt University in Berlin, the Friedrich-Schiller-Universität Jena, the Philosophy and Social Science Conference in Prague, the Université de Strasbourg, the University of Southampton, the Lichtenberg-Kolleg in Göttingen, and the Sorbonne. I am indebted to the discussions at these events and many more conversations with colleagues. For helpful recommendations and critique I wish to thank in particular Bruce Ackerman, Amy Allen, Chris Armstrong, Albena Azmanova, Richard Bernstein, Thomas Biebricher, Jean Cohen, Maeve Cooke, Erin Cooper, Ciaran Cronin, Eva Erman, Alessandro Ferrara, Estelle Ferrarese, Nancy Fraser, Dorothea Gädeke, Pablo Gilabert, Klaus Günther, Mark Haugaard, Malte Ibsen, Rahel Jaeggi, Jane Mansbridge, Christoph Möllers, Dmitri Nikulin, David Owen, Paul Patton, Hartmut Rosa, Martin Saar, Bill Scheuerman, Ian Shapiro, Holmer Steinfath, David Strecker, James Tully, Martin van Gelderen, Lea Ypi, Eli Zaretsky, and Michael Zürn. The paper appeared in the *Journal of Political Philosophy* (23/2 (2015): 111–27) and I am grateful to three anonymous reviewers for their comments. For the present volume, the article has been slightly edited.

[2] There are of course exceptions, such as Philip Pettit's work—see his recent book *On the People's Terms* (Cambridge University Press 2012)—as well as Ian Shapiro's writings, in particular *Democratic Justice* (Yale University Press 1999) and *The Real World of Democratic Theory* (Princeton University Press 2011). The work of Iris Young also remains essential in this context, especially *Justice and the Politics of Difference* (Princeton University Press 1990) and *Responsibility for Justice* (Oxford University Press 2011). An important contribution is also Frank Lovett, *A General Theory of Domination and Justice* (Oxford University Press 2010). I discuss the difference between my discourse-theoretical and Pettit's neo-republican conception of domination in my "A Kantian Republican Conception of Justice as Non-Domination," in Andreas Niederberger and Philipp Schink (eds.), *Republican Democracy* (Edinburgh University Press 2013) 154–68 and Rainer Forst, "Transnational Justice and Non-Domination: A Discourse-Theoretical Approach," ch. 10 in this volume.

The title "noumenal power" might suggest that I am going to speak about a certain form of power in the world of ideas or of thought, and that this will be far removed from the reality of power as a social or institutional phenomenon. In Joseph Nye's words, one might assume that I have only the "soft power" of persuasion in mind and not the "hard power" of coercion.[3] Real and hard power, a "realist" might say, is about the empirical world, it is made of material stuff, like political positions, monetary means or, ultimately, military instruments of force.

However, this would be a misunderstanding. For I want to claim that the *real* and *general* phenomenon of power is to be found in the noumenal realm, or better—to avoid misunderstandings about Platonic ideas or a Kantian metaphysics of "things in themselves"—in the "space of reasons," to borrow Wilfrid Sellars's famous phrase, understood as the realm of justifications. Here is what Sellars says: "The essential point is that in characterizing an episode or a state as that of *knowing*, we are not giving an empirical description of that episode or state; we are placing it in the logical space of reasons, of justifying and being able to justify what one says."[4] To adapt this insight to my purposes, I suggest that the essential point about power is that, in characterizing a situation as an exercise of power, we do not merely give an empirical description of a state of affairs or a social relation; we also, and primarily, have to place it in the space of reasons, or the normative space of freedom and action.[5] Power is not only exercised by and over free agents; it is also the term for what is going on when someone acts for certain reasons for which others are responsible—that is, reasons that he or she would not otherwise have had and that still characterize him or her as an agent for whom alternative ways of acting remain open, although possibly fewer than before (but the number of options may also have increased). To be a subject of power is to be moved by reasons that others have given me and that motivate me to think or act in a certain way intended by the reason-giver. Hence, while in political philosophy we usually inquire into the *justification of power*, in what follows I am interested in the *power of justifications.*

It is important to note that my use of the term "justification" in the following will be primarily descriptive. When I speak of justifications as "moving" persons through "acceptance," I do not imply that they are "acceptable" from a critical perspective. Likewise, my analysis is a cognitivist one; but that does not mean that the reasons and beliefs that I refer to are reflexively constructed or tested. Ideological justifications also count as justifications when it comes to understanding how power works. The noumenal space that I think is relevant here is an "impure" space that includes what persons see as justified, for good *or* bad reasons.[6] We need criteria to distinguish between good and bad justifications, but the general concept of power itself does not contain these criteria.

[3] Joseph S. Nye, Jr., *The Future of Power* (Public Affairs 2011) pt. 1.

[4] Wilfrid Sellars, *Empiricism and the Philosophy of Mind*, ed. Robert Brandom (Harvard University Press 1997) 76.

[5] On the idea of such a normative space see Robert Brandom, "Freedom and Constraint by Norms," *American Philosophical Quarterly* 16 (1979): 187–96, as well as Robert Brandom, *Reason in Philosophy: Animating Ideas* (Harvard University Press 2009) chs. 1 and 2.

[6] This is discussed in Amy Allen, Rainer Forst, and Mark Haugaard, "Power and Reason, Justice and Domination: a Conversation," *Journal of Political Power* 7 (2014): 7–33.

2. Where it is addressed, the concept of power is heavily contested and there is a huge panorama of strikingly different views and definitions of power in the literature—if we compare, for example, Weberian, Foucauldian, Habermasian, or Arendtian approaches. Steven Lukes in his important discussion argued that power is an "essentially contested" concept, for it is irreducibly evaluative and is thus a matter of political debate. Every definition of power, Lukes argues, has some normative notion of social relations and non-dominated interests in mind—including his own "radical view."[7] But here I would like to take issue with Lukes; for, while I agree that his definition is a normative and contestable one, I think a better definition is available that avoids essential contestation.

Here is Lukes's original definition: "A exercises power over B when A affects B in a manner contrary to B's interests."[8] Yet, in line with his own subsequently revised view, I believe that this is much closer to a definition of *domination*, which is "only one species of power," as Lukes now acknowledges.[9] What his analysis revealed were the many ways of exercising power as the "imposition of internal constraints" that lead to the acceptance of certain forms of domination—thereby neglecting "the manifold ways in which power over others can be productive, transformative, authoritative and compatible with dignity."[10] Thus, we need a definition of power that is broader than the notion of domination.

Most definitions of the concept of power either explain it as a negative phenomenon, as a form of domination; or, failing that, they at least follow Max Weber's lead in using a conflictual model. Weber famously defined power as "the probability that one actor within a social relationship will be in a position to carry out his own will despite resistance, regardless of the basis on which this probability rests."[11] Weber took this notion to be "sociologically amorphous" and preferred the more precise notion of *Herrschaft*, by which he meant the possibility that an order is being followed by a defined set of persons.[12] Yet while an imposition of the will in a given conflict of wills is clearly an exercise of power, it need not serve as the paradigm for power; it is in fact closer to a certain form of domination. Power is a more inclusive concept that can also refer to the formation of and rule by a common will.

Approaches which focus on the exercise of power as an imposition of will, or as constraining others by external or internal means, often have equally one-sided positive counterparts that focus on communicative forms of power. An example is Hannah Arendt's conception of power as "acting in concert," as being based on free and equal consent, and hence as different from violence or force.[13] Arendt's insights are important, but the conceptual contrast she draws is too stark; we should reserve

[7] Steven Lukes, *Power: A Radical View* (2nd edn., Palgrave 2005) 29 ff. and 123 ff.

[8] ibid 30. [9] ibid 12. [10] ibid 109.

[11] Max Weber, *Economy and Society*, ed. and trans. Guenther Roth and Claus Wittich (University of California Press 1978) 53.

[12] It is unfortunate that *Herrschaft*—which means rule—is usually translated as "domination," which corresponds to the German *Beherrschung*. To identify rule with domination in this way would seem to imply that the exercise of power is invariably a matter of domination, thus ruling out the possibility that legitimate rule is also an exercise of power (which is, of course, what Weber meant).

[13] Hannah Arendt, *Crises of the Republic* (Harvest Books 1972) 143 and 140.

the concept of power neither for a negative nor for a purely positive phenomenon. Power can be either constraining or liberating.[14]

The most important insight of Arendt's that needs to be preserved for a conception of noumenal power is derived from her analysis of revolutionary events. Here one can see that the power of a government is not reducible to the means of institutional, or ultimately military, power at its disposal; for there may come a time when people no longer obey the law or fear the tanks, and when those who drive the tanks are no longer willing to obey orders to shoot at people in the street. What reasons people have to act in a certain way at that precise moment is a complicated issue. But any analysis of power must leave room for a distinction between the cases where you welcome a tank as liberating, where you fear it, and where you see it as an enemy but nonetheless no longer fear it. In the latter case, the tank can still be a means of force and an objective threat when viewed from an observer's perspective, but it has lost its power over you. It has physical force over you, but no longer any human, normative power to guide your thoughts. So if we want to explain whether it has power over others or not, we need to understand what goes on in the heads of those who are subjected to its power or who have freed themselves from it—and that is where the noumenal realm of power lies. Noumenal power is thus, to reiterate, not a separate form of power alongside threats of force; rather, it is the very core of such threats as exercises of power. The latter can be successful only if they have the intended mental effects.

3. In order to understand how an exercise of power moves persons, we need a cognitive account of power that is neutral with regard to its positive or negative evaluation. Let us begin by defining power as *the capacity of A to motivate B to think or do something that B would otherwise not have thought or done.*[15] Power exists as the capacity ("power to") to be socially effective in this way—that is, to "have" power—which leads to power as being *exercised* over others ("power over"), where it is open whether this is done for (and by using) good or bad reasons and whether it is done for the sake of or contrary to B's interests—and by what means.[16] The means in question can be

[14] For a very clear discussion of the ethical neutrality of the concept of power see Robert E. Goodin, *Manipulatory Politics* (Yale University Press 1980) 1–7.

[15] The definition has affinities with the "formal definition of power" suggested by Robert A. Dahl, "The Concept of Power," *Behavioral Science* 2 (1957): 201–15, at 202 ff.: "A has power over B to the extent that he can get B to do something that B would not otherwise do." In his analysis of the use of a certain "base" of power, such as institutional positions or resources, as a means of exercising power, Dahl focuses on the extent or "scope" of a change in the behavior of others and does not thematize, as I do, the mode of any such exercise of power—that is, that it involves a change in the space of justifications for a person or group of persons.

[16] Since I do not think that "power over" should be defined negatively as "the ability of an actor or set of actors to constrain the choices available to another actor or set of actors," as Amy Allen does in her book *The Power of Feminist Theory: Domination, Resistance, Solidarity* (Westview 1999) 123, I do not see any need to introduce the notion of "power with" as the "ability of a collectivity to act together for the attainment of an agreed-upon end or series of ends" (at 127) either. This ability is a case of a collective "power to," generated through consent and common aims, whereas the attainment of the end, if achieved in political conflict, requires a form of "power over." Democratic rule (sometimes also defined as "power with"), as I will explain below, is a form of "power over" based on generally justified norms. For further discussion see Allen, Forst, and Haugaard, "Power and Reason, Justice and Domination: a Conversation" (n. 6).

a "powerful" speech, a well-founded recommendation, an ideological description of the world, a seduction, an order that is accepted, or a threat that is perceived as real. All of these are exercises of noumenal power. A threat gives the person who is threatened a reason to do something; but as long as a relation of power exists, at least one alternative way of acting is open to the person threatened. Otherwise this person would be a mere object, like a stone or a tree that is being moved. Thus, a case of pure force, where A moves B purely by physical means, by handcuffing him or her and carrying him or her away, is no longer an exercise of power, for the handcuffed person doesn't "do" anything; rather, something "is done" to him or her. Thus, the above definition no longer applies. At that point, power as a relation between agents turns into brute physical force and violence, and the noumenal character vanishes. The person moved by sheer force is thus completely under the control of the other, as a mere physical object, and so, seen in isolation from noumenal-social contexts, is no longer an agent in the relevant sense. But such isolation is artificial, for most of the time an exercise of physical force is meant to have a noumenal effect either on the person subjected to it (e.g., instilling fear) or on others who witness what is going on (e.g., intimidating them).

In contrast to the use of physical force or violence, power rests on recognition. This is, to repeat, not necessarily a reflexive or consensual form of recognition, for the threat that is perceived as real is, at that very moment, also recognized and gives one a reason for action as intended by A—in that sense, to point a gun at someone is to "give" him or her a reason. But if, as sometimes happens, the threat by the blackmailer or the kidnapper is no longer taken seriously, then their power disappears. They can still use brute force and kill the kidnapped person, but that is rather a sign of having lost power (either over those who are not willing to pay or over the kidnapped person, who refuses to recognize the kidnapper as dominant and in turn threatens or ridicules him or her). The exercise and effects of power are based on the recognition of a reason—or better, and more often, of various reasons—to act differently than one would have acted without that reason. This recognition rests on seeing a "good enough" reason to act; it means that you see a *justification* for changing how you were going to act. Power rests on recognized, accepted justifications—some good, some bad, some in between. A threat (or a gun) can be seen as such a justification, as can a good argument. But power exists only when there is such acceptance.

Even though the kinds of acceptance sufficient for subjection to power all have a cognitive character, there is a spectrum of kinds of acceptance ranging from explicit acceptance based on critical reflection and evaluation, through cases where one feels "forced" to accept a certain argument, although one would prefer not to, or cases where one is forced to accept a threat or an order by a superior as a reason for compliance, up to, finally, cases where one accepts certain justifications almost blindly without further question—for example, by conforming to social meanings of what "befits" a woman, a "decent" or "deviant" person or someone who is supposed to play a certain social role as demanded by tradition. All of these forms of being moved by justifications are "noumenal" in the relevant sense insofar as they involve a certain relation in the space of justifications. But the cognitive and normative character and quality of these justifications varies greatly. An analysis (and critique) of power must reconstruct these different modes and their possible combinations in a given social situation. As the major theorists of power like Machiavelli knew, it is useful to combine some of these modes when it comes to generating power and support for a particular kind of rule.[17]

Thus the phenomenon of power is noumenal in nature: *to have and to exercise power means to be able—in different degrees—to influence, use, determine, occupy, or even seal off the space of reasons for others.*[18] This can occur in the context of a single event, such as a powerful speech or an act of deceit, or of a sequence of events or in a general social situation or structure in which certain social relations are regarded as justified, whether reflexively or not, so that a social order comes to be accepted as an *order of justification.* Relations and orders of power are relations and orders of justification; and power arises and persists where justifications or social relations arise and persist, where they are integrated into certain *narratives of justification.*[19] In the light of such narratives, social relations and institutions and certain ways of thinking and acting appear as justified and legitimate, possibly also as natural or in accordance with God's will. These can be relations of subordination or of equality, whether political or personal, and the corresponding justifications can be well founded and collectively shared with good reasons; alternatively, they can be merely "overlapping," or they can be distorted and ideological—that is, they can justify a social situation of asymmetry and subordination with bad reasons that could not be shared among free and equal justificatory agents in a practice of justification free from such asymmetry and distortion.[20] Such a notion of ideology does not necessarily involve a conception of "objective" or "true interests"; all it implies, normatively speaking, is a *right to justification* of social and political relations between free and equal persons.[21] This right implies that all those who are subjected to a normative order should be its co-authors as equal participants and normative authorities in adequate justificatory practices that critically reflect on and constitute that order. In the present context, this means that those subjected to forms of power have the

[17] See especially Niccolò Machiavelli, *The Prince*, ed. and trans. Quentin Skinner and Russell Price (Cambridge University Press 1988) ch. 17.

[18] I leave the issue of having power over oneself undiscussed.

[19] For the notions of orders or narratives of justification see Rainer Forst and Klaus Günther, "Die Herausbildung normativer Ordnungen," in Rainer Forst and Klaus Günther (eds.), *Die Herausbildung normativer Ordnungen: Interdisziplinäre Perspektiven* (Campus 2011) 11–30, and Rainer Forst, "On the Concept of a Justification Narrative," ch. 3 in this volume.

[20] Here I am in agreement with the central insight of Jürgen Habermas's version of critical theory. See especially Jürgen Habermas, *The Theory of Communicative Action*, trans. Thomas McCarthy, 2 vols. (Beacon 1984 and 1987).

[21] I discuss the moral foundations and political implications of this right in Rainer Forst, *The Right to Justification: Elements of a Constructivist Theory of Justice*, trans. Jeffrey Flynn (Columbia University Press 2012), and Rainer Forst, *Justification and Critique: Towards a Critical Theory of Politics*, trans. Ciaran Cronin (Polity 2014). In an historical perspective, I discuss the dynamic of justification in Rainer Forst, *Toleration in Conflict: Past and Present*, trans. Ciaran Cronin (Cambridge University Press 2013). The relation between power and toleration is the main topic of Wendy Brown and Rainer Forst, *The Power of Tolerance: A Debate* (Columbia University Press 2014).

right and the requisite "normative powers"[22] (i.e., social and institutional discursive power) to make implicit or "tacit" justifications explicit, to question given justifications (as well as dominant or hegemonic ways to construct justifications),[23] to reject faulty ones, and to construct better ones, as well as to demand the existence of proper practices and institutions of justification in the first place. This is the first demand of justice of those subjected to a normative order: to have standing as equal normative authorities within such an order.

In general, an account of power need not accord a central role to the notion of interests, be it the interests of the power-holders or of those who are subject to power. An account of reasons for beliefs is better suited to explaining why people act in a certain way and how power functions. Religion, for example, is a very powerful motivating force in many societies and for many people. Religiously based reasons are often combined with other considerations and they often lead people to act in certain ways and to see social relations as more or less justified; but it is not always clear what kinds of "interests" someone pursues when he or she is motivated by religion. In any case, reasons explain beliefs, and beliefs explain interests and actions; thus the deeper one digs, the more one needs to inquire into people's reasons. This is the basic level of explanation of their actions as *their* actions—as what they see as justified. Justifications are basic, not interests or desires.[24]

A noumenal account of power relations is more "realistic" than theories which locate power in material or physical means, be it money or weapons. For, on the one hand, it explains all those forms of power that cannot be explained by recourse to such means—the power of speech, of (again, good or bad) arguments, of seduction, of love, of "acting in concert," of commitments, of morality, of personal aims, and so forth. More importantly, on the other hand, it also explains the power of such means, since money only motivates those who see its use as being justified in general and in a particular case, and who have aims which make money necessary; and weapons, as I explained above, only serve their function if they are seen as reason-giving.[25] If they are not, one can still use them to shoot, but then power is transformed into physical force, and the real intention for using them—being recognized as superior

[22] James Bohman, *Democracy across Borders: From Demos to Demoi* (MIT Press 2007) 5 and *passim*, uses this term for the capacity of persons or groups or states to influence their legal and political standing in a political system to which they are subject.

[23] For a discussion of the aspects of critique (and critical theory) relevant here see Rainer Forst, *Justice, Democracy and the Right to Justification: Rainer Forst in Dialogue* (Bloomsbury 2014), including in particular in that volume: Amy Allen, "The Power of Justification," 65–86; Kevin Olson, "Complexities of Political Discourse: Class, Power and the Linguistic Turn," 87–102; Anthony Simon Laden, "The Practice of Equality," 103–26; and my reply "Justifying Justification: Reply to My Critics," 178–205.

[24] From the perspective of a particular social theory, this is stressed by Luc Boltanski and Laurent Thévenot, *On Justification: Economies of Worth*, trans. Catherine Porter (Princeton University Press 2006). From a philosophical point of view, compare Thomas Scanlon, *Being Realistic About Reasons* (Oxford University Press 2014).

[25] Thus, it is not the case that political power must ultimately be backed by means of sanctions and force, as many argue. See e.g. Talcott Parsons, "Power and the Social System," in Steven Lukes (ed.), *Power* (New York University Press 1986) 94–143, and John Searle, *Making the Social World: The Structure of Human Civilization* (Oxford University Press 2010) 163. In his general analysis of various forms of power, however, Searle stresses its reasons-based character.

and threatening—may remain unrealized. Punishment, by using violence, is often a sign of the failure of power, not of its successful exercise.

4. An important test of the realism of the theory of noumenal power is whether it can explain the power of "structures," be it general social structures or more particular organizational structures within, say, a university or a school. Every social order consists of such structures, and in modern societies they are highly differentiated and complex, if one thinks, for example, of the components of an economic structure, from a property regime to a certain organization of production and distribution of goods through a (more or less regulated) market, and so forth. It is often assumed that such structures causally determine the actions of those who "function" within them and are subject to the "structural forces" (or even the "structural violence") of institutionalized social systems. Thus, Habermas analyses the development of such systems in terms of the establishment of social spheres of strategic or instrumental, rather than communicative, action that work through the non-discursive media of money and power.[26] The subsystems of the modern economy and the administrative state increasingly leave the normative contexts of the communicative lifeworld behind and "congeal into the 'second nature' of a norm-free sociality that can appear as something in the objective world, as an *objectified* context of life."[27]

If we inquire further into what this process of objectification involves, the role that noumenal power plays within social structures of that sort becomes apparent and we arrive at a different picture from the one presented by Habermas. A "second nature" of acting (or "functioning") within certain structures presupposes acceptance of the rules of these structures, as well as of certain justifications offered for them, such as ideas about property, cooperation, or efficiency, but also notions of fairness, desert, and the like (and again, it must be added that such acceptance need not be based on critical reflection but can also be of an ideological kind). Thus, such structures are not "norm-free";[28] rather, the norms and justifications they rest on allow for certain forms of strategic action that disregard traditional and ethical norms, potentially "colonizing" the lifeworld (in line with Habermas's analysis).

We can distinguish four aspects of noumenal power when it comes to social structures:

(1) Every social order in general, and every social subsystem in particular, is based on a certain understanding of its purpose, aims, and rules—in short, it is a normative order as an *order of justification*. An economy rests on very general ideas of value, labor, nature, and productivity, but also on notions of fair exchange, for example, and as a result it is open to criticism in how it interprets and realizes such values or norms.[29] Thus there are certain justification narratives on which such an order

[26] Jürgen Habermas, *Theory of Communicative Action*, vol. 2, (n. 20) 183 and 196.

[27] ibid 173.

[28] See Axel Honneth and Hans Joas (eds.), *Communicative Action: Essays on Jürgen Habermas's The Theory of Communicative Action* (MIT Press 1991).

[29] One such model of immanent critique can be found in Axel Honneth, *Freedom's Right: The Social Foundations of Democratic Life*, trans. Joseph Ganahl (Columbia University Press 2014) ch. 3, sect. 2.

or system is founded. One could think here of the great reconstructions of such narratives by social theory, such as Max Weber's analysis of the contribution of a Protestant ethic to the development of the spirit of capitalism. However, a modern economy is not based on a single grand narrative alone but on many others as well; and even though they form an order as part of a more comprehensive social order, there are many possible tensions and contradictions between its components, such as ideas of fairness of opportunity, on the one hand, and libertarian freedom, on the other, or the idea of personal desert, to name but a few.[30] So, even though a social structure can be reduced neither to its narrative foundations nor to a narrow set of such justifications, it does rest on such foundations.

(2) Structures that are accepted on the basis of such narratives and justifications often find their main support in the idea that, despite tensions in their justificatory basis and despite perceived shortcomings, there is no available alternative to them. So these structures not only rely on certain noumenal power constellations; they also *produce and reproduce* such constellations by affirming them and suggesting that how they function is "natural," so that a "second nature" can develop. Through their everyday workings, these structures limit what can be imagined as possible and—*pace* Habermas—themselves attain a certain lifeworld status as the way things are and will be. The normative power of the factual is reproduced by these structures, and it is a form of noumenal power—namely, justification through everyday practice and socialization into a certain frame of mind.

(3) In this way, structures that rest on and reproduce noumenal power have a certain *influence* over persons that appears to be a form of power. Within a patriarchal structure, for example, women may conform to patriarchal rules even where the patriarch leaves things implicit or is absent, or no longer tries to dominate. That means that the noumenal power structure that supports social power relations is still in place, with the result that a certain order of action is upheld. It is, however, more appropriate to speak of "influence" rather than "power" in cases where power is not intentionally exercised by persons over others. Structures do not "exercise" power as persons do; rather, they rely on and provide opportunities for exercising it.

(4) This brings us to the way in which power is *exercised within* structures. Given that the essential power of such structures is of a noumenal kind, defining values, norms and rules and social positions, such power structures enable persons with sufficient *noumenal capital*[31] in the appropriate sphere—such as a priest, an officer, or an entrepreneur—to use their social recognition and standing[32] within the structure as a *resource* to exercise power over others who duly follow an admonition, obey an order, or accept an employment contract and its implications. In this way, structures serve as important background resources for the exercise of power, because within

[30] See Boltanski and Thévenot, *On Justification* (n. 24).

[31] This concept is broader than the related one of "symbolic capital" coined by Pierre Bourdieu, since it applies to all forms of power, including "material" ones. See Pierre Bourdieu, *Practical Reason: On the Theory of Action*, trans. Randall Johnson (Stanford University Press 1998).

[32] This is also the point where a discursive notion of *authority* can be developed: having authority means having a certain standing within a normative order, such that one disposes over particular

them persons have a power status that is perceived as implying the justifications that lead others to do certain things. Normative roles, offices, and functions are noumenal power statuses that facilitate the exercise of certain forms of power over others by "unburdening" social action within such institutional spheres from the explicit requirement of justification, so that justification can be taken as a given. However, the question of justification can reappear as soon as someone is seen to overstep the limits of his or her function or role.

To illustrate the four aspects of noumenal power within social structures—the aspects of grounding, reproduction, influence, and resource—a brief look at Marx's analysis of the fetish character of commodities is helpful. In his critique of social alienation, Marx tries to show how a certain "mystical"[33] idea of commodities dominates the noumenal realm of the capitalist economy and transforms social relations into relations between things, thereby veiling the truth of social relations and establishing a false justification narrative for them. Furthermore, this narrative makes it impossible to gain collective control over the system of production and distribution:

> The value character of the products of labour becomes firmly established only when they act as magnitudes of value. These magnitudes vary continually, independently of the will, foreknowledge and actions of the exchangers. Their own movement within society has for them the form of a movement made by things, and these things, far from being under their control, in fact control them.[34]

Founded on a particular notion of value, the capitalist economy produces a second nature of persons who see each other as market participants and are held captive by certain conceptions of commodity, labor, and exchange. The latter form a justification complex that influences and controls people's lives and, ultimately, enables some to exploit others and leads those exploited to accept their position as natural or unavoidable. Therefore, a critique of that kind of political economy must begin in the noumenal realm by describing social life differently and dispelling the "whole mystery of commodities, all the magic and necromancy that surrounds the products of labour on the basis of commodity production . . ."[35] Any social structure can thus only be as firm as its justifications are firmly grounded—and a critique of power has to target the core of these justifications.[36]

The real site of power struggles, as all of the great theoreticians (and practitioners) of power recognized, is the discursive realm—the realm where justifications are formed and reformed, questioned, tested, and possibly sealed off or reified. It is the site where interests and preferences are formed, and where ideological acceptance of subordination finds its hegemonic justification, as Gramsci emphasized and as

noumenal capital with regard to certain areas of social life—e.g., in exercising the function or role of a teacher or a judge.

[33] Karl Marx, *Capital: A Critique of Political Economy*, vol. I trans. Ben Fowkes (Penguin Books 1990) ch. 1, sect. 4, 164.

[34] ibid 167–8. [35] ibid 169.

[36] On the role of the concept of justice in this context see Forst, "Justice after Marx," ch. 7 in this volume.

Lukes addressed with his third dimension of power.[37] But we need not assume that such acceptance is based on only one narrative, and we need not assume that such a formation is without "cracks," that is, that it is accepted without doubt or partial resistance. Also, in most cases the social situation cannot be reduced to a single set of antagonistic class interests;[38] an analysis of power can allow for more social and discursive pluralism of reasons, interests and—often temporary—social alliances.

5. There are important parallels and differences between a theory of noumenal power and Michel Foucault's theory of discursive power. Parallels consist in his attempt to define power as a general social phenomenon that is not modeled on the paradigm of domination and in his emphasis on power as operating on free subjects,[39] his insight that power can be productive as well as disciplining, and, most of all, that power works by way of truth regimes, that is, in the cognitive realm:

> What makes power hold good, what makes it accepted, is simply the fact that it doesn't only weigh on us as a force that says no, but that it traverses and produces things, it induces pleasure, forms knowledge, produces discourse.[40]

However, by focusing on large-scale truth regimes (*epistemes*) or constellations of power (*dispositifs*), Foucault had a (neo-, rather than post-structuralist) tendency to describe such regimes as much more homogeneous than they in fact are. In any given historical epoch, a mixture of religious, scientific, and institutional practices constitutes certain forms of "subjectivation"; but every such form comes in a number of versions and is reproduced in multiple ways in the minds of subjects that leave much room for variation—and critique.[41] Furthermore, despite many avowals to the contrary, Foucault did favor a negative view of power as disciplining and as governing subjects—as structuring, and thereby also limiting, possibilities of thought and action, and thus (often) prompting reactions of resistance:

> This form of power that operates directly on everyday life and categorizes individuals, designates them by their identity, assigns them their individuality, imposes a law of truth on them that they must recognize and others have to recognize in them. It is a form of power that turns individuals into subjects.[42]

[37] Lukes, *Power* (n. 7) 143f., defines the third dimension as the "capacity to secure compliance to domination through the shaping of beliefs and desires, by imposing internal constraints under historically changing circumstances."

[38] As has been shown by feminist criticism; see Nancy Fraser, *Fortunes of Feminism: From State-Managed Capitalism to Neoliberal Crisis* (Verso 2013).

[39] "Power is exercised only over free subjects, and only insofar as they are 'free'." Michel Foucault, "The Subject and Power," in Michel Foucault, *Power*, ed. James Faubion, trans. Robert Hurley *et al.*, *Essential Works* (New Press 2002) vol. 3, 342.

[40] Michel Foucault, "Truth and Power," interview with Alessandro Fontana and Pasquale Pasquino, in Michel Foucault, *Power/Knowledge: Selected Interviews and Other Writings 1972–1977*, ed. Colin Gordon (Pantheon 1980) 119. See also Michel Foucault, *The History of Sexuality*, vol. I, trans. Robert Hurley (Vintage 1978) pt. 4. Compare also the analysis of "pastoral power" in "The Subject and Power" (n. 39) 333: "Finally, this form of power cannot be exercised without knowing the inside of people's minds, without exploring their souls, without making them reveal their innermost secrets. It implies knowledge of the conscience and an ability to direct it."

[41] This is discussed by Wendy Brown and myself in Brown and Forst, *The Power of Tolerance* (n. 21).

[42] Foucault, "The Subject and Power" (n. 39) 331 (translation amended).

Power forms the self-image of the subject, but it remains an "imposition." But why, we may ask, does this have to be the case? Why not think of forms of power that *empower* and ground a different practice of freedom that is powerful because it leaves the definition of freedom up to the individuals themselves, a freedom that is not "free from power" but is more free from given forms of subordination and normalization? This is very much in line with important arguments of the later Foucault, although he did not offer a comprehensive theoretical account of the forms of "counter-power" he envisioned, usually referring to them as an "ethos" of critique.[43]

There is another important point that needs to be made with respect to Foucault. Whereas his stress on the linkage between power and truth makes a cognitivist analysis of power necessary—as an analysis of the justifications that are accepted for ordering society and "forming" subjects—his emphasis on the discipline of the body as the site of subjectivation may speak against a cognitivist approach. Foucault showed, according to some interpreters, how power "imprints" itself "directly on the bodies and affective investments" of subjects.[44] But that would be an incorrect conclusion to draw. For, as Foucault pointed out in his genealogy of sexuality, for example, the body is "normalized" only through the adoption of certain categorizations and "truths" about the "inner" self. Thus, the body should not be seen as a reality beyond justification, as on a neo-Cartesian or Freudian conception, for example; rather, it is the result of a certain order in the realm of social justifications that makes persons think *and* feel about themselves in a certain way. Viewed from this perspective, bodies (and feelings) are not separate, non-cognitive entities with a truth of their own. They are products of discursive power. Otherwise the critical approach of genealogy[45] favored by Foucault would not be appropriate, since it reconstructs the history of subject-formation in order to understand and reject the self-images and truth-constructions that have been imposed on "docile" subjects: "We have to promote new kinds of subjectivity through the refusal of this kind of individuality that has been imposed on us for several centuries."[46]

6. So how should the analysis of power relations proceed? It needs to operate on at least two levels: first, it should provide a discursive analysis of the dominant or possibly hegemonic justifications for certain forms of thought and action that eventually materialize into a social order as an order of justification; and, second, it should identify the power positions within a society: Who has which possibilities to influence

[43] See especially Michel Foucault, "What is Enlightenment?" in *The Foucault Reader*, ed. Paul Rabinow (Pantheon, 1984) 32–50. Also, Foucault's later work on ancient ethical practice has to be seen in this light. See Paul Patton, "Foucault's Subject of Power," *Political Theory Newsletter* 6 (1994): 60–71. For an elaboration of an ethos of freedom along Foucauldian lines see James Tully, *Public Philosophy in a New Key*, vol. 1 (Cambridge University Press 2008).

[44] Thus Amy Allen in Allen, Forst, and Haugaard, "Power and Reason, Justice and Domination" (n. 6) 17.

[45] For an analysis of that method see Martin Saar, *Genealogie als Kritik* (Campus 2007) and David Owen, "Criticism and Captivity: On Genealogy and Critical Theory," *European Journal of Philosophy* 10 (2002): 216–30.

[46] Foucault, "The Subject and Power" (n. 39) 336.

the dominant order of justification? What is the current arrangement of the *relations of justification* within various social spheres and in political life generally?[47]

In order to perform such an analysis, we need to keep in mind the different degrees of the exercise of noumenal power that I referred to above. We call *power* generally the capacity of A to influence the space of reasons for B and/or C (etc.) such that they think and act in ways they would not have without the interference by A; moreover, the move by A must have a motivating force for B and/or C (etc.) that corresponds to A's intentions and is not just a side effect (i.e., a form of influence). Such power can be the power of a good or a bad teacher, it can be the power of a liberating revolutionary or a dictator who convinces or seduces the masses, and it can be the power of a kidnapper whose threat is taken seriously. The concept of power itself determines neither the evaluation nor the means used to move someone to think or to do something.[48]

Rule I call a form of power where the power-holder not only uses his or her capacity to decisively influence the space of justifications for others, but where certain comprehensive (religious, metaphysical, historical, or moral) justifications (and usually a mixture thereof) determine the space of reasons within which social or political relations are being framed—relations which form a structured, durable, and stable social order of action and justification. Again, this rule can be well justified or it can rest on bad justifications (that are perceived as good by those who are governed). Democratic rule exists where those subject to a normative order are at the same time the normative authorities who co-determine this order through democratic justification procedures. Thus, their standing as justificatory equals is secured by the rights and institutions of a democratic political order. Democratic power is exercised through the rule of reciprocally and generally justifiable reasons when it comes to basic questions of justice.[49] Further political issues are decided through fundamentally just (and legitimate) justificatory procedures in which all subjected can participate as justificatory equals.

In cases of unjustifiable asymmetrical social relations which rest on a closing off of the space of justifications such that these relations appear as legitimate, natural, God-given, or in any way unalterable and leave hardly any alternative for those who are subjected, we encounter forms of *domination.* These are backed by a combination of one-sided, hegemonic justifications and do not give those who are subjected the possibility of or, normatively speaking, the right to reciprocal or general justification and critique. The realm of reasons is sealed off, either because the situation of domination is (more or less) accepted as legitimate or because it is backed by serious threats. This means that *coercion* or *force* looms in the background—that is, forms of power which increasingly deny the right to contestation and justification and

[47] For the idea of relations of justification see my *Justification and Critique* (n. 21) especially 1–13.

[48] An important further case of the exercise of power should be mentioned here, namely influencing the space of reasons of someone by withholding important information with the aim of steering him or her in a particular direction. This is a form of interference that is included in my definition. I am grateful to Pablo Gilabert and to an anonymous reviewer for alerting me to this case.

[49] See Forst, *The Right to Justification* (n. 21) ch. 7.

severely restrict the space of reasons. Thus, a discourse-theoretical notion of (non-) domination, unlike a neo-republican version, does not focus on the robustness of the protection of secured spheres of individual freedom of choice.[50] Instead, it focuses on the normative standing of persons as justificatory equals and normative authorities within a political and social order understood as an order of justification. Political domination has two important dimensions: the rule by unjustifiable norms and, reflexively speaking, the lack of appropriate discursive arenas and institutional structures of justification to contest given justifications and discursively to construct generally and reciprocally acceptable justifications that lead to authoritative norms.

We encounter *violence*, finally, where the exchange of justifications is denied entirely and the space of reasons is supplanted by means of sheer physical force.[51] When this happens, a relation of noumenal power turns into a relation of overwhelming physical facticity: the person subjected to violence is not made to do something any longer; he or she is a mere object. At that moment, power as a normative force moving an even minimally free agent fades away; it might reappear when those subjected to violence begin to act as the power-wielder wills, either out of fear or because they are traumatized, but in any case no longer as mere physical objects.[52] Power is a way of binding others through reasons; it breaks down when the other is treated as a mere "thing" and no longer as an agent of justification whose compliance rests on some form of recognition. Thus we have to analyze power relations along a spectrum extending from its exercise through the justificatory quality of reasons shared among deliberating persons, at one end, to the limiting case of its exercise by way of physical force, at the other, which in its extreme form lies outside of the realm of power, being instead a reflection of the lack of power.[53] The reality of the exercise of power usually falls somewhere in between, and the main object of analysis is the noumenal character of the social relations or events in question: What are the justifications that move persons?

To analyze power relations, we thus need to develop a method of analysis in the two dimensions named above: the level of discourse and its specific content (dominant reasons and narratives of justification) and the different positions and normative powers (or "noumenal capital") of agents with respect to their ability to generate and use discursive power (status, competence, institutional structures, etc.).[54] This is a complicated matter for a number of reasons. First, the reasons why certain rules or normative orders are accepted and followed are most often plural and cannot be subsumed under just one category of reasons. Think, for example, of the variety

[50] See Pettit, *On the People's Terms* (n. 2) ch. 1. I elaborate on this in my "A Kantian Republican Conception of Justice as Non-Domination" (n. 2) and in "Transnational Justice and Non-Domination: A Discourse-Theoretical Approach" (n. 2).

[51] The same hold for psychological violence, which I cannot discuss further here.

[52] Power, of course, as remarked above, remains present in acts of violence when they have a certain effect on others who witness it.

[53] Here I agree with Arendt in her remark about "sheer violence": "Rule by sheer violence comes into play where power is being lost . . .," in *Crises of the Republic* (n. 13) 152.

[54] On this see the analysis of structural inequalities in access to public discourses by Bernhard Peters, "Deliberative Öffentlichkeit," in Lutz Wingert and Klaus Günther (eds.), *Die Öffentlichkeit der Vernunft und die Vernunft der Öffentlichkeit: Festschrift für Jürgen Habermas* (Suhrkamp 2001) 655–77, at 670 ff.

of reasons for accepting patriarchal authority—reasons of love, admiration, self-interest, convention, religious upbringing, fear, or despair, for example. Usually, it is a mixture of these, and the question of the entry of critique along one or more of these lines is complex as well. However, in order to do justice to the power formations in a society, an appropriate matrix must be worked out.

Second, even though I warned at the outset against the metaphysical idea of noumenal "things in themselves," there is some truth to this way of speaking. For, as Kant remarked, we cannot look into the heads of people in order to discover which reasons actually motivate them. Thus, in a way, any analysis of noumenal power has to accept ambivalence and contestation; it can never be final and completely objective.

Third, when it comes to positions of discursive power and their holders, we also need to construct a matrix for such positions, whether they be in the media, the church, politics, education, and so forth. In all of these contexts, justifications are produced and questioned. But again, there is indeterminacy here, for a public position of discursive power need not correspond to an institutional position. There are institutionally "weak" persons or groups who can generate a lot of power (the phenomenon of "charisma" is important in this context), and there are people in strong positions whom hardly anyone takes seriously. They lack noumenal power. In other words, they are not sufficiently capable of maneuvering within or influencing the public space of reasons. But even the most powerful individuals or groups cannot determine or close off the space of reasons entirely—that would be a task for the gods or a Leviathan as Hobbes imagined it. To have power means to rule in the space of reasons; but, given the plurality of human life, this is not absolute rule.

If we want to develop our analysis of power into a critique of power, we need to develop a *critical theory of relations of justification* along the lines I mentioned.[55] This theory has a material component—namely, a critical understanding of dominant justifications for particular social relations—and critique aims specifically at false, or at least one-sided, justifications for asymmetrical social relations that fall short of the criteria of reciprocity and generality, in short, relations of domination. In the political sphere, to repeat, domination should be defined as rule without adequate justifications, and, reflexively speaking, as rule without adequate structures of justification being in place. Hence a critique of relations of justification aims at a survey of the various social and political positions of generating and exercising discursive power in different social and political spheres. Normatively speaking, such a critique aims to establish a basic structure of justification among free and equal persons as the first demand of justice, or fundamental justice, as I call it.[56] The question of power is the first question of justice.

[55] Cf. Forst, *Justification and Critique* (n. 21).

[56] See Forst, *The Right to Justification* (n. 21) chs. 4, 8, and 12, and Forst, *Justification and Critique* (n. 21) chs. 1 and 5. See also Simon Caney, "Justice and the Basic Right to Justification" in Forst, *Justice, Democracy and the Right to Justification* (n. 23) 147–66, and my "Justifying Justification" (n. 23) 205–15.

PART II

JUSTIFICATION NARRATIVES AND HISTORICAL PROGRESS

3

On the Concept of a Justification Narrative

1. To understand human beings as beings endowed with reason, as *animalia rationalia*, is to view them as *justifying beings*. Reason is the ability to take justifying reasons as one's guide in interactions with the world and when accounting for one's actions. This practice of orienting and accounting for oneself is a social practice of culturally and historically situated beings who, on the one hand, are free to choose their reasons but, on the other, are bound by the reasons that are available to them. The space of the reasons[1] is a space of justifications that legitimize not only individual actions, but also complex systems of thought and action, hence social relations and political institutions.

But human beings are also beings *who tell stories*. The space of the reasons in which they orient themselves is not a bare space of individual sentences, or even norms, but one populated by narratives. Such beings are situated in a spatiotemporal context of interrelated meanings in which individual events and experiences are connected with collective orientations and historical classifications. In Reinhart Koselleck's words, they find themselves in the nexus of the "space of experience and horizon of expectations"[2] in which historical time is structured by narratives. Human beings identify themselves and others through narratives that connect them, while also making them identifiable as individuals. "What is his story?" is a question that asks about an individual's personality, and answers to it point to many other stories.[3] If we want to understand how a collective evolved and developed a self-understanding, we must understand its history as something that is narrated—or, better, its histories, because neither a person nor a community has only one history.

But what exactly is the relationship between justification and narration? On a Platonic conception, narratives would be primarily conceived as illusions that must be viewed critically and overcome along the path leading to pure insight into the truth about the world. In the context of the Frankfurt research institute on the formation of normative orders this would mean that the narratives in which the justifications of actions, social relations, and institutions are embedded represent, at

[1] Wilfrid Sellars, *Empiricism and the Philosophy of Mind*, ed. Robert Brandom (Harvard University Press 1997).

[2] Reinhart Koselleck, "'Space of Experience' and 'Horizon of Expectation': Two Historical Categories," in Reinhart Koselleck, *Futures Past: On the Semantics of Historical Time*, trans. Keith Tribe (MIT Press 1985) 267–88.

[3] See Hannah Arendt, *The Human Condition* (University of Chicago Press 1958) §25, on the narrative constitution of the human "web of relationships."

best, embellishments and at worst obfuscations or detours; our task would then be to look for normative distillation apparatuses, as it were, to separate out the legitimation essence from the superfluous aspects and make it visible.

But that this search will be in vain becomes apparent once we reflect that justifying reasons for normative orders are not simply connected with stories, but cannot even be fully understood without them.[4] Reasons and justifications spring from historical constellations and experiences. When asked why a particular political institution exists, one will usually respond with a story that led to certain conclusions. Although the latter must appear rational and acceptable according to general standards, it is doubtful whether these standards suffice to provide descriptive explanations of orientations and to render them normatively intelligible. Stories provide the supporting basis for reasons, but the reasons also tower above any given story and raise it from the idiosyncratic level into a universal space of justifications. In other words, these kinds of narratives raise the claim to be part of a *learning process*—and what is learned in such a process has to emerge from the situation and to be open to evaluation in general terms. Narratives and justifications are connected, therefore, but they do not merge.

In our research we do not start from a notion of "pure" justifications free from contextualized situation and genesis, nor do we think that justifications can occur and be valid only in singular narrative contexts.[5] Although they arise in specific contexts, narratives also point beyond and serve as a basis for criticizing such contexts. Normative orders that claim to be just and, for example, to guarantee human rights, do so in specific ways; but with their normative self-descriptions they open themselves up to criticism—and to a dynamic of justification that can always call established social standards of legitimacy into question.

2. These initial reflections are connected with a series of research questions that cluster around the concept of a *justification narrative* that we employ in our research.[6] An essential aspect of our research is the reconstruction of the *internal* perspectives involved in the formation of systems of thought and action. "Normative orders" are based on fundamental justifications and correspondingly serve to justify social rules, norms, and institutions; they ground claims to power and justify a certain distribution of goods and life chances. As such, a normative order must be regarded as an *order of justification*: it presupposes justifications and at the same time generates them.

[4] See Charles Tilly, *Why?* (Princeton University Press 2006) 16 ff.

[5] This latter view is defended, for example, by Alasdair MacIntyre, *Whose Justice? Which Rationality?* (University of Notre Dame Press 1988); for criticism see Rainer Forst, *Contexts of Justice: Political Philosophy beyond Liberalism and Communitarianism*, trans. John M. M. Farrell (University of California Press 2002) ch. IV.3.

[6] To recount the genesis of this term would be a narrative in its own right. Even though I am to a certain extent responsible for its specific formulation, I am certainly not responsible for all of the underlying ideas. Others have contributed to this, in particular Klaus Günther, with whom I have worked out the basic ideas of the research program in Rainer Forst and Klaus Günther, "Die Herausbildung normativer Ordnungen: Zur Idee eines interdisziplinären Forschungsprogramms," in Rainer Forst and Klaus Günther (eds.), *Die Herausbildung normativer Ordnungen* (Campus 2011) 11–30. In this section, I draw on (also in part the wording of) this account.

Orders of this kind are embedded in justification narratives that arise in historical situations and are handed down and modified over long periods of time. The concept of a justification narrative correspondingly serves as a heuristic device to connect the normative dimension of justification that aims at rational persuasion with the dimension of socially effective justifications which are recognized and practiced by those involved as persuasive and are constituted by their respective experiences and expectations. We regard justification narratives as embodiments of contextual rationality. In them, images, individual stories, rituals, facts, and myths are condensed into powerful grand narratives that serve as a resource for generating a sense of order. Insofar as normative orders are framed in narratives—in particular those of a religious nature (divine right versus natural rights), and those which can be traced back to political achievements such as revolutions or victories (e.g., in wars of liberation) or also to processes of coming to terms with a past collective injustice (as in the case of twentieth-century criminal violations of human rights)—they have a special binding power and authority; they acquire historical significance and at the same time the emotional power to inspire identification. The historical experience of the breakdown in civilization caused by the Shoah, for example, defines the context of our recent understanding of human dignity and human rights; and the recollection of the diverse struggles against colonial domination by Europeans heightens the sensibility for the claims of cultural and religious identities and ways of life. Telling a story of destruction, persecution, and torture, of humiliation and discrimination, then seems to be sufficient to justify normative claims. But perhaps it is not quite sufficient, because not only must the story be told in the right way, which is hard enough, but the one who tells it with the intention of providing a justification must also be able to show whether the right conclusions were drawn from it.

However, what constitutes an appropriate interpretation of a current conflict that is always embedded in a historically, materially, and socially localized context and how each existing normative order should be interpreted and applied in light of this, is generally a matter of dispute among those involved—just think of the many controversial historical comparisons that are drawn when judging the legality of humanitarian intervention, or also when interpreting the basic right to religious freedom in the face of crucifixes in classrooms or teachers wearing headscarves.[7] An essential requirement for understanding social conflicts and orders, therefore, is an understanding of the relevant, historically saturated narratives. Equally indispensable, however, is in addition the recognition that the narrative reference to "a" or to "the" history alone is not sufficient to justify whether the correct conclusion was drawn from it. What is called "correct" here must be open to justification in the culturally "thick" context as well as in the argumentatively pointed and "thin" context of considerations of principle. The relationship between the two components of the concept of a justification narrative remains a complicated matter.

[7] On this see Rainer Forst, "One Court and Many Cultures: Jurisprudence in Conflict," ch. 6 in this volume.

3. The following remarks are not primarily concerned with how social justification narratives develop and change in concrete historical terms, a topic studied extensively in the research cluster with reference to different historical eras.[8] My primary interest, by contrast, is in the diverse justification narratives that can be found in political philosophy and their structure. Such narratives serve as a *frame* for more specific historical justification narratives. The point of analyzing them is to provide a more detailed account of the relationship between narrative and justification. Here, I would like to cite some central justification narratives by way of example.

(a) In Plato's *Republic* we encounter the *paradoxical political* type of narrative. The most well-known example is the so-called allegory of the cave. At first sight it may seem contradictory that Plato should fall back on a story in the passage where he depicts the pure philosophical contemplation of the Ideas and of "true being." But in his eyes the counterfactual narrative is necessary to represent the conflict between *doxa* and *episteme* in a graphic way; only thus can he clarify the bitter truth that the best state constitution cannot be realized because the mass of the people are incapable of understanding those who are fit to rule, the philosophers. In order to render intelligible the paradox that the good state cannot be realized, Plato has to resort to the power of imagination in narrative form—only the death of the individual who wants to liberate the ignorant from their shackles brings the argument forth with full force. The story is thus an epistemic means that enables finite minds to grasp the dramatic nature of their bias.

Here an essential structural element of political-philosophical narratives becomes apparent: they arise in order to transform narratively representable reality into a second possible world, so that a third world can appear—that of the Ideal or at least of better order—in the light of this confrontation. In Plato's case, this third world is the world of the Ideas and of the best political constitution. If you will, the de facto normativity and its justifications are extrapolated and confronted with a counterfactual normativity from which different, in this case aporetical, conclusions are drawn.

At the same time Plato's *Republic* also shows what holds for all narrative structures in political philosophy, even when they paint ideal images or have a utopian orientation: they are always reflections on real history, in this case, the history of Athens and of Socrates. There are no "worldless" narratives that are not also reflections of reality.

(b) This also applies to another highly influential story, Augustine's *transcendent-dialectical* narrative of "the city of God." Following the conquest of Rome and the disintegration of the Empire, Augustine defines the divine state which transcends the real state and stands in a dialectical relationship to it. In this way, Augustine preserves the purity of Christ's teachings and of his kingdom—in short, of the Christian normative order—while at the same time emphasizing its connection with the earthly kingdom, whose normative order can neither reproduce nor imitate the

[8] The collection of essays edited by Andreas Fahrmeir and Annette Imhausen, *Die Vielfalt normativer Ordnungen* (Campus 2013) illustrates the role played by the concept in the historical and anthropological research of the Cluster of Excellence "Normative Orders."

divine order, although it can align itself with the latter, even if it necessarily remains afflicted with the faults of all earthly things. For subsequent political thought, this bipartite or tripartite division of normative orders into an empirical, an ideal, and a mixed order would remain definitive, even when, as in Kant, the ideal was understood in secular terms. The Lutheran two-kingdoms doctrine is no different in this respect than other conceptions of a dialectical relationship between reality and ideal, whereby the Christian notion of transcendence opens up a deep normative divide between earthly and divine citizenship that can be traced back to different origins within the narrative: "Two cities, then, have been created by two loves: that is, the earthly by love of self extending even to contempt of God, and the heavenly by love of God extending to contempt of self. The one, therefore, glories in itself, the other in the Lord."[9] The principle of justice that differentiates political orders from "bands of robbers" is in this context a central bond connecting both forms of citizenship, even if it can be realized only imperfectly on earth.[10]

(c) Justice is also what separates the two worlds in a different form of political justification narrative, the *ironic utopian* one. In More's *Utopia*, for example, the England of his time is subjected to severe criticism as a topsy-turvy world in which injustice prevails, while with the abolition of private property the distant land of Utopia seems to have found the key to eradicating all social evils. But More portrays Utopia, with all of its social controls and strict regimentation of social life, in turn as an at least in part topsy-turvy world, thereby creating a play of mirrors that in fact leaves the reader in "Nowhere," neither here nor there. This is the true meaning of the utopian narrative whose ironic distancing applies not only to those who accept the existing world unquestioningly, but also to those who imagine that they are engaged in establishing the perfect world or who think they know how to get there.[11]

(d) The early modern period brought forth a revolutionary new justification narrative, the *contractualist* narrative. It launches a polemical attack on the *paternalistic* narrative that was predominant at the time. The paternalistic narrative can be found in its pure form in Robert Filmer, for example, who in his work *Patriarcha* traces the "natural" and absolute claim to power of the king back to divine will in direct succession to Adam. John Locke attacks this paternal political authority in his treatises on government, contradicting it point by point: individuals, Locke argues, were created by God as free and equal, and political authority comes into existence only through a free contract in which the conditions of its exercise are laid down. The narrative of a state of nature, conflict, and state formation is not a historical narrative, but, as a fictional-historical legitimation narrative, it is succinct and open to interpretation, as is shown by the many versions of this narrative developed since Hobbes,

[9] Augustine, *The City of God against the Pagans*, ed. and trans. R. W. Dyson (Cambridge University Press 1998) Book XIV, ch. 28, 632.

[10] ibid Book IV, ch. 4, 147.

[11] See Rainer Forst, "Utopia and Irony: On the Normativity of a Political Philosophy of 'Nowhere,'" in Rainer Forst, *Justification and Critique: Towards a Critical Theory of Politics*, trans. Ciaran Cronin (Polity 2014) 177–90.

whether positive, as in Rousseau's *Social Contract*, or negative, as in his *Discourse on Inequality.* Even the most radical concepts of social criticism cannot do without a narrative, whether it be one in which the state is founded freely or one in which it is founded in the wrong way by property owners.

(e) The religious conflicts that rocked European societies between the sixteenth and the eighteenth centuries (and beyond) gave rise to a series of political-religious justification narratives whose message is either the dominance of one religion or denomination or, on the contrary, a doctrine of toleration and pluralism.[12] In Pierre Bayle, in particular, we find a specific form of a *fictional polemical* narrative, which—for example, in his *Historical and Critical Dictionary*[13]—offers counter-narratives to traditional assumptions about the virtues of Christians and the vices of non-Christians. These culminate in his book on the comet (1682), in which he presents the narrative, which can neither be confirmed nor refuted by experience, of an atheistic people who are no less capable of morality and justice than a God-fearing people, but whose lack of a certain taint—namely, the propensity to religious fanaticism—is of great advantage.[14]

(f) The eighteenth century exhibits a series of important justification narratives whose central characteristic is the idea of human progress along the path toward self-perfection stretching indefinitely into the future.[15] From Lessing through Condorcet up to Kant, the idea was developed that the human race is progressively perfecting itself through the cultivation of its rational faculties. Enlightenment was understood as a dialectical, but nevertheless teleological, process. Hegel would develop this *progressive* justification narrative into a philosophy of mind in an all-encompassing, world-historical sense, whereas the Left Hegelians up to Marx interpreted it as a dynamic process of development toward overcoming capitalist society.

It was not only critics like Herder or Mendelssohn who problematized the progressive Enlightenment narrative and called for *counter-narratives.* The imperialist implications of these narratives, which differentiated human beings according to "race" and to levels of and potentials for development, were denounced at different times and their consequences, from colonization to slavery, were demonstrated.[16] Today's "post-colonial" discourse testifies to the continued presence of this past.[17]

(g) Any list of examples of important political justification narratives cannot fail to include the narrative of *nationalism* which dominated the nineteenth century. Nationalist narratives invent communities of solidarity and shared destiny; they

[12] See Rainer Forst, *Toleration in Conflict: Past and Present*, trans. Ciaran Cronin (Cambridge University Press 2013); on Bayle see ch. 5, §18.

[13] Pierre Bayle, *Historical and Critical Dictionary: Selections*, ed. and trans. Richard H. Popkin (Hackett 1991).

[14] Pierre Bayle, *Various Thoughts on the Occasion of a Comet*, trans. Robert C. Bartlett (SUNY Press 2000) para 145.

[15] On this see Rainer Forst, "The Concept of Progress," ch. 4 in this volume.

[16] See Thomas McCarthy, *Race, Empire, and the Idea of Human Development* (Cambridge University Press 2009).

[17] Dipesh Chakrabarty, *Provincializing Europe: Postcolonial Thought and Historical Difference* (Princeton University Press 2007).

emphasize the differences from other communities and demarcate themselves by imagining a history and identity of their own.[18] The specificity of the nation is defined through difference and its value is underlined, which can lead to claims to domination no less than to claims to liberation. Nationalism is a special form of collective identity formation that clusters a variety of characteristics (language, religion, shared history and origin, shared beliefs and experiences) into a narrative whose normative power is manifested in particular in the *topos* of self-assertion and self-determination—for example, in the struggle against colonial domination and subordination, but sometimes also against a purely imaginary form of rule or "inundation by foreigners." At this point, the discourse of self-assertion becomes inverted into aggression and often degenerates into destructive rage.

Here it should be noted that, on the one hand, the justification narratives briefly sketched acquire their normative power from the specific way in which they combine human experiences and expectations and form them into ideals, but that, on the other hand, they are directed essentially toward relatively abstract principles such as those of justice, of freedom, or collective self-determination, whose validity constitutes the quality of the respective justification and transcends specific contexts.

4. Political justification narratives of the kind mentioned seldom occur in pure form in reality; for the most part they are associated with specific narratives that arise out of particular situations. The United States of America is an example of this. The dominant justification narratives in the US context are connected with Christian topoi of citizenship in God, for example when John Winthrop's expression the "city upon a hill" of 1630 is used to stress the exceptionalism of the Puritan colonization of the "New World" and the religiously charged missionary idea that informed the foundation of this community, and which continues to shine through in the self-understanding of this political order to the present day. Conversely, the Augustinian idea is also at work when doubts are expressed whether a refulgent city such as the one spoken of in the Sermon on the Mount can exist on earth. Increasing expectation goes hand-in-hand with self-doubt. So, to recall More, the beautiful Utopia is always at the same time the vulnerable and in part failed, in essence unattainable, Utopia.

From an early date, the motif of the "Mayflower Compact" of 1620, in which the pilgrims founded a political community in Plymouth by contract, took its lead from the contractualist justification narrative that Locke also associates with America when he says that "in the beginning all the world was America,"[19] a land which was not used properly and made productive by the indigenous peoples (a classical *topos* of the legitimization of colonialism). The natural law-based, contractualist self-understanding was fully developed in the American war of independence against England, in which the contractualist language acquired revolutionary force

[18] Benedict Anderson, *Imagined Communities: Reflections on the Origins and Spread of Nationalism* (Verso 1991).

[19] John Locke, *Two Treatises of Government*, ed. Peter Laslett (Cambridge University Press 1989) 97.

and at the same time served the purpose of nation-building. Thomas Jefferson's Declaration of Independence testifies to this.

At the same time, there developed counter-narratives that not only denounced the violent land seizure and the destruction of indigenous cultures. In addition, there were disputes within the newly independent colonies over what kind of state should arise and whose interests should prevail. The so-called "Antifederalists" advocated a loose alliance of the separate states, and in some states attempts were made to change the ownership structure in favor of the poorer classes. From this perspective, the constitution founding of 1787 appears as a "coup" by the wealthy and capital-owning class and not as the fulfillment of a liberating revolution.[20] This critical narrative also persists to this day.[21]

The fact that the liberal contractual idea nevertheless dominated the justification narrative of the new nation is attributed to a peculiarity already highlighted by Tocqueville, namely, that this society became a bourgeois society without first having to overcome a feudal phase; the assumption is that as a result it adopted a liberal self-description almost as a matter of course.[22] Viewed in this light, the continued existence of slavery until the Civil War appears as an anomaly. Opposed to this are narratives that emphasized not just the economic but also the cultural factors that upheld slavery and that divide American society up to the present day. This example also draws attention to the dark side of liberal society and its idea of progress, which ascribed the leading role in the civilizing process to the Europeans.

The complex relationship between liberalism and nationalism played an especially important role where, in the course of the waves of Catholic immigration during the second half of the nineteenth century, the question of identity and religion was raised, afterwards also in relation to other ethnicities. "Nativists" set themselves apart from the new immigrants and sought to uphold a specific national identity, a debate that persists to the present day in which aggressive demarcations face off against polemical challenges in the style of Bayle.[23] Here again it becomes apparent that the narrative construction of the "true America(n)" is an unfinished and controversial process and how very different justification narratives and counter-narratives overlap. Such narratives spring from social conflicts and continue to refer to them, even where they strive to represent them as being completed. These comprehensive stories form the indispensable reservoir for the narrative construction of the legitimacy of American politics, not only as fodder for inauguration speeches by

[20] See Horst Dippel, *Die Amerikanische Revolution 1763–1787* (Suhrkamp 1985).

[21] See Eli Zaretsky, *Why America Needs a Left* (Polity 2012).

[22] See Louis Hartz, *The Liberal Tradition in America* (Harvest 1955); for a differentiated account see James P. Young, *Reconsidering American Liberalism: The Troubled Odyssey of the Liberal Idea* (Westview 1996).

[23] See Lawrence H. Fuchs, *The American Kaleidoscope: Race, Ethnicity, and the Civic Culture* (Wesleyan University Press 1990); Kenneth L. Karst, *Belonging to America: Equal Citizenship and the Constitution* (Yale University Press 1989); Michael Walzer, *What it Means to Be an American* (Marsilio 1992).

American presidents, but also in everyday culture and in artistic representations of the past and the present.[24]

5. This would not be the case if the way justification narratives exercise effects did not point to the nature of social and political *power*. Here I must limit myself to some incomplete remarks.[25] If we understand intersubjective, social power as the ability of an agent A to bring another agent B to think or do something that B would not otherwise have thought or done, then it is at first an open question whether this is a result of a good and convincing discourse, a recommendation, a lie, an act of seduction, a command, or a threat. This understanding of power is evaluatively neutral. In all of these cases, the effect of power depends on B recognizing a reason for behaving in accordance with A's intention. Power exists between people as long as they influence each other through their ability to motivate others to do something in all of these different ways; power disappears when it is replaced by sheer physical force. A kidnapper, for example, has power over his victim and those who are supposed to pay the ransom only as long as his threat is taken seriously; if it is not, then he can still exert brute force, but he no longer has the power to achieve his goal. An example of this phenomenon in the political domain is the fate of despots who beyond a certain point—albeit one difficult to determine—cease to have power; even the tanks they may still have at their disposal can become blunt instruments of power if they no longer inspire fear. The results may be a spiral of violence, but also a nonviolent revolution.

Thus, the true phenomenon of power is noumenal or intellectual in nature: having power means being able to influence, determine, occupy, or even close off the space of reasons and justifications of other subjects—and here the degrees to which this can be done are important. This can occur in a single case, through a good speech or through deception; but the locus of power can also be a social structure that rests on specific justifications or condensed justification narratives. An order of justification is therefore always an order of power, although this does not say anything about the justifications in question or about the power constellation as such. Justifications can be imposed or they can be freely shared, and between these extremes there are many other modalities. Therefore, power always unfolds in the space of communication, which does not necessarily mean that it is well founded. It is always discursive in character and the struggle for power is a struggle over the possibility of structuring, or even dominating, the store of justifications on which others can draw. Its modus operandi is cognitive but not necessarily reflective. There is no realm of "reason" beyond "power," therefore, but there are better and worse,

[24] See Martin Seel, "Narration und (De-)Legitimation: Der zweite Irak-Krieg im Kino," in Andreas Fahrmeir (ed.), *Rechtfertigungsnarrative: Zur Begründung normativer Ordnung durch Erzählung* (Normative Orders, vol. 7) (Campus 2013) 45–57. In this context it is important to point out that cinematic justification narratives participate in, and hence are based on and continue and change, more inclusive narratives.

[25] For a more detailed account see Rainer Forst, "Noumenal Power," ch. 2 in this volume.

reasonable and unreasonable, justifications besides more and less effective ones. So we have to distinguish the normative *force* of justifications and justification narratives from their *quality*.

As for the definition of power: let us define *power* (*Macht*) in general as the ability of A to influence the space of reasons of B such that how B thinks or acts is a result of A's influence, where the influence in question must be intentional, since otherwise one could only speak of an effect and not of power. Then *rule* (*Herrschaft*) designates a particular form of the exercise of power in which social or political relations are joined into an order that rests on specific supporting justifications and narratives. We speak of *domination* (*Beherrschung*) when the relations in question are asymmetrical ones based on restricting the space of justifications in favor of particular legitimations that are not well-founded and represent such an order as, for example, just, willed by God, or unalterable. Then the space of justifications may be sealed off ideologically or be occupied by effective threats, which means that illegitimate *coercion* (*Zwang*) is present. Finally, we encounter pure *violence* (*Gewalt*) when a relationship of justification, even an asymmetrical one, is replaced by a physical effect. Then power is on the wane, although this does not mean that freedom is on the advance; rather, it is disappearing. For freedom and power belong together, as long as the latter acts upon cognitively motivated subjects. Power is the art of binding others through reasons; it is at the core of normativity. The spectrum of relations of power, therefore, extends from conditions based on freely shared, reciprocally general reasons at the one end, to those situated in the transitional zone where power is replaced by violence at the other. It should be noted in this context that power also exists where cognitive effects are achieved through lies or deception.[26]

Anyone who is interested in an analysis of power, therefore, must employ a differentiated method that explores the discursive space as a space of good or bad justifications. Furthermore, it must analyze how these justifications evolved and the complex effects they exercise, and it must examine the positions and structures in a given society that are decisive for discourse. It understands—however imperfectly, given that it is analyzing an intelligible phenomenon—the discursive space as a space of power. Thus, the primary issue here is not so much the justification of power as the power of justifications.

Justification narratives develop normative power to the extent that they cast the political and social world in a certain light, connect the past, present, and future, reality and ideals, as well as individuals and a collective, and form them into an accepted order of justification. This normative power or force says nothing about the normative quality of the justifications and the historical coherence of the narratives, since these could also be ideological. But even in that case, a narrative derives its power not only from the collective perception of its cogency, but also from acceptance of the overarching principles and values expressed by the justifications generated. The

[26] This is an essential difference from the account of power presented in Hannah Arendt, *On Violence* (Harcourt, Brace & World 1970).

power of a justification narrative follows from its historical explanatory power and from its normative acceptance; power is the capacity to bind. The quality of a justification narrative consists in turn in its historical correctness, as judged by the best standards, and ultimately in its normative acceptability, as tested by reflection.

6. The criteria for such reflexive examination are not imposed on orders of justification from the outside, but are a result of internal critical questioning of prevailing justifications. Here, however, an overhasty distinction between "immanent" and "transcending" criticism would be misplaced. For example, it is difficult to determine the point at which the questioning of Filmer's patriarchal story by the contractualism of the Levellers or Locke ceased to be an immanent controversy over England's self-understanding or the biblical foundations of the legitimation of rule and became a radically new way of thinking about politics and justification.

The concept of an order of justification or of a justification narrative allows us, in addition, to localize a normative structure or a principle in the concept of justification, which is as much imminent as it is transcendent (and transcendental), because, no matter what concrete form the practice of questioning an existing justification assumes, it always involves claiming the right to ask such a question. In doing so, individuals or groups enter the political space of justifications, they share in constituting it, they change it, and they claim the right to be respected as justification authorities. Historical actors always make concrete demands. But a critical and emancipatory dynamic is triggered within existing orders of justification when a *right to justification* is claimed and demanded. The content of this right, expressed in Kantian terms, is the claim to be recognized as free and equal justification authorities and the right not to be subjected to any norms or institutions except those to which one could have freely consented.[27] To this corresponds, in abstract terms, the principle of justification as a recursive principle of practical reason which states that norms that lay claim to general and reciprocal validity must be justifiable with reasons that cannot be generally and reciprocally rejected. In practical contexts, this principle and the corresponding right to justification constitute the essential structural element in terms of which the legitimacy of an order of justification must be measured.

The principle of justification and the demand to be respected in one's dignity as a justification authority are not pallid ahistorical truths of reason, but express historically effective normative claims of persons or groups who question the justification of a given order. This lends concepts such as justice, human rights, and democracy a reflexive point that corresponds to their historical genesis: the core political and normative content of these concepts is the demand that the justifications of a normative order can withstand the scrutiny of those for whom they are supposed to be valid.

[27] For a detailed account see Rainer Forst, *The Right to Justification: Elements of a Constructivist Theory of Justice*, trans. Jeffrey Flynn (Columbia University Press 2012) and Rainer Forst, *Justification and Critique* (n. 11). In addition, Rainer Forst, "The Right to Justification: Moral and Political, Transcendental and Historical. Reply to Seyla Benhabib, Jeffrey Flynn and Matthias Fritsch," in *Political Theory* 43/6 (2015): 822–37.

With this, the justification requirement itself becomes practical. The basic claim of human rights, for example, is that there are certain fundamental rights to have one's status as a free and equal justification authority guaranteed, and that being a member of a democratic legal community is an essential part of this.[28] And the first requirement of justice consists, reflexively speaking, in the claim that the establishment of a basic structure of justification is required to ensure that generally valid norms can discursively acquire and merit this validity in corresponding practices of justification.

Although history should not be viewed as a linear and progressive sequence in which successively higher and more egalitarian justification structures are established, the historical dynamic of ever more wide-ranging demands for justifications can nevertheless be reconstructed, as can the (often successful) attempts to fend off these demands by sealing off spaces of justification.[29] Progress manifests itself in such a dialectical conception of history in the overcoming of inadequate justifications for social relations and in the establishment of improved discursive relations of justification; but the persistence of asymmetric justification narratives and corresponding orders likewise becomes apparent. The struggle over the power of justifications cannot be brought to a close. Once a certain level has been reached, internal pressure develops to go beyond this level; and how radical the corresponding demands for justification can or must be depends on the existing relations of justification. No narrative can immunize itself completely against criticism; but as a general rule it can shield itself temporarily against specific criticisms that are perceived as inappropriate, arcane, or incomprehensible.

Justification narratives are in essence neither good nor bad; descriptively speaking, they have different normative force and, normatively speaking, they differ in their quality. They can be better ordered or be full of contradictions, and they can be more or less comprehensive. By contrast, they cannot generate their criteria of validity out of themselves in an autonomous way. However specifically the dominant language of justification narrows them down discursively—for example, to certain religious foundations—they can always be measured radically against their own claim to justification by questioning whether the dominant language is in fact the right one. Thus, for example, instead of a father ordained by God, the king becomes an employee appointed by contract and the corresponding order of justification is turned on its head—or, rather, on its feet.

What this ultimately means for our understanding of normative orders is that we must work with two different meanings of normativity. The normative force and power of actually accepted justification narratives points to a descriptive understanding of normativity, whereas their problematization, including their reflexive examination in accordance with the criteria of generality and reciprocity, amounts

[28] See Forst, *Justification and Critique* (n. 11) ch. 2.

[29] I have explored this in *Toleration in Conflict* (n. 12) through a systematic, historical analysis of the demand for toleration and legal equality.

to a critical understanding in terms of a theory of validity that always transcends existing justifications.[30] Normatively speaking, any order of justification and any justification narrative can count as well-founded only when it leaves sufficient room for this reflexive examination. A narrative cannot surmount this normativity of criticism by itself; this normativity is fundamental.

[30] On this see Rainer Forst, "Critique of Justifying Reason: Explaining Practical Normativity," ch. 1 in this volume.

4

The Concept of Progress

1. Viewed from a historical vantage point, the concept of progress which has shaped the Western tradition is a highly specific one and a result of a series of developments.[1] First, the idea that time unfolds in a linear way had to take shape and become established in contrast to cyclical conceptions. Subsequently, the assumption that the *saeculum* would come to an end with the return of Christ was replaced by the idea that the future is in principle open—and in particular that its inherent telos is the unlimited perfectibility of human capabilities. In one of the founding works of modernity, the *Oratio de hominis dignitate* of 1486, Pico della Mirandola depicts God addressing the first man as follows:

> We have given to thee, Adam, no fixed seat, no form of thy very own, no gift particularly thine, that thou mayest feel as thine own, have as thine own, possess as thine own the seat, the form, the gifts which thou thyself shalt desire. .... Thou canst grow downward into the lower natures which are brutes. Thou canst again grow upward from thy soul's reason into the higher natures which are divine.[2]

However, the subject of such progress was not primarily the individual, but humanity as a whole. In Kant's formulation: "In the human being (as the only rational creature on earth), those predispositions whose goal is the use of his reason should develop completely only in the species, but not in the individual."[3]

The question of which societies and forces should lead and direct this process, and how it could be conceived as universal advancement given the diversity of cultures, religions, and ways of life, was and is a much-discussed subject since the Enlightenment, if we think of the contrasting teleologies of history offered by Lessing and Herder, for example, or of the skepticism of Mendelssohn. We are still part of this history, and we know the disastrous consequences, especially in the

[1] This text is based on a lecture I delivered as part of the series "Vielfalt der Moderne—Ansichten der Moderne" [Forms of Modernity—Views of Modernity] held in October 2009 in Berlin at the initiative of German President Horst Köhler. It appeared in a volume with the same title edited by Hans Joas (2012). On that occasion Ashis Nandy delivered a trenchant critique of the concept of progress; see Ashis Nandy, "Fortschritt," in Hans Joas (ed.), *Vielfalt der Moderne: Ansichten der Moderne* (Fischer, 2012) 53–66.

[2] Pico della Mirandola, *On the Dignity of Man*, trans. Charles Glenn Wallis and Paul J. W. Miller (Hackett, 1998) 4–5.

[3] Immanuel Kant, "Idea for a Universal History with a Cosmopolitan Aim," trans. Allen W. Wood, in Immanuel Kant, *Anthropology, History and Education*, ed. Robert B. Louden (Cambridge University Press 2007) 109 (Ak. 8: 18) (translation amended).

context of colonialism, of the idea that European societies reflected the advanced stage of culture that was to be reached, with the Europeans playing an educational role in this process.[4] In our "post-colonial" age, this problem also shapes our attitude to the concept of progress. For its reverse side was economic exploitation, political oppression, and cultural domination.

But however critical we should be of the one-sided technological or social ideals of progress that entailed as well as obscured practices of power and control over "backward" or "underdeveloped" peoples by the supposedly "advanced" cultures, we must nevertheless recognize from the perspective of participants in social practices that it is very difficult for human beings not to conceive of themselves as progressive beings—as beings who encounter natural and social obstacles which hinder their development and which they seek to overcome in order to improve their individual and collective lives. In the final analysis, the critique of false notions of progress also rests on such striving for progress. Viewed in dialectical terms, the critique of progress is sustained by thinking in terms of progress that seeks clarity about itself. No society can dispense entirely with the imperative of progress, because this imperative has deep social and normative roots: it is a demand that comes from those who suffer oppression or abuse or whose lives are marked by the lack of resources or possibilities. The idea of progress is not an alien power imposed from the outside, therefore, but first and foremost has an internal source—namely, the desire for social improvement. The first and original locus of progress is not a global stage on which political and technological fantasies of omnipotence are played out, but the infrastructure of a society in (conflictual) motion because its members want to improve their situation.

2. When we engage in an intercultural dialogue about the concept of progress, we must rid ourselves of some false images that hold our imagination captive. One such image is the construction of the "West" as a culture of technological and social development, while the "rest" remain trapped in ancient traditions, perspectives, and social systems. Not only should such crude reifications be avoided in principle; this viewpoint also tends to blind us to the fact that Western history itself is marked by constant controversies over what progress means and whether it is a good thing. There were no unilinear developments in Western societies, and there was no consensus on the direction progress should take. This was not only or primarily a question of "progressives" versus "conservatives"; on the contrary, here the dialectic of progress, which would later be thematized by Critical Theory, was noticed from an early date. One of the most powerful and constantly revived narratives of Western philosophy was that of "diremption" [*Entzweiung*], the notion that technological and social progress came at the price of loss, moral decline, and cultural

[4] Philipp Lepenies traces this idea through European history from the invention of the linear perspective in the Renaissance to present-day discourses regarding development cooperation in Lepenies, *Art, Politics, and Development: How Linear Perspective Shaped Policies in the Western World* (Temple University Press 2014). For a comprehensive critical theory of the idea of development see Thomas McCarthy, *Race, Empire, and the Idea of Human Development* (Cambridge University Press 2009). On the interpretation of Kant in this context, see Katrin Flikschuh and Lea Ypi (eds.), *Kant and Colonialism: Historical and Critical Perspectives* (Oxford University Press 2014).

impoverishment or one-sidedness. We need only recall Rousseau's *Discourses*, we need only think of Herder, Hegel, Nietzsche, Weber, Adorno, and Horkheimer, to recognize that every "Western" stage of progress and development was accompanied by serious doubts. The question of what had been lost and who were the winners and losers of the new age was always raised. "We have Physicists, Geometricians, Chemists, Astronomers, Poets, Musicians, Painters," wrote Rousseau, "we no longer have citizens; or if we still have some left, dispersed in our abandoned rural areas, they waste away indigent and despised."[5] For Rousseau, the modern, progressive human being is only driven by self-interest, outward appearance, and the drive to dominate; he has lost his authentic, inner nature.

If we ask today on a larger scale what price non-Western societies pay for supposed progress, therefore, we should not pretend that Western societies are one-dimensional formations, and we should not forget the Romantic, Marxist, and Christian critics of modernity, among others. Yet in doing so we should be careful to avoid an error of transference. For, just as a concept of progress and related practices that are unacceptable to its members must not be imposed upon a society, so, too, its criticism of (false) progress should not be rashly assumed to be one that we already know from the West. Nevertheless, the language of progress is unintelligible apart from criticism of progress. Environmental movements, which have a long tradition, are proof of this, as are the social movements that cite growing poverty and lawlessness as counterarguments against increasing wealth. In one of the most important modern philosophical reflections on the concept of progress, Walter Benjamin interpreted Paul Klee's "Angelus Novus" as the angel of history who, his gaze turned toward the past, recognizes "one single catastrophe" that "keeps piling wreckage upon wreckage and hurls it in front of his feet. The Angel would like to tarry, to awaken the dead, and make whole what has been destroyed. But a storm is blowing from Paradise; it has got caught in his wings with such violence that the Angel can no longer close them.... It is *this* storm that we call progress."[6]

3. A correct understanding of the contemporary discussion about the concept of progress presupposes a distinction between two major fields of debate. On the one hand, in many societies there is a debate over the appropriate definition of technological progress as qualitative progress: How much environmental destruction does unfettered economic growth bring with it? What is our stance on genetically modified foods? What is and is not permitted in medical research? These are genuine evaluative questions concerning progress in specific areas of science, technology, and economics that examine its social costs. Here it is important to recognize that the dynamics of these debates, which develop into political conflicts, compel all parties

[5] Jean-Jacques Rousseau, *Discourse on the Sciences and Arts*, in Jean-Jacques Rousseau, *The Discourses and Other Early Writings*, ed. and trans. Victor Gourevitch (Cambridge University Press 1997) 1–28, at 24.

[6] Walter Benjamin, "Theses on the Philosophy of History," in Walter Benjamin, *Illuminations*, ed. Hannah Arendt, trans. Harry Zohn (Schocken 1969) 253–64, at 257–8 (emphasis in original) (translation amended).

to adopt a political-ethical or a moral language: it must be shown which social benefits certain controversial developments bring with them—and those who dispute these benefits likewise have to use normative arguments. In pluralistic societies, it is not unusual that such debates involve clashes between very different value systems, so that the search for shared norms proves to be difficult.

On the other hand, there are debates about progress that also call for a normative language, but one of a different kind. In such cases resistance to certain conceptions of progress is fueled less by ethical evaluations of a desirable way of life than by an impulse of justice. For what is deplored are forms of social or economic change that are enforced; what is revealed is a desire for emancipation which should not be confused with a general form of skepticism concerning progress. The targets of criticism are unilateral and externally imposed conceptions of development that in a certain sense colonize the lifeworlds in question or whole societies—also in an effort to "develop," "modernize," and sometimes even to "liberate" these societies.[7] Whether it is powerful states, associations of states, or international organizations that are accused of neo-colonialism does not change the fact that here it is essentially a matter of how power is distributed and of relations of domination—and of how much social self-determination is possible in a globalized society. These conflicts are not simply a matter of being for or against "globalization," however, because many of the global political and economic relations that are criticized as asymmetrical cannot be changed other than through global coordination.

Both debates, but especially the latter, show that the discussions about the concept of progress should not be viewed in terms of a simple Pro and Contra. Instead, we must keep the social dimension of these controversies in mind. Then the question is often not whether a society should "develop," but who determines this process and defines the corresponding goals. The decisive question raised by the concept of progress remains how the power to define progress and the paths leading to it is distributed. Properly understood, this is the question of justice.

4. With this we arrive at an important insight. Although the concept of progress is used normatively in the two fields of debate mentioned, it is not itself a normative concept in its own right. Technological progress cannot count as progress without social evaluations of what it is good for, who benefits from it, and what costs it generates, nor can true social progress exist where the changes in question are enforced and experienced as colonization. Technological progress must be socially accepted, and socially accepted progress is progress which is determined by those affected themselves. Therefore, democratic political forms and procedures are not only goals also but essential conditions of social advancement. Of particular importance in this regard are the many "empowerment" initiatives, such as political initiatives in civil society forums and organizations or economic empowerment measures, for example through microcredits or more comprehensive social policy measures, and especially where underprivileged groups—in many countries, first and foremost

7 See James Tully, "On Law, Democracy and Imperialism," in James Tully, *Public Philosophy in a New Key, Volume 2: Imperialism and Civic Freedom* (Cambridge University Press 2008) 127–65.

women—win participation rights through struggles. Increasing the scope for action of individuals and collectives, as Amartya Sen emphasizes, is the central means and goal of development and progress.[8]

As the example of contemporary China demonstrates, in an age of multiple modernities there is no universally valid script for the linkage between economic, cultural, and political modernization in the sense of democratization. But in the long run it is doubtful whether the one can succeed without the other. A regime is strengthened by increases in prosperity but is simultaneously tested and placed in question by technical capabilities and by new upwardly mobile social groups. Social dynamics lead to political dynamics. However, such processes do not unfold along a single, predictable path. That may be unsettling for those who hope to derive prognostic wisdom from sociological research; normatively speaking, it is also a good thing, because every process that deserves to be called progress should be one which those affected initiate or at least control themselves. This is difficult enough. But once again it becomes apparent that the evaluative criteria for progress refer to the concept of self-determination—as a fundamental requirement of justice.

This potentially gives rise to a dilemma. We began by emphasizing the critique of unilateral Western notions of social development and progress; but now a whole series of normative concepts such as autonomy, democracy, or justice, which owe their existence to a Western political and cultural background, come back into play. Have we reverted from the criticism of a form of particularism that disguises itself as universalism to this very particularism? With this we must contrast a different logic. For the critique of the unilateral or imposed, of the dominant and oppressive idea of progress or of the corresponding practice is, to repeat, itself normative, and it calls for nothing less than self-determined forms of social development. This language is the authentic language of progress, therefore, and what critics as well as proponents of the idea of progress must recognize is that progress is a *reflexive* concept: every progressive process must be constantly questioned as to whether it is in the social interest—correctly understood—of those who are part of this process. Thus, every criticism is itself also part of progress, and the principle that progressive developments must always be open to justification is both inherent in practice and transcends it.

5. The true logic of progress not a historical, a social-technical, scientific, or technological logic; rather, it is a social logic in the sense that it must be supported and defined by a society itself. There are no predetermined blueprints for this, although there is a reflexive principle which states that only those who are affected may define the steps that constitute "progress." This principle does not authorize anyone to serve as the teacher of others; rather, it refers to a normative structure of social self-determination according to which no one may be subjected to specific rules or institutions which cannot be adequately justified to him or her as a free and equal subject. That is the core meaning of self-determination central to social progress. It expresses

[8] Amartya Sen, *Development as Freedom* (Oxford University Press 2001).

a basic human "right to justification," which is as much a right to the protection of individuals as to equal participation in social processes.[9] A society in which this principle is put into practice in a non-dominating way can be called progressive. Progress means that a society strives for new levels of justification which not only ensure that political and social relations can be justified in a reciprocal and general way, but also that there are institutions for producing such justifications in discursive practice.[10]

Therefore, it is not only a question of peace, stability, and mutual respect when intercultural dialogue about progress emphasizes the right to remain free from colonizing interventions, even well-intentioned ones.[11] But it should likewise be noted that the core of human rights, which finds expression in a right to justification, is not negotiable. What constitute human rights is not specified in the diplomatic domain of intergovernmental negotiations or in the "overlapping consensus" of the major religions, but in the reflexive determination of rights that no one can deny others for good reasons.[12] Thus, neither at the international nor at the national level may anyone determine for others what progress means for them. This is a basic requirement of justice.

If the language of human rights, self-determination, and justice is the language of progress, therefore, then this is not primarily a historical or a sociological insight or demand. Rather, it follows as a moral imperative from the critique of false ideas of progress and from the critique of the prevention of social progress. For emancipation from a situation of oppression and disenfranchisement is a human right, now and at all times. Therefore, we are bound to adhere to this concept of progress—normatively for the sake of those who need it, and descriptively as a concept which expresses that societies are not rigid housings beyond change, even if at times they appear to be. The same Benjamin who makes a radical criticism of progress also defends it when he writes: "Only for the sake of those bereft of hope have we been given hope."[13]

[9] Rainer Forst, *The Right to Justification: Elements of a Constructivist Theory of Justice*, trans. Jeffrey Flynn (Columbia University Press 2012) and Rainer Forst, *Justification and Critique: Towards a Critical Theory of Politics*, trans. Ciaran Cronin (Polity 2014).

[10] I trace such a logic of progress with reference to the question of toleration in Rainer Forst, *Toleration in Conflict: Past and Present*, trans. Ciaran Cronin (Cambridge University Press 2013).

[11] See Jürgen Habermas, *The Postnational Constellation*, trans. Max Pensky (Polity 2001) ch. 5.

[12] See Forst, *Justification and Critique* (n. 9) ch. 2 and Rainer Forst, "The Point and Ground of Human Rights: A Kantian Constructivist View," in David Held and Pietro Maffettone (eds.), *Global Political Theory* (Polity 2016) 22–39.

[13] Walter Benjamin, "Goethe's Elective Affinities," trans. Stanley Corngold, in Walter Benjamin, *Selected Writings, Volume 1: 1913–1926*, ed. Marcus Bullock and Michael W. Jennings (Harvard University Press 1996) 297–360, at 356 (translation amended).

PART III

RELIGION, TOLERATION, AND LAW

5

Religion and Toleration from the Enlightenment to the Post-Secular Era

Bayle, Kant, and Habermas

Since the turn of the millennium, Jürgen Habermas has engaged in wide-ranging reflections on religion as a continuing, productive normative force in modern and "post-secular" societies. Central to his approach is the classical question of the relationship between enlightenment and religion, which I will address in what follows in the light of the problem of toleration. In doing so, I compare Habermas's thought to that of Pierre Bayle and Immanuel Kant. For, although Habermas undoubtedly stands in a tradition founded by Bayle and Kant, he develops a number of important orientations within this tradition and has changed his position in his recent work.[1] Whereas in his earlier work he leaned toward a more neo-Kantian position on the relationship between faith and reason, in recent times he has developed a neo-Baylean view (section 3). When it comes to the question of an "autonomous" grounding of morality, by contrast, he (increasingly) defends a guarded position by comparison with both of these thinkers (section 2).

The comparison between these perspectives enables us not only to understand Habermas's position better but also draws attention to a fundamental question raised by the modern world: what common ground can human reason establish in the practical and theoretical domain between human beings who are divided by profoundly different religious (including antireligious) views? In conclusion, I will discuss not only the resulting political consequences (section 4) but will also formulate the thesis that a post-secular society must exhibit a complex reflexive character when it comes to defining faith and reason, to the autonomy of morality, and to the politics of toleration (section 5), where the reflexivity in question continues the process of secularization in the right way.

[1] In what follows, I draw upon the more detailed presentation in Rainer Forst, *Toleration in Conflict: Past and Present*, trans. Ciaran Cronin (Cambridge University Press 2013), in particular §18 (Bayle) and §21 (Kant). I developed the comparison between Bayle and Kant in "Toleranz, Glaube und Vernunft: Bayle und Kant im Vergleich," in Heiner Klemme (ed.), *Kant und die Zukunft der europäischen Aufklärung* (de Gruyter 2009) 183–209, which serves here as a template. An earlier version of the present text appeared in French under the title "Lumières, religion et tolérance," trans. Tristan Coignard and Maïwenn Roudaut, *Lumières* 19 (2012): 15–48.

1. Toleration: Concept and Conceptions

In order to clarify the systematic meaning of the problem I want to examine in connection with Bayle, Kant, and Habermas, let me begin by making a couple of preliminary remarks on the concept of toleration.[2] This concept comprises the following three components:

The first is the so-called *objection component*. This states that the beliefs or practices that are tolerated are considered to be false or are condemned as bad. Without this component, we would be dealing with indifference or affirmation, not with toleration.

Second, toleration involves a positive *acceptance component* that specifies reasons for why it is right, or is even required, to tolerate the false or bad beliefs or practices. This does not mean that the reasons for objecting are annulled, only that they have been counterbalanced and overridden.

Finally, third, toleration also involves a *rejection component* that contains reasons for specifying the much-debated limits of toleration. Here a clearly negative evaluation predominates that calls for an end of toleration and, if necessary, for intervention.

This brief analysis shows that we are dealing with three kinds—or three functions—of reasons, so that the exercise of toleration faces the task of connecting these reasons in the right way. Moreover, it is apparent that toleration is a *normatively dependent concept* in need of substantive normative justification—from resources that it itself does not possess. These resources must be able to explain how "good" reasons for objection, acceptance, and rejection are constituted. Furthermore, it is important, starting from this core concept of toleration, to be able to distinguish different conceptions of toleration. Here I will sketch, at least briefly, the two most important of them.

The first, classical understanding of toleration I call the *permission conception*. On this conception, an authority permits one or several minorities to live in accordance with their beliefs, which are characterized as "deviant," provided that they do not challenge the supremacy of this authority. What sets the minorities apart is supposed to remain a "private matter," confined within a narrowly circumscribed and clearly defined framework laid down unilaterally by the side that wields power. Toleration is something that is bestowed and it can be revoked at any time if the minorities violate certain conditions. Objection, acceptance, and rejection are in the hands of the authority, which in principle is not under any institutional pressure to justify itself. This conception of toleration can be found in the classical toleration laws, for example the Edict of Nantes (1598), which speaks a clear language:

> [N]ot to leave any occasion of trouble and difference among our Subjects, we have permitted and do permit to those of the Reformed Religion, to live and dwell in all the Cities and places

[2] For a more in-depth discussion and references see Forst, *Toleration in Conflict* (n. 1) ch. 1.

of this our Kingdom and Countreys under our obedience, without being inquired after, vexed, molested, or compelled to do any thing in Religion, contrary to their Conscience . . .[3]

This kind of toleration is exceedingly ambivalent. Whereas, on the one hand, it grants persecuted minorities a certain degree of security and specific liberties, it is, on the other hand, a continuation of domination by other means. The tolerated minorities have to purchase their liberties with obedience and loyalty, because they are dependent on the protection of the authority and they are marked out as second-class citizens who deviate from the norm. This is the kind of toleration that Kant has in mind when he speaks of the "arrogant name of tolerance" in his answer to the question "What is enlightenment?"[4] Goethe expressed it as follows: "Tolerance should be a temporary attitude only; it must lead to recognition. To tolerate means to insult."[5]

In the course of a long and conflict-ridden modern development, by contrast, a second, horizontal rather than primarily vertical conception of toleration developed that I call the *respect conception*. The underlying idea is that tolerance is a mutual attitude that persons exhibit toward one another: they are at once tolerating and tolerated. Although they differ sharply in their respective notions of the good and of salvation, they accord each other a status as equals which states that generally valid norms must rest on reasons that all those affected can accept *equally* and do not favor one side, not even the majority. The "authority" to "bestow" liberties is no longer located exclusively in a power center. It resides, rather, in a process of general legitimation that provides for a special level of justification in questions of principle. When it is located in the political-legal domain, this mode of justification is called "democracy," but with strong protection of the status of minorities as legal and political equals.

2. An Autonomous Conception of Morality

(1) Without wanting to be unjust toward important precursors like Castellio, Bodin (the Bodin of the *Colloquium Heptaplomeres*), or Grotius, Pierre Bayle was the first thinker to develop the appropriate moral argument for a consistent respect conception at the social level. This argument essentially draws on three insights. First, as a Huguenot who suffered persecution in France and an undogmatic thinker who later also became a target of the hostility of his fellow-believers, Bayle was convinced that, given the excesses of superstition and religious fanaticism of his time, a false—as we would now say "fundamentalist"—conception of religion represented the greater

[3] Quoted from Roland Mousnier, *The Assassination of Henry IV*, trans. Joan Spencer (Scribner, 1973) 316–47.

[4] Immanuel Kant, "An Answer to the Question: What is Enlightenment?" in Immanuel Kant, *Practical Philosophy*, ed. and trans. Mary Gregor (Cambridge University Press 1996) 21 (8:40). References to translations of Kant's works are followed in parentheses by the volume and page numbers of the edition of the Königlich-Preußische Akademie der Wissenschaften (1903–11) (de Gruyter 1968).

[5] Johann Wolfgang von Goethe, *Maxims and Reflections*, trans. Elizabeth Stopp, ed. Peter Hutchinson (Penguin Books 1998) 116 (translation amended).

evil compared to atheism. Second, his study of the arguments of the late Augustine, the source of the doctrine that there is a duty to be intolerant for the sake of the salvation of the errant, had convinced him that the two most influential arguments for toleration—namely, that the individual conscience *cannot* and *should not* be forced to embrace the true faith—were not convincing. As Bayle's contemporary Jonas Proast also showed in his controversy with Locke, the first argument could be empirically refuted by citing examples of successful conversions that were more or less directly "assisted"; and the second argument lost its basis once salvation, as conceived by Christianity, was at stake. Who could stand idly by and watch a deluded man rushing toward the abyss of damnation when one could hold him back?[6]

Bayle recognized, thirdly, that a justification of toleration had to include a *reciprocal duty of tolerance* that could be morally justified independently of specific articles of faith. Otherwise the never-ending dispute over who was in the right and was allowed to coerce others in the name of the "true religion" could never be resolved. At the same time, however, such a justification could not come at the expense of the beliefs of each party to the dispute that they were advocating the true faith. According to Bayle, it had to be possible to arrive at an independent moral insight that it is "childish" always to insist only on one's own truth in religious conflicts, since that is precisely what is in dispute.[7] Moreover, there had to be a form of practical reason which made it clear that, without independent principles, any act of violence could be deemed agreeable to God. But, according to Bayle, this should appear inadmissible not only to every true Christian but also to anyone who thinks clearly and is enlightened by the *lumière primitive et universelle* of a "natural equity."[8]

Bayle develops these ideas in detail in his important work, the *Commentaire philosophique* (1685). There, he argues that the "natural light" of reason (*raison universelle*) implanted by God in all human beings independently of their religion reveals the "most general and infallible principles" of morality. Bayle puts the point in proto-Kantian terms:

> But since passions and prejudices only too often obscure the ideas of natural equity, I would advise a person who intends to know them well to consider these ideas in general and as abstracted from all private interest and from the customs of his country.[9]

Then, Bayle continues, one should ask oneself whether a certain practice could meet with general agreement in a particular society:

> Is such a practice just in itself? If it were a question of introducing it in a country where it would not be in use and where he would be free to take it up or not, would one see, upon examining it impartially that it is reasonable enough to merit being adopted?[10]

Using the argument for the autonomy of morality, Bayle tried to convince proponents of forced conversions that they were completely inverting the requirements of

[6] On this see Forst, *Toleration in Conflict* (n. 1) §5.
[7] Pierre Bayle, *Pierre Bayle's Philosophical Commentary: A Modern Translation and Critical Interpretation*, ed. and trans. Amie Godman Tannenbaum (Peter Lang 1987) 13 ff.
[8] ibid 30. [9] ibid. [10] ibid.

morality and turning virtues into crimes. The reason for this was the presumption that one had the right to impose the true religion by force, so that violence suddenly became "good" or "salutary." According to Bayle, this is "the most abominable doctrine that has ever been imagined."[11] With this argument, anyone could turn any position on its head:

If one would say, "it is very true, Jesus Christ has commanded His Disciples to persecute, but that is none of your business, you who are heretics. Executing this commandment belongs only to us who are the true Church," they would answer that they are agreed on the principle but not in the application and that they alone have the right to persecute since truth is on their side ... When one reflects on all this impartially, one is reduced necessarily to this rare principle, *I have truth on my side, therefore my violences are good works. So and so errs: therefore his violences are criminal.* To what purpose, pray, are all these reasonings? Do they heal the evils which persecutors commit, or are they capable of making them reconsider? Is it not absolutely necessary in order to cure the furor of a zealot who ravages a whole country or to make him comprehend his doings, to draw him out of his particular controversies and remind him of principles which are common to both parties such as the maxims of morality, the precepts of the Decalogue, of Jesus Christ and of His Apostles, concerning justice, charity, abstinence from theft, murder, injuries to our neighbor, etc.?[12]

Here the two key components of Bayle's argument for toleration are clearly discernible: the *normative* component of the independent morality of reciprocity and the *epistemological* component of the non-demonstrability of the true faith. For violence, judged in accordance with "natural" moral concepts, is nothing but violence, Bayle argues, and the claim to speak for the unquestionably true religion cannot be redeemed by means of "natural" reason on grounds that *cannot be reasonably rejected*. According to Bayle, it is not just a matter of appealing to an independent, rational sense of morality *as morality* common to all human beings that is free from fanatical distortions, in order to be able to differentiate moral from religious truths; rather, it is also a matter of undercutting religious disputes by showing that, although they are not entirely pointless, they cannot be resolved here on earth by rational means alone. This calls for a conception of the *finitude of reason* which states that, in matters of faith, disagreements among finite rational beings are unavoidable. (I will return to this point in the next section.)

With this argument for the autonomy of morality, Bayle takes up a line of thought developed in an earlier treatise, the *Pensées diverses sur la Comète* (1682/3). There he developed the thesis, which would later become famous as *Bayle's Paradox*, that even a society of atheists could be fair and stable, and perhaps even more peaceful than a religious society. The reason why atheism is considered to be the worst crime is "the false prejudice concerning the lights of the conscience, which are imagined to be the rule of our actions in the absence of a proper examination of the true springs that make us act."[13] The mistaken assumption is that a conscience that believes in providence and that virtue will receive divine reward and vice divine punishment

[11] ibid 47. [12] ibid 84–5.

[13] Bayle, *Various Thoughts on the Occasion of a Comet*, trans. by Robert C. Bartlett (SUNY Press 2000) §133 (165).

acts morally out of fear of God. This, Bayle argues, is completely at variance with experience. In the real world, it seems to be more the case that the very people who ardently profess their faith are capable of the worst crimes.

From a philosophical perspective, the numerous examples of religious fanaticism prove, according to Bayle, that human beings often fail to act in conformity with the principles of "natural equity" that they all share irrespective of their religion. On the contrary, they act in accordance with other motives; in particular, they succumb to the negative influence of passions and habits and to the positive influence of countervailing reflections, such as the fear of legal punishment and the fear of losing social recognition. And the same reflections can also be found among atheists, Bayle argues, so that, when it comes to morals, a society of atheists is potentially as stable as any other. In both negative and positive senses, atheists and religious believers are equals—"Jew and Mohammedan, Turk and Moor, Christian and Infidel, Indian and Tartar, the inhabitant of the firm earth and the inhabitant of the isles, nobleman and commoner."[14] From this perspective, the fear expressed by Locke and by many later eighteenth-century Enlightenment thinkers that morality would lack any basis without belief in divine justice is groundless. Human beings do not live in accordance with their principles of conscience but with other passions and considerations shared by all human beings.

However, this is only one aspect of Bayle's reflections. For atheists and religious believers are equals not only in their negative and positive passions but also in their autonomous faculty of moral insight (which Bayle conceives in almost Kantian terms):[15]

> Reason dictated to the ancient sages that it was necessary to do what is good for the love of the good itself, that virtue was its own reward, and that it belonged only to a vicious man to abstain from evil for fear of punishment ... This makes me believe that reason without the knowledge of God can sometimes persuade a man that there are decent things which it is fine and laudable to do, not on account of the utility of doing so, but because this is in conformity with reason. ... For one must know that although God does not reveal himself fully to an atheist, he does not fail to act upon the latter's mind and to preserve for him that reason and intelligence by means of which all men understand the truth of the first principles of metaphysics and morals.[16]

With this, Bayle takes the decisive step toward his justification of toleration. For if atheists and religious believers of all kinds are not only capable of positive passions of moral conformity and of self-interest, but also have the capacity to grasp the basic principles of theoretical and practical reason and to act accordingly, then the way is open for a conception of toleration based on mutual respect and on the justification of one's own claims with a shared rational foundation that is no longer tied to particular religious assumptions.

[14] Bayle, *Various Thoughts* (n. 13) §136 (169).

[15] This is also stressed by Ludwig Feuerbach, *Pierre Bayle: Ein Beitrag zur Geschichte der Philosophie und Menschheit*, in Feuerbach, *Gesammelte Werke* 4, ed. Werner Schuffenhauer (Akademie Verlag 1967) 103.

[16] Bayle, *Various Thoughts* (n. 13) §178 (221–2).

Bayle's thought thus makes the breakthrough to the insight that the question of mutual toleration calls for an *autonomous conception of morality* based on an independent faculty of practical reason to act on the basis of shareable justifications. Moreover, it also recognizes that toleration (in accordance with the respect conception) is conceivable only by means of what can be called the *deontological difference*—the difference between the unconditional principle of respect for the other as an equal, on the one hand, and all of the conceptions of the good, on the other, which may be "wider" or even "deeper" than morality, but nevertheless are and may be the focus of reasonable disagreement and constitute the objects of toleration.

(2) In a corresponding reconstruction of the logic of the "rationalization of morality" that is characteristic of the discourse of toleration, Kant's moral philosophy must count as the culmination of this rationalization. According to Kant, the ability to judge and act morally should be located exclusively in the faculty of practical reason. Moral action presupposes not only moral autonomy—the freedom to determine one's will in accordance with self-imposed laws—but also the autonomy of morality from heteronomous determinations of its principle and "incentives," be they doctrines of earthly happiness or heavenly blessedness. Thus, Kant connects the question of which actions are morally justifiable with a procedure that tests their universalizability such that no moral person serves "merely as a means" to someone else's end. For, as Kant explains using the example of a false promise, "he whom I want to use for my purposes by such a promise cannot possibly agree to my way of behaving toward him, and so himself contain the end of this action."[17]

For the problem of toleration it should be noted that Kant interprets the need to justify actions that affect the moral interests of others in relevant ways such that restricting individual freedom on religious grounds counts as unjustified because it would amount to restricting the autonomy of the person affected in favor of positing the truth in a unilateral way. Thus, not only must happiness not serve as a motive for acting morally; in addition, a person's happiness, assuming that he or she is a responsible adult, must not be made into the end of action against that person's will. Happiness is an object of irreducible conflicts of opinion, "not an idea of reason but of imagination":

> But it is a misfortune that the concept of happiness is such an indeterminate concept that, although every human being wishes to attain this, he can still never say determinately and consistently with himself what he really wishes and wills. The cause of this is that all the elements that belong to the concept of happiness are without exception empirical, that is, they must be borrowed from experience, and that nevertheless for the idea of happiness there is required an absolute whole, a maximum of well-being in my present condition and every future condition. Now, it is impossible for the most insightful and at the same time most powerful but still finite being to frame for himself a determinate concept of what he really wills here.[18]

[17] Immanuel Kant, *Groundwork of the Metaphysics of Morals*, ed. and trans. Mary Gregor (Cambridge University Press 1998) 38 (4:429 ff.).

[18] ibid 28 (4:418).

Therefore, the duty to promote the happiness of others must take its cue from *their* conception of happiness, even though this does not have to be accepted as binding and it does not represent the reason for moral action: "It is for them to decide what they count as belonging to their happiness; but it is open to me to refuse them many things that *they* think will make them happy but that I do not, as long as they have no right to demand them from me as what is theirs."[19] Neither imposing my notions of happiness on them nor, conversely, imposing theirs on me would be reconcilable with the dignity of a moral person endowed with reason and capable of self-determination. Thus, the dignity of the person, which must be respected unconditionally, can also be understood in such a way that every moral person has a basic *right to reciprocal and general justification* of all action-legitimating norms that claim reciprocal and general validity.[20] Here it is important that respect for the autonomy of the other person is *not* grounded in enabling him or her to lead a "good life" as a result. Rather, it is a matter of respect for the dignity of the other person as a morally self-determining being who offers and receives reasons. This is the meaning of the requirement to respect personal responsibility [*Mündigkeit*] and the right to make an independent use of one's reason, which, for Kant, is the hallmark of enlightened morality. In the history of morality, therefore, it is he who spelled out in detail Bayle's original idea that human beings, in addition to all of the particular ethical, and especially religious, identities that they possess and that divide them, have a common identity that binds all human beings morally *qua* human beings—namely, that of being a moral person.

Kant was the first to develop a rational conception of morality that makes such a clear separation between norms and principles that acquire categorical moral validity in virtue of being strictly justifiable and universalizable, and those values or notions of happiness that are not strictly justifiable and universalizable, and hence are not suitable for defining a universally binding morality—although they are suitable for orienting people in their lives. The morally good and the happy life, according to Kant, are two different things.[21] Moreover, among the conceptions that pervert morality by putting something else in the place of unconditional respect for others Kant counts conceptions based on anthropology and ones based on theology.[22] An ethical doctrine of happiness, whether it is based on religious or materialist assumptions, cannot ground moral obligation. Here the categorical distinction between ethical doctrines and universally valid moral norms is developed explicitly and it is of cardinal importance for a moral-philosophical perspective on the discourse of toleration. It enables us to differentiate between profound *ethical objection* and *moral acceptance* (to recall the components of toleration identified at the beginning) and at the same time to bring them together in a single conception. In this way it becomes clear how such a form of toleration could become a generally binding *requirement*

[19] Immanuel Kant, *The Metaphysics of Morals, Doctrine of Virtue*, ed. and trans. Mary Gregor (Cambridge University Press 1996) 151 (6:388).

[20] For a detailed account see Forst, *The Right to Justification*, trans. Jeffrey Flynn (Columbia University Press 2012) pt. I, and Rainer Forst, *Justification and Critique: Towards a Critical Theory of Politics*, trans. Ciaran Cronin (Polity 2014) ch. 4.

[21] See Kant, *Groundwork of the Metaphysics of Morals* (n. 17) 48 (4:442).

[22] ibid 22 (4:410).

of reciprocal respect—specifically among persons with not only divergent but also conflicting ethical convictions.

(3) Without a doubt, the discourse ethics of Jürgen Habermas is situated in this tradition. At its center is the deontological distinction between *moral* norms that can claim validity in a universalistic sense because they are justifiable in practical discourses, and *ethical* values that can claim only particular validity.[23] This represents a further development of the Kantian understanding of morality, with the important difference that, instead of a reflective procedure for examining norms, now an intersubjective, discursive procedure of norm justification is proposed. Moreover, this discursive procedure is not grounded in transcendental reflection but is based on a reconstruction of the normative content of discursive presuppositions of argumentation. According to Habermas, the procedural conditions inscribed in rational practical discourses can be captured by the principle of universalization (U). This states that a norm can claim validity only if "all affected can *freely* accept the consequences and the side effects that the *general* observance of a controversial norm can be expected to have for the satisfaction of the interests of *each individual*."[24] From this follows the principle of discourse ethics (D) as a moral principle. (D) states that "only those norms can claim to be valid that meet (or could meet) with the approval of all affected in their capacity as participants in a practical discourse."[25] The parenthetical qualification underlines the counterfactual character of moral validity, according to which every concrete justification remains criticizable in the light of better reasons.

Aside from the difference between a transcendental and a reconstructive, pragmatic justification of the moral principle and between a "monological" and a "dialogical" version of the norm justification procedure, there is another important difference from Kant that is bound up with the problem of morality and religion. Whereas Kant's thesis of the autonomy of morality attributes morally binding and motivating power to the moral law of practical reason itself, Habermas no longer thinks that "detranscendentalized" reason is capable of such autonomous binding power and motivation: "Unlike the classical form of practical reason, communicative reason is not an immediate source of prescription."[26] Habermas does not regard either the insight into the discourse principle or the insight into justified norms as an independent justification endowed with autonomous motivating power. Rather, discursive morality relies on "accommodating" forms of life and corresponding learning processes[27] that give rise to postconventional attitudes. But morality is in danger

[23] See Jürgen Habermas, "Discourse Ethics: Notes on a Program of Philosophical Justification," in Jürgen Habermas, *Moral Consciousness and Communicative Action*, trans. Christian Lenhardt and Shierry Weber Nicholsen (MIT Press 1990) 43–115, at 103 ff.

[24] ibid 93. [25] ibid.

[26] Jürgen Habermas, *Between Facts and Norms: Contributions to a Discourse Theory of Law and Democracy*, trans. William Rehg (MIT Press 1996) 4. See also Jürgen Habermas, "Communicative Reason and the Detranscendentalized 'Use of Reason,'" in Jürgen Habermas, *Between Naturalism and Religion: Philosophical Essays*, trans. Ciaran Cronin (Polity 2008) 24–76.

[27] Habermas, "Treffen Hegels Einwände gegen Kant auch auf die Diskursethik zu?," in Habermas, *Erläuterungen zur Diskursethik* (Suhrkamp 1991) 9–30, at 25.

of losing its validity as a result—specifically, at the moment the question of moral validity is seen as being "intertwined" with ethical and pragmatic motives in order to express the "self-understanding of subjects acting communicatively" as a whole.[28] This implies that non-moral motives—in particular, ethical considerations of the good life—are supposed to support morality, at least in part, so that morality would enjoy only hypothetical validity contingent on each person's self-understanding.

This danger is most acute where Habermas takes up the bioethical problem of the "future of human nature," the problem that led him to adopt a new approach to religious validity claims in the social domain in the first place. In a critique of certain eugenic measures and perspectives that challenge the inviolability of human nature and the human person and can extend to "human breeding"[29] he sees essential presuppositions of the modern morality of mutual respect in jeopardy. According to Habermas, however, these presuppositions themselves *cannot* be defended on purely moral grounds, but are instead embedded in a "species ethics" that is prior to morality. This leads him to the following thesis: "An assessment of morality as a whole is itself not a moral judgment, but an ethical one, a judgment which is part of the ethics of the species."[30] If morality as a whole were jeopardized because the assumption of moral autonomy was challenged and persons were "programmed," then, according to Habermas, this species ethics would have to remind us what we would lose as a result. From a consistently deontological perspective, however, respect for moral autonomy and for its indispensable preconditions (insofar as it can be shown which these are) is—in my view, at least—*morally* and not ethically required. Otherwise, moral respect would become a matter of what we "want,"[31] which is conditioned by ethics, by the ethical desire to preserve a certain form of life that supports morality. But actions and decisions that threaten morality, whether in specific cases or in principle, are morally impermissible, as can be argued with Kant against Habermas. Here responsibility toward those affected does not allow any leeway for *ethical* decisions about what "we" do or do not want as a species.[32]

Therefore, a position beholden to Bayle and Kant must insist that a post-secular society also cannot dispense with a secular conception of morality that is capable of motivating out of its own resources. Otherwise the only kind of obligation that could be produced in the conflict between religious doctrines would be one based on ethical overlaps or compromises. But this would place in question a clear moral language, such as the one Bayle demands. Thus, a reflection made by Habermas in the context of the genealogy of the secular distinction between ethics and morality in the light of religious pluralism is open to doubt:

[28] Jürgen Habermas, "Rightness versus Truth: On the Sense of Normative Validity in Moral Judgments and Norms," in Jürgen Habermas, *Truth and Justification*, trans. Barbara Fultner (MIT Press) 237–76, at 274.

[29] Jürgen Habermas, *The Future of Human Nature*, trans. Hannah Beister, Max Pensky, and William Rehg (Polity 2003) 72.

[30] ibid 73. [31] ibid.

[32] On my critique of Habermas see Forst, *The Right to Justification* (n. 20) chs. 3 and 4.

Aware of the normatively shaped relations in cultures influenced by religion, Kantians had good "ethical" reasons—not "moral" reasons, mind you, but a "need"—neither to withdraw to ethnocentric relativism concerning values nor to fall back on compassion or egocentric calculations of utility in the face of the epistemic problems posed by religious pluralism.[33]

This need is not in dispute. But the reason for assuming a categorically valid morality is insight into the capability and duty of practical reason to regard every person as a free and equal justificatory authority, whatever conception of the good he or she may or may not share. This ethical pluralism must not be transcended again in an overarching ethics of the "species" or be endowed with special validity. Reflection on the independence of morality in view of deep-seated ethical differences cannot be reconciled with Habermas' view that the "reflexive decision whether we still even 'want' to see ourselves as persons who act responsibly . . . is no longer a moral question that can be clearly answered in accordance with standards of moral obligation."[34] To introduce the plurality of species ethics here in such a way that morality would depend on one of them would be to draw the wrong conclusion from the conflict between ethical doctrines. Reflection on this conflict in particular makes morality not only desirable but strictly binding.

3. Faith and Reason

(1) If Bayle appears to be a precursor of Kant when it comes to developing an autonomous conception of morality, the situation is different as regards the relationship between faith and reason. Bayle defends a conception of finite practical and theoretical reason whose guiding assumption is that reason must recognize its own limits with regard to "speculative truths." This opens up the space of metaphysical or religious conflict between positions that can be reasonably held but can also be reasonably rejected. The reason for this is that "evidence is a relative quality,"[35] especially in religious matters. Habit, training, or other factors mean that rational individuals arrive at very different evaluations and judgments and differences may arise that cannot be resolved based on a clear rational judgment. A reasonable person is aware of the "burdens of reason" (to borrow a term of Rawls's)[36] and, according to Bayle, knows that "difference in opinion [is] man's inherent infelicity, as long as his understanding is so limited and his heart so inordinate."[37] Therefore, the desire for a single religion that unites all human beings will remain unfulfilled, and the best response to this is to espouse toleration. Rational human beings recognize that their reason is finite and that religious differences are unavoidable. Yet at the same time they recognize that it does not follow that they should mistrust their faith, since this insight by no means refutes their faith nor does it reduce it to something merely subjective.

[33] Jürgen Habermas, "A Symposium on Faith and Knowledge," in Jürgen Habermas, *Postmetaphysical Thinking II: Essays and Replies*, trans. Ciaran Cronin (Polity 2017) 135.
[34] ibid. [35] Bayle, *Pierre Bayle's Philosophical Commentary* (n. 7) II.1, 93.
[36] John Rawls, *Political Liberalism* (Columbia University Press 1992) ch. 2.
[37] Bayle, *Pierre Bayle's Philosophical Commentary* (n. 7) II.6, 141.

This is the central theme of Bayle's *Dictionnaire historique et critique* (1696). Bayle's main concern in this work is not, as many of his readers assumed, to reject faith as "irrational"—but neither is it to espouse an extreme form of fideism[38] in the tradition of Montaigne and Pascal that affirms faith even against reason. He wants to create room for religious answers to metaphysical questions by placing limits on the negative force of reason—answers that reason alone can neither provide nor demand nor can it prohibit them. This cuts the ground out from under dogmatic disputes about and proofs of the "true faith," without religious belief that remains within the boundaries of what can be rationally debated becoming empty or irrational as a result. Both sides, reason and faith, must heed their respective limits: reason recognizes its limitations in speculative questions to which faith alone can provide further answers; and faith does not try to present and impose its "truths" as conclusive matters that are beyond reasonable dispute. Although faith is situated *beyond* reason, it is not *irrational.* At the same time, (theoretical and practical) reason remains the faculty shared by all human beings that unites them despite all religious differences and continues to be a corrective to superstition. Reasonable faith knows that it is a *faith*.

In two articles in the *Dictionnaire* devoted to the "Manichaeans" and the "Paulicians"—hence to those "heretics" who trace the existence of good and evil in the world back to two different conflicting sources—Bayle develops the thesis that the negative arguments of the Manichaeans cannot be refuted by rational means. For one cannot provide an adequate explanation of how God can be the author of evil or, if he is not its author, of how the existence of evil in creation is to be accounted of if one does not *believe*—beyond all experience—the story of the Fall of Man.[39] Bayle should not be understood as claiming that revelation is believed entirely without reasons; rather, his position is that revelation offers "the best solution" to the problem posed, although this cannot be demonstrated by purely rational and empirical means. The "natural light of philosophy," he argues, ties the "Gordian knot" of the need for explanation ever tighter;[40] but an answer can be found on the basis of faith. This answer will always remain contested in the realm of reason, according to Bayle. As a result, the dogmatists should show as much restraint in their claims to absoluteness as the philosophical sceptics who only manage to pose riddles. Questions such as that concerning the reason for the existence of evil exceed the metaphysical possibilities of human beings.[41] Therefore, reason should recognize that this is where the realm of faith begins and that acrimonious disputes over demonstrations of the

[38] Thus Richard Popkin, "Pierre Bayle's Place in 17th Century Skepticism," in *Pierre Bayle: Le philosophe de Rotterdam*, ed. Paul Dibon (Vrin 1959) 1–19, at 1, who qualifies this only in relation to Bayle's later work. Craig B. Brush, *Montaigne and Bayle: Variations on the Theme of Skepticism* (Nijhoff 1966) 300, by contrast, characterizes Bayle correctly as a "semi-fideist" insofar as he does not think that the truth of faith can be demonstrated, but does not think it is irrational either.

[39] Pierre Bayle, *Historical and Critical Dictionary: Selections*, ed. and trans. Richard H. Popkin (Hackett 1991) article "Manicheans," remark D, 151 f.

[40] Bayle, *Historical and Critical Dictionary: Selections* (n. 39) article "Paulicians," 268.

[41] ibid article "Paulicians," remark M, 191.

truth are pointless. Questions of this kind are, to use a different vocabulary, objects of "reasonable agreement," matters of dispute among reasonable human beings.

He makes this point even clearer in his second "clarification," which was necessary because Bayle himself was suspected of Manicheanism. There he uses formulations that trace the fine line between, on the one hand, his reduction of the claim to truth of the Christian religion to the domain of pure faith, which made him into a spoiler and sceptic in the eyes of those who wanted to unite philosophy and theology under the supremacy of theology, and, on the other, his restriction of the claim to authority of philosophy in the religious domain, which turned him into an obdurate fideist in the eyes of those who wanted to unite both under the supremacy of philosophy. He emphasizes "that all articles of the Christian faith, maintained and opposed by the weapons of philosophy alone, do not emerge in good shape from the battle," and hence that they must abandon this battlefield and look for a different fortress—namely, Holy Scripture.[42] This is not an admission of weakness but instead a result of the insight that "*the mysteries of the Gospels are above reason* [*dessus de la Raison*]," that "it is impossible to solve the difficulties raised by philosophers; and, consequently, a dispute in which only the natural light will be employed will always end to the disadvantage of the theologians; and they will find themselves forced to give ground and take refuge under the protection of the supernatural light." That is an insight, Bayle continues, into the "limits" of reason which "can never attain to what is above it."[43] At the same time, it is also a self-limitation of religion, which as a result abandons the scene of the battle over absolute truth that could justify faith rationally.[44]

The message of this way of defining the boundary between reason and faith for toleration is clear: the truths of religion become accessible only through inner faith. The implication for sects such as the Manichaeans is that there is no reason not to tolerate them. Moreover, with regard to unbelievers who remain trapped in the confusion of reason, this view implies that there is no reason for intolerance, because the natural light remains a reliable guide in moral matters.[45] Although the disputes between Catholics and Protestants do not become empty, they are relativized as regards the prospect of resolving them.[46] At the same time, there is no justification for a reverse form of intolerance on the part of reason that would represent all forms of faith as superstitious and irrational. Faith has its own domain in which it provides answers to metaphysical questions that cannot be found by rational means alone:

> [A] true Christian, well versed in the characteristics of supernatural truths and firm on the principles that are peculiar to the Gospels, will only laugh at the subtleties of the philosophers, and especially those of the Pyrrhonists. Faith will place him above the regions where the tempests of disputation reign. He will stand on a peak, from which he will hear below him the thunder of arguments and distinctions; and he will not be disturbed at all by this—a peak, which will be for him the real Olympus of the poets and the real temple of the sages, from which he will see in perfect tranquility the weaknesses of reason and the meanderings of mortals who only follow that guide. Every Christian who allows himself to be disconcerted

[42] ibid Second Clarification, 409. [43] ibid 410 ff. (French, 1223). [44] ibid 414.
[45] ibid 411. [46] ibid 413.

by the objections of the unbelievers, and to be scandalized by them, has one foot in the same grave as they do.[47]

This is a subtle response to the accusation of making philosophical concessions to the Manichaeans and Sceptics and thereby casting doubt on the foundations of religion as a result. Bayle accepts the first part of the accusation, only to charge those who see this as a challenge to religion not only with having a falsely grounded faith that confuses the domain of reason with that of faith, but also with being of weak faith. He rescues the possibility of faith at the cost of relativizing the claim to absolute, rationally redeemable truth. Anyone who has "witnessed the mighty contests between reason and faith"[48] will not fall back into the dogmatic slumber in which the boundary between these two domains is forgotten.

(2) Bearing in mind how Bayle portrays the relationship between practical and theoretical reason and faith, we find a different path in Kant—and with it the key difference between two forms of Enlightenment thought. Bayle assigns faith and reason to separate domains, which makes him into an "intellectual flagellant," according to critics like Feuerbach, who at the same time praises Bayle as Kant's precursor in matters of morality.[49] Kant, in contrast to Bayle, does not proceed from moral philosophy to a conception of "reasonable religion," but instead to the notion of a "religion of reason" (*Vernunftreligion*).

The path to this conception leads through the idea of the "supreme good," which Kant formulates in response to the question of how "supreme ends" that enable reason to "find peace" can be conceived, if not from a speculative, then from a *practical* point of view.[50] The two questions that concern the practical interest of pure reason—namely "What should I do?" and "What may I hope?"—should, accordingly, be viewed in such a way that the answer to the first is: "Do that through which you will become worthy to be happy," from which follows the second question, which asks: "If I behave so as not to be unworthy of happiness, how may I hope thereby to partake of it?"[51] The question of hope, according to Kant, necessarily aims at happiness. However, if morality is to remain free from empirical motives of happiness, it can be referred only to the "worthiness to be happy" as an answer to the first question. Hence, it becomes the question of how this worthiness is possible—that is, the question of happiness "proportionate" to morality. According to Kant, such a "system of self-rewarding morality"[52] is possible only on the basis of the idea of a "highest reason" that "commands in accordance with moral laws, as at the same time the cause of nature."[53] Thus, the two questions concerning morality and hope that guide the practical interest of reason come together in an "ideal of the highest good," the ideal of a perfect harmony of the morally perfect will with the "highest blessedness" conceivable only through a divine "author and regent" of the world.

[47] ibid Third Clarification, 429. [48] ibid 435.

[49] Feuerbach, *Pierre Bayle* (n. 15) 163.

[50] Immanuel Kant, *Critique of Pure Reason*, ed. and trans. Paul Guyer and Allen W. Wood (Cambridge University Press 1998) 673 (B 825 ff./A 797 ff.) and 675 (B 830/A 802).

[51] Kant, *Critique of Pure Reason* (n, 50) 679 (B 836f./A 809f.). [52] ibid (B 837/A 809).

[53] ibid 680 (B 838/A 810).

At the limit of finite reason, therefore, only the idea of a transcendent being, according to Kant, can make the unity of the ends of morality and happiness conceivable. And pace Kant's insistence that he remains within the architectonic of his critique of reason, with this he transgresses the boundaries of reason toward a form of "moral theology." Even though the latter is not purely speculative, it nevertheless leads from the question "What can I hope for?" into the realm of speculation, or at least into the realm of faith, although Kant sees this as a purely "rational faith"—namely, the belief in the creator of a world in which moral action, although still categorically required, will not have been in vain.

This is reinforced in the *Critique of Practical Reason*, where Kant believes that he can resolve the "antinomy of practical reason" only through the idea of worthiness to be happy. And although he describes the supreme good in this context as the "whole *object* of a pure practical reason," he insists that it is not the *determining ground* of moral action, since that would lead to heteronomy.[54] The idea of the supreme good arises from the "need of reason"[55] that happiness in proportion to morality "can at least be thought as possible."[56] This is the key point for Kant: while morality founded on human autonomy is strictly binding for reason, the faith that corresponds to the postulates of the immortality of the soul and the existence of God is not, "for there can be no duty to assume the existence of anything." The "morally necessary" assumption that God exists is thus merely a "subjective" need, albeit also a need of consistent reason.[57] Thus, when Kant speaks in the *Critique of Judgment* of a "moral proof of the existence of God," he means not only that this follows from the primacy of practical reason, but also that morality is in the first instance an autonomous obligation of reason, whereas belief in a moral creator is only an implication of the notion of happiness that can correspond to this morality alone.[58]

This is not the place for a detailed discussion of what this limitation means for the status of the "supreme good" or whether it fits well—or even could fit well—with the architectonics of Kantian philosophy, in particular his moral philosophy. In short, with the idea of the supreme good, Kant, in my view, makes too many concessions to a legitimate, but not necessary need of finite rational beings to invest their actions with a transcendent meaning from a moral-ethical point of view when he recognizes this *need* as an *interest* of practical reason, although not one on the same level as the interest in the question of knowledge or of morality. Here he goes a step too far in the endeavor to transgress the boundaries of finite reason when he regards

[54] Immanuel Kant, *Critique of Practical Reason*, ed. and trans. Mary Gregor (Cambridge University Press 1997) 91–2 (5:109).

[55] As Kant also puts it in "What does it mean to orient oneself in thinking?," in Immanuel Kant, *Religion within the Bounds of Mere Reason*, ed. and trans. Allen W. Wood and Giorgio Di Giovanni (Cambridge University Press 1998) 1–14, at 8 (8:139) and in "On the Common Saying: That May be Correct in Theory, but it is of no Use in Practice," in Kant, *Practical Philosophy* (n. 4) 279–309, at 282 n. (8:279 ff. n.).

[56] Kant, *Critique of Practical Reason* (n. 54) 99 (5:119).

[57] ibid 105 (5:125 ff.).

[58] Immanuel Kant, *Critique of the Power of Judgment*, ed. Paul Guyer, trans. Paul Guyer and E. Matthews (Cambridge University Press 2000) 316 (5:450 ff.).

the faith that corresponds to the supreme good as something that is *postulated* by reason.[59] It could at most be *permitted* within the bounds of finite reason.

Decisive for the issue of toleration is Kant's assumption that here he has discovered the kernel of a rational, purely moral faith according to which morality remains valid for its own sake, although it nevertheless presents moral duties as "divine commands" and affirms that the harmony between nature and morals corresponds to a "kingdom of God."[60] How this conception comes closest to Christianity while nevertheless going beyond it, Kant explains in detail in *Religion within the Boundaries of Mere Reason* (1793). With this, in spite of all the difference from the tradition of rational religion that as a general rule founds morality on a deistic conception of natural religion, Kant reverts to this tradition insofar as he thinks that the differences between the positive religions—and the associated intolerance—can be reconciled through a "rationalization" of religion that ultimately treats all religious differences as incidental matters (*adiaphora*).[61]

Kant's rational religion is not only founded on morality. As regards its exercise, it also consists essentially in a moral outlook, specifically "the heart's disposition to observe all human duties as divine commands."[62] It strives to create an "ethical community," a "people of God," that lives only under laws of virtue and could ultimately form the one "true church," the Kingdom of God on earth, without any splits over doctrine or rites.[63] In contrast to the "pure religious faith" that does not allow any pluralism, Kant can see in the diversity of positive religions that appeal to revelation only a multiplicity of "forms of faith," of mere "ecclesiastical faiths," that are basically morally indifferent:

> *Different religions*: an odd expression! just as if one could also speak of different *morals*. There can indeed be historically different creeds, [to be found] not in religion but in the history of means used to promote it, which is the province of scholarship, and just as many different religious books ... but there can be only one single religion holding for all human beings and in all times.[64]

According to Kant, it is "more appropriate" to say that someone is "of this (Jewish, Mohammedan, Christian, Catholic, Lutheran) faith, than: He is of this or that religion."[65] "Religious struggles," according to Kant, always turned exclusively on "ecclesiastical faith." They consisted in one side declaring that their inessential doctrines and practices were religious necessities and that people of other faiths were

[59] Immanuel Kant, *Religion within the Bounds of Mere Reason*, ed. and trans. Allen W. Wood and Giorgio di Giovanni (Cambridge University Press 1998) 35 (6:6), where Kant asserts that morality leads "inevitably" to religion.

[60] Kant, *Critique of Practical Reason* (n. 54) 107 (Ak. 5:128 ff.).

[61] As he argues in "The Conflict of the Faculties," in Immanuel Kant, *Religion and Rational Theology*, ed. and trans. Allen W. Wood and Giorgio di Giovanni (Cambridge University Press 2008) 233–328, at 266 (7:40).

[62] Kant, *Religion within the Bounds of Mere Reason* (n. 59) 98 (6:84).

[63] ibid 109–10 (Ak. 6:98–101).

[64] Immanuel Kant, "Toward Perpetual Peace: A Philosophical Project," in Kant, *Practical Philosophy* (n. 4) 317–51, at 336 n. (8:367 n.).

[65] Kant, *Religion within the Bounds of Mere Reason* (n. 59) 116 (6:107 ff.).

unbelievers or heretics.[66] However, this does not mean that for Kant every ecclesiastical faith is equally inessential and unimportant. Because human beings demand "something that the senses can hold on to" in matters of faith, and ecclesiastical faith is therefore to some extent unavoidable, that faith is to be preferred whose teaching harmonizes best with the "original" or "natural" rational religion. This conception not only sets narrow limits on the claim to validity of revealed religions in order to put an end to all religious disputes. It also leads Kant to a position that passes judgment on these religions, confirming, for example, Mendelssohn's fear that the rational religion of the Enlightenment not only casts fundamental doubt on positive religion but also involves new kinds of bias.[67] In this context, Kant shows a clear preference for Christianity over Judaism. He considers the latter to be a purely political rather than a moral faith, "a collection of merely statutory laws," so that Judaism "strictly speaking . . . is not a religion at all" or a church but a political community.[68] The history of moral religion began only with Christianity, according to Kant, with its emphasis on inner, moral belief that is the essence of a pure moral disposition, although it later fell prey to the intolerant sectarianism of ecclesiastical faith; only in "the present" is there the prospect of overcoming these enmities and returning to the "true religious faith," which leads to religious unification.[69]

Thus, the humanist idea of religious unity returns in the guise of moral religion. And, even though Kant repeatedly stresses the primacy of rational morality that is open to and unites all human beings over all forms of revelation, he nevertheless continues the tradition of attempts to overcome intolerance between religions (or "forms of faith") by also transcending their essential differences, yet without being able to shake off the prejudices of his own Christian tradition in the process. Kant first detached human beings as autonomous moral persons from the religious horizon of both tradition and the Enlightenment, only to relocate them within the reconstructed horizon of a universalistic religion. On a critical examination, however, the latter proves to be neither universalistic nor to follow from morality and, in its striving for unity, it does not do sufficient justice to the problem of toleration. From a Baylean perspective, the argument for rational religion does not take the insight into the limits of reason seriously enough.

(3) Until the 1990s, Jürgen Habermas dealt with the topic of religion primarily within the framework of the Weberian theory of societal rationalization. According to that conception, the differentiation of value spheres displaces the older forms of religious normative validity and transforms them over the course of modernity, which advances toward a "postmetaphysical" mode of thinking. In particular, in the discussion of the "linguistification of the sacred" in the *Theory of Communicative Action*, Habermas draws on Mead and Durkheim to show how, as society evolved, "the archaic core of the normative" connected with religious worldviews gave way to the "universalization of law and morality" and the associated rationalization of

[66] ibid 117 (6:108 ff.).

[67] On this see Forst, *Toleration in Conflict* (n. 1) §20.

[68] Kant, *Religion within the Bounds of Mere Reason* (n. 59) 130 (6:125).

[69] ibid 135–6 (6:131 ff.).

society.[70] According to Habermas, communicative action takes the place of the normativity founded on the sacred:

> The disenchantment and disempowering of the domain of the sacred takes place by way of a *linguistification of the ritually secured, basic normative agreement*; going along with this is a release of the rationality potential in communicative action. The aura of rapture and terror that emanates from the sacred, the *spellbinding* power of the holy, is sublimated into the *binding/bonding* force of criticizable validity claims and at the same time turned into an everyday occurrence.[71]

In this way, religious communities become secularized into cooperative communities and the complexes of law and morality absorb the normative contents of religious systems and reconfigure them on the basis of rational critique and validity. Reaching consensus through language replaces traditional normative thought obedient to an authority and real normative worlds are transcended through an appeal to a more inclusive discourse community. As a result, the historical genesis of the discourse theory of morality and of the constitutional state becomes apparent. This general conception is situated within the Enlightenment tradition to which Kant also belongs, according to which the forces of reason replace religion. And even though Habermas, unlike Kant, does not develop a notion of "rational religion," he nevertheless agrees with Kant that the traditional form of religious faith has become obsolete in the modern era and is replaced by the rationality of discursive legislation. On this view, social progress marginalizes religion and turns it into a force that still has ethical relevance in the lives of individuals but no longer in the moral and political life of secular political communities as a whole.

To be sure, this view is counterbalanced in Habermas by another one that emphasizes that religion preserves a productive moment in modernity as well. This emphasis is especially apparent in his texts on philosophers such as Bloch, Benjamin, and Scholem and their relationship to Judaism. In these writings, Habermas stresses the potentials of religious traditions that, although they have to be transmitted and translated, nevertheless cannot (or at least cannot as yet) be completely exhausted in modern normative orders. In his readings of the aforementioned thinkers, Habermas places particular emphasis on the figures of thought of messianic hope that transcends social reality and of salvation from a derelict and fallen rationalized world—for example, in Benjamin he highlights the recollection of the possibility of a "fulfilled" or, better, "not misspent" life[72] and, in Scholem, reflection on the human beyond the horizon of a one-sided modernized society: "Among modern societies, only those that are able to bring essential elements of their religious traditions which point beyond the merely human into the spheres of the profane will also be able to rescue the substance of the human."[73]

[70] Jürgen Habermas, *The Theory of Communicative Action*, Vol. 2, trans. Thomas McCarthy (Beacon Press 1987) 46.

[71] ibid Vol. 2, 77 (first emphasis added).

[72] Jürgen Habermas, *Philosophical-Political Profiles*, trans. Frederick G. Lawrence (MIT Press 1983) 157 (translation amended).

[73] ibid 210 (translation amended).

In his recent writings on religion, Habermas returns to these motifs informed by the critique of society and of rationality of the *Dialectic of Enlightenment*. Now, however, he connects them not only with a vehement critique of the excesses of the "uncontrolled process of modernization,"[74] but also develops a new account of the relationship between faith and knowledge that in important respects is closer to Bayle than to Kant, insofar as it sees the fact that religion remains a productive social force in modernity as a hallmark of a "post-secular society."[75] Here a variety of motives play a role. In the controversy alluded to above with bioethical developments and risk scenarios up to and including perfectionistic human breeding programs, Habermas is convinced that it is necessary to preserve and invoke in discourse semantic and ethical contents of religious traditions that express reservations against such developments. Secular and religious citizens must simultaneously perform the corresponding "work of translation" because, even though the secular state calls for a secular justification of generally valid norms, it must respect and make optimal use of the wealth of possible viewpoints. Reason must remain public and free from religion. But, mindful of its own limitations, it can help in the "appropriation of the particularistic semantic potentials contained in the languages of specific communities,"[76] such as those that can be found in religious traditions. Habermas thinks that Kant's philosophy of religion in certain respects provides a model for this because, on the one hand, it insists on the independence of reason but, on the other, it pursues the "goal of redeeming religious contents through translation."[77] However, Habermas correctly emphasizes that this conflicts with the intention—in my view, the dominant one in Kant—that reason should adjudicate over the truth and falsity of religion and integrate and supersede it.[78]

Therefore, Habermas is actually led by a reflection that is closer to Bayle to view the continued existence of religion as a characteristic of modern society and as a result of the finitude of reason in the domain of what Rawls calls "comprehensive doctrines." The controversy with the ethical pluralism emphasized by Rawls in *Political Liberalism* was a major factor in leading Habermas to rethink the role of religion in the public discourse of secular, democratic societies.[79] Thus, Habermas writes, very much in line with Bayle:

> The religious side must accept the authority of "natural" reason as the fallible results of the institutionalized sciences and the basic principles of universalistic egalitarianism in law and morality. Conversely, secular reason may not set itself up as the judge concerning truths of

[74] Jürgen Habermas, "The Boundary between Faith and Knowledge," in Jürgen Habermas, *Between Naturalism and Religion: Philosophical Essays*, trans. Ciaran Cronin (Polity 2008) 209–47, at 238.

[75] Jürgen Habermas, "Faith and Knowledge," in Jürgen Habermas, *The Future of Human Nature*, trans. Hannah Beister, Max Pensky, and William Rehg (Polity 2003) 101–15, at 114.

[76] Habermas, "The Boundary between Faith and Knowledge" (n. 74) 240.

[77] ibid 230.

[78] ibid.

[79] On this see the controversy with Rawls originally published in the *Journal of Philosophy* and reprinted in Jürgen Habermas, *The Inclusion of the Other*, trans. Ciaran Cronin (MIT Press 1998) chs. 2 and 3. On my own attempts on this see Rainer Forst, *Contexts of Justice: Political Philosophy beyond Liberalism and Communitarianism*, trans. John M. M. Farrell (University of California Press 2002) and *The Right to Justification* (n. 20) ch. 4.

faith, even though in the end it can accept as reasonable only what it can translate into its own, in principle universally accessible, discourses.[80]

In his recent work, Habermas situates this within a broad historical framework. Against a "blinkered Enlightenment which is unenlightened about itself,"[81] he stresses the connections reaching back into the "Axial Age" between religious and moral transcendence of social reality and founding social integration. Moreover, he highlights the importance of a continued, complementary learning process between the two sides (which is connected in turn with the reference to the motivational weaknesses of "rational morality" criticized above).[82] In this context, Habermas revises the thesis of the linguistification of the sacred. According to this revised position, the comprehensive religious worldviews that arose during the Axial Age were essential in the development of social normativity by facilitating, in combination with religious observances, an "extraordinary form of communication"[83] that generated a "strong normativity" of social solidarity.[84] In the process of social development, these overarching justification narratives come under normative pressure, as postulated by the theory of linguistification. However, according to Habermas, it is possible that they contain "still vital semantic potentials"[85] that reason must take seriously: "We may ask whether we must take religion seriously in a philosophical sense as a *contemporary* intellectual formation, where by 'religion' I understand religious observances in connection with conceptions of redemptive justice."[86]

Here I cannot discuss this complex reconstruction of the formation of social normativity in greater detail. In the context of the discussion of toleration, it should be noted that the redefinition of the relationship between faith and reason leads Habermas to a conception of toleration—developed in dialogue with my proposal in *Toleration in Conflict*—that explicitly appeals to Bayle. It ultimately boils down to a (in my terminology) respect conception that rests on an interplay between universally binding moral judgments and respect for and tolerance of ethical and religious diversity.[87] It is important in this context that Habermas (as I proposed in *Contexts of Justice*) employs the concept of the "translation" of religious arguments in public political discourses, at least when it comes to discourses that lead to legally and politically binding decisions (I will return to this point), where translation calls

[80] Jürgen Habermas, "An Awareness of What is Missing," in Jürgen Habermas, *An Awareness of What is Missing: Faith and Reason in a Post-Secular Age*, ed. Michael Reder and Josef Schmidt, trans. Ciaran Cronin (Polity 2010) 15–23, at 16.

[81] ibid 18.

[82] Habermas, "An Awareness of What is Missing" (n. 80) 19. See also Jürgen Habermas, "The New Philosophical Interest in Religion. An Interview with Eduardo Mendieta," in Jürgen Habermas, *Postmetaphysical Thinking II: Essays and Replies*, trans. Ciaran Cronin (Polity 2017) 66: "After all, ritual has been a source of social solidarity for which neither the enlightened morality of equal respect for all nor the Aristotelian ethics of virtue and the good life provides a real, motivational equivalent."

[83] Jürgen Habermas, "The Lifeworld as a Space of Symbolically Embodied Reasons," in Jürgen Habermas, *Postmetaphysical Thinking II: Essays and Replies*, trans. Ciaran Cronin (Polity 2017) 28–42.

[84] ibid; see also Jürgen Habermas, "Linguistification of the Sacred. In Place of a Preface," in Jürgen Habermas, *Postmetaphysical Thinking II: Essays and Replies*, trans. Ciaran Cronin (Polity 2017) vii–xiv.

[85] ibid xiv.

[86] Habermas, "The Lifeworld as a Space of Symbolically Embodied Reasons" (n. 83), 42.

[87] See Habermas, *Between Naturalism and Religion* (n. 26) chs. 5 and 9.

for reciprocal and general justifications for general norms on grounds of justice.[88] He also sees this as a political and moral duty to provide justifications. Against the background of his redefinition of the role of religion in social life, however, he adds the idea, which extends this conception, of a "cooperative"[89] and *mutual* translation. Not only do citizens with religious beliefs have a duty to translate them into a generally acceptable, secular language in order to avoid unfair domination of others through insufficiently legitimized beliefs. In addition, non-religious citizens also have the task of understanding and respecting the positions of people who think in religious terms and of developing the potentials of these beliefs in a mutual learning process: "A liberal political culture can even expect its secular citizens to take part in efforts to translate relevant contributions from religious language into a publicly intelligible language."[90]

It should be noted concerning this, however, that the political and moral duty to translate claims and arguments into a language that cannot be reciprocally and generally rejected (which might be called "secular") and the duty to treat religious positions with hermeneutic sympathy are not strictly reciprocal. Aside from the fact that this could lead to a paternalism of "translation assistance," the public reason of justification remains something independent and shared. It cannot assign duties of justification symmetrically in such a way that all those involved must travel the same distance in order to arrive at general norms.[91] For example, someone who wants to forbid same-sex marriages or the construction of mosques on religious grounds must travel a longer distance in order to reach a formulation in reciprocal and general reasons—which according to this conception of justification is not sufficiently possible—than someone who calls for equal rights for minorities. Duties to offer justifications are addressed to all equally and according to the issues at stake, not in accordance with considerations of proportionality.[92] The principle that the state should be neutral with regard to religion is based on a conception of justice that stands outside of the dispute between religious doctrines.

4. The Politics of Toleration

(1) While Kant's philosophy of religion represents a step backward by comparison with Bayle's conception from the perspective of a systematic theory of toleration,

[88] See Forst, *Contexts of Justice* (n. 79) 99 and 129–30; also, *Toleration in Conflict* (n. 1) §37. Jürgen Habermas, "Religion in the Public Sphere: Cognitive Presuppositions for the 'Public Use of Reason' by Religious and Secular Citizens," in Habermas, *Between Naturalism and Religion* (n. 26) 114–47, at 131 ff.

[89] Habermas, "Faith and Knowledge" (n. 75) 109.

[90] Jürgen Habermas, "Prepolitical Foundations of the Constitutional State?" in Jürgen Habermas, *Between Naturalism and Religion: Philosophical Essays*, trans. Ciaran Cronin (Polity 2008) 101–13, at 113.

[91] Jürgen Habermas, "Religious Tolerance as Pacemaker for Cultural Rights," in Jürgen Habermas, *Between Naturalism and Religion: Philosophical Essays*, trans. Ciaran Cronin (Polity 2008) 251–70, at 263 ff.

[92] On this see Forst, *Toleration in Conflict* (n. 1) §§37 and 38.

Kant, in contrast to Bayle, makes an immanent connection between his moral-philosophical argument and his political theory. Habermas clearly follows Kant in this regard. In both thinkers we find a translation of the moral principle of respect and justification into a theory of political legitimation in the medium of "public reason." Bayle, by contrast, remains a child of his time in drawing a clear boundary between toleration at the social level and toleration at the level of the state. Unlike Calvinist monarchomachs such as Pierre Jurieu, Bayle clung steadfastly to the idea that a strong ruler is an indispensable guarantor of toleration at the state level. Bayle stands in the line of political thought extending back to Marsilius of Padua that sees a sovereign temporal state and ruler as a necessary counterweight to the power of the church(es). He remains a follower of the *politiques*, especially of de l'Hôpital, whom he describes in the corresponding article in the *Dictionnaire* as one of "the greatest men of his time." He likewise praises Henry IV, who, in the Edict of Nantes, had for the first time accorded the Huguenots a certain level of protection against prosecution, calling him in the relevant article the "greatest among princes." In the articles on Bodin, Grotius, and Hobbes, Bayle also leaves the reader in no doubt about his preference for an absolutist regime that is tolerant of religion over the "confusion" of democracy.[93] Only a sovereign who stands above the religious and civil disputes of his time can keep the peace, according to Bayle.

(2) Kant, by contrast, develops a theory of law that contrasts law, as regards its content, with all ethical doctrines of happiness and, as regards its form, with moral imperatives, because positive law refers only to external actions and not to inner motivation. The essential difference between legality and morality for Kant resides less in the content of the respective laws than in the "incentives."[94] Thus the moral prohibition on the coercion of conscience finds its way into the law in such a way that the supreme principle of law already stipulates that restrictions on freedom of choice have to be justified: "Right is therefore the sum of the conditions under which the choice of one can be united with the choice of another in accordance with a universal law of freedom."[95] The foundation of this definition of law, which states that all forms of legal coercion must be justified in a reciprocal way among free and equal persons, is a moral basic right and human right to freedom understood in terms of natural law: "Freedom (independence from being constrained by another's choice), provided that it can coexist with the freedom of every other in accordance with a universal law, is the only original right belonging to every man by virtue of his humanity."[96] This (on my interpretation) is what follows for law from the moral basic right to justification—that is, from the basic right to unconditional respect as an "end in oneself." The protection accorded individual freedom by no means rests on a conception of the good life for which legally protected and socially enabled forms of autonomy would be necessary. Kant's conception is, rather, that

[93] See, in particular, Pierre Bayle, "Hobbes," in Bayle, *Political Writings*, ed. and trans. Sally L. Jenkinson (Cambridge University Press 2000) 79–92, remarks C and E, 81 ff. (This article from the *Historical and Critical Dictionary* is not included in either of the abridged English translations.)

[94] Kant, *Groundwork of the Metaphysics of Morals* (n. 17) 21–2 (6:220).

[95] ibid 24 (6:230). [96] ibid 30 (Ak. 6:237).

the inviolability of persons—that is, their dignity—already excludes interference by others. Whether this helps those who are not "violated" to live a good life is an entirely different matter. The barrier of the need to justify restrictions on freedom is raised earlier, according to Kant, and it is stricter than that allowed by such an alternative conception of ethical autonomy:

> But the concept of an external right as such proceeds entirely from the concept of freedom in external relations between people and has nothing at all to do with the end that all of them naturally have (their aim of happiness) and with prescribing means for attaining it, so that also the latter absolutely must not be mixed with that law as its determining ground.[97]

Against the background of the original right of human beings and the corresponding basic definition of law, Kant arrives at the formulation of different conceptions of the "person."[98] For, in addition to the autonomous *moral person* who acts in accordance with the categorical imperative and is owed moral respect, Kant distinguishes three "a priori principles" in the "civil condition" and, correspondingly, three further conceptions of the person—namely, ethical, legal, and political conceptions. The three principles are: "1. The *freedom* of every member of the society as a *human being*. 2. The *equality* of every member as a *subject*. 3. The *independence* of every member of a commonwealth as a *citizen*."[99] The first means: "No one can coerce me to be happy in his way (as he thinks of the welfare of other human beings); instead, each may seek his happiness in the way that seems good to him ..."[100] According to Kant, this excludes "paternalistic government" which treats its subjects as "minor children." This ensures that the legal autonomy of the person is protected against external interference. Internally, the law functions as a "protective cover" for the *ethical person* to live her life in accordance with the conceptions of the good that, for whatever reason, seem right to her.[101] Correspondingly, the second principle, that of equality, means that individuals as *legal persons*, as "subjects" (*Unterthanen*) who are subjected to the authority of the law and, irrespective of their social status, stand under laws that apply to everyone in the same way and place equal limits on everyone's freedom of choice.

Finally, the third principle spells out the role of the person as a *citizen*—that is, as a "colegislator."[102] This follows from the fact that, according to the principle of right, only "general laws" can be laws of freedom, and they can be general only if they are in accordance with the "united will of the people."[103] In this role alone can citizens be politically autonomous, as Kant argues drawing on Rousseau's notion of autonomy. As a matter of principle, they obey only laws that they have given themselves—that

[97] Kant, "Theory and Practice" (n. 55), 290 (8:289).

[98] On the following fourfold differentiation of conceptions of the person and conceptions of autonomy see Forst, *Contexts of Justice* (n. 79) in particular ch. 5, sections 2 and 3, and *The Right to Justification* (n. 20) ch. 5.

[99] Kant, "Theory and Practice" (n. 97) 291 (8:290); see also Kant, *Groundwork of the Metaphysics of Morals* (n. 17) 91 (8:314).

[100] Kant, "Theory and Practice" (n. 97) 291 (8:290).

[101] See Forst, *Contexts of Justice* (n.79) ch. 2.

[102] Kant, "Theory and Practice" (n. 97) 294 (8:294).

[103] Kant, *Groundwork of the Metaphysics of Morals* (n. 17) 91 (6:313).

is, no law other "than that to which [they have] given [their] consent."[104] As an active member of the polity, as a voting citizen, the person is a *citoyen*, not just (as in his role as a legal person) a *bourgeois*: he is simultaneously author and addressee of the law (to the extent that, as Kant adds in the spirit of his time, he is of the male sex and is a property owner). Hence, generally and reciprocally valid law can be legitimate only if it was agreed upon in procedures of general and reciprocal justification; the "mere idea of reason," "which, however, has its undoubted practical reality," states that "the touchstone of any public law's conformity with right" is its ability to command general agreement.

(3) A distinguishing feature of Jürgen Habermas's political theory ever since *Structural Transformation of the Public Sphere* is its quest for a social and political locus of the collective, discursive use of public reason. Here I must leave to one side the different phases of his work that would have to be taken into consideration in this connection and will focus instead exclusively on his recent work. In the mature version of his legal and democratic theory developed in *Between Facts and Norms*, Habermas stresses the Kantian distinction between different roles of the person and, in particular, the difference between law and morality. According to this theory, legitimate law is not justified in moral terms. Rather, it is justified in a process that connects liberal human rights and democratic popular sovereignty in such a way that the form of modern law yields the principle of democracy in combination with the discourse principle. This explains "the performative meaning of the practice of self-determination on the part of the legal consociates who recognize one another as free and equal members of an association they have joined voluntarily."[105] Out of this core idea Habermas develops a system of individual rights understood as rights of legal persons and citizens. These include rights to the "greatest possible measure of *equal liberties*."[106] However, unlike natural individual rights, they are not prescribed to the legislative process in advance but are conceived as conceptual implications of this process. Then elaborating these rights means that they must be interpreted in democratic procedures, although they may not be questioned in principle: they have the status of enabling conditions of democracy.

Although, according to Habermas, with regard to fundamental issues such as individual rights, legal norms must "be in accord with moral norms,"[107] they themselves are not justified in moral terms. At the same time, their elaboration must not conflict with moral reasons, which is why, when it comes to questions of principle, a corresponding level of justification must be achieved. For the question of toleration in the context of the interpretation of individual liberties, this means that procedures must be developed that realize this level of justification. Here the neutrality of the procedure and the relevant constitutive principles play an important role. Habermas argues with Ackerman and Larmore that political norms must remain neutral toward contested ethical teachings, so that their justification must be based on general, not on particular ethical reasons.[108] This ensures the priority of justice over the good.

[104] ibid 91 (6:313). [105] See Habermas, *Between Facts and Norms* (n. 26) 110.
[106] ibid 123. [107] ibid 155. [108] ibid 307 ff.

As a result, tolerance becomes a *democratic virtue* that is called for when ethical positions clash and a norm that can be justified in reciprocal terms has to be found, whether in the mode of discursive justification or of a compromise that satisfies requirements of fairness. Tolerance is a virtue of justification for which it is illegitimate to subject others to norms that cannot be justified reciprocally but only in a one-sided ethical manner. In this way individual freedom is secured.[109] This freedom is a form of communicative freedom in a twofold sense: it is the freedom to form particularistic bonds and to live in the corresponding forms of life that enjoy legal protection even if they are unconventional; at the same time, it is the freedom to demand justifying reasons for restrictions on liberty, reasons that can show why such restrictions can be legitimized among free and equal persons.

On my interpretation, this freedom is based on a moral *right to justification* of others that, in political contexts, turns democratic toleration into a duty. But, as a result, I use a stronger moral—specifically, a Kantian—concept of the duty (to justify) and of the moral individual right (to justification) than Habermas's reconstructive theory allows. The latter does not ascribe moral validity of its own to the discourse principle and also regards the legal form as a mere historical fact.[110] In my view, this not only contradicts the moral meaning and justification of the form of law; it also fails to satisfy the autonomy of the morality (called for in connection with Bayle and Kant in sect. 2 above) which provides an *independent* foundation for the possibility and duty of mutual toleration. Here, too, we get a glimpse of the problems created by the weakening of claims to moral validity in Habermas's recent approach—on the one hand, as discussed above, in the relationship between morality and ethics and, on the other, as discussed here, in the relationship between morality and law.

5. Concluding Observations

This synopsis of Kantian arguments shows that Kantian moral philosophy and Kant's philosophy of religion and political philosophy provide arguments for religious freedom: freedom of religion is a direct expression of respect for the dignity of the person. Thus, according to the *respect conception* first worked out fully by Kant, toleration is required primarily for *moral* reasons. However, it also follows from the principle of *rational religion* that religion should prevail by "rational means" alone, without having to resort to force. In addition, from the *legal principle* it follows that restrictions on freedom must be justified in reciprocal terms and that other people's notions of happiness do not provide legitimate reasons to coerce. And, finally, from the corresponding *political principle* it follows that all coercive laws must stem from "public reason," so that the latter must itself already be pluralistic. In this way, Kant,

[109] See Habermas, *Between Naturalism and Religion* (n. 26) chs. 5 and 9.

[110] See Forst, *The Right to Justification* (n. 20) ch. 4, and Habermas's reply in "Rawls's Political Liberalism: Reply to the Resumption of a Discussion," in Jürgen Habermas, *Postmetaphysical Thinking II: Essays and Replies*, trans. Ciaran Cronin (Polity 2017) 189–209.

if we compare his approach to that of Bayle, raised the latter's position to a new normative level.

Where Kant deviates sharply from Bayle, however, is in his conception of the implications of the finitude of reason for religious questions. Here, as I have shown, two main paths of the Enlightenment diverge: the Baylean path, which makes a clear (although not absolute) separation between reason and faith, and the Kantian path, which aims at an extensive abolition of religious differences under the primacy of practical reason. Regarding the issue of toleration, the path taken by Bayle is in my view to be preferred. It is more consistent and leads to a conception of reasonable ethical differences that nevertheless *cannot* be overcome by rational means. Bayle saw more clearly than Kant the limits of finite, human reason in questions of religion.

Kant's key advance over Bayle was his political translation of the moral principle of justification through which he transposed the respect conception from the horizontal, civil level to the vertical dimension of political toleration. If reciprocal and general justification among moral persons is required in order to justify actions, it is also required among citizens who have to decide which positive laws should regulate their shared social life. Then tolerance is not just a civil, interpersonal virtue but also a political virtue of democratic lawgivers who respect each other as free and equal persons. It ensures that the laws that are justified in the medium of public reason involve the level of toleration and freedom implied by the limits of justification: in exchanging their positions and reasons, citizens recognize what they *cannot* force each other to do. Therefore, they will pledge each other fundamental freedoms in the form of basic rights that guarantee freedom of choice and they will recognize that *mutual* tolerance is an important virtue of equitable lawgivers *and* of reasonable legal subjects who respect these laws. In this way, the *one-sided*, authoritarian permission conception of toleration, which Kant castigates as "arrogant," is overcome.

Habermas follows Kant in making this connection between civil and democratic toleration under the premises of discourse theory. However, he differs in two important respects from Kant. The "detranscendentalized" approach does not allow Habermas a strong deontological theory in the Kantian sense that would interpret the discourse principle itself (in moral contexts) as a moral principle. Despite the basic deontological approach of discourse ethics, this leads to ambivalences concerning the thesis of the autonomy of morality defended by Bayle and Kant. Regarding the two main paths pursued by the Enlightenment in defining the relationship between reason and religion, Habermas, who originally leaned toward a Kantian position, in his recent work clearly follows Bayle. On this view, Enlightenment reason entails an enlightenment of reason that leads it to recognize its own finitude and thereby accords faith a legitimate place in a modern society. This is how we should understand Habermas's plea for an Enlightenment that is enlightened about its own biases:

> Faith remains opaque for knowledge in a way that can neither be denied nor simply accepted. This reflects the inconclusive nature of the controversy between self-critical reason that is willing to learn and the contemporary reality of religious beliefs. This controversy can

sharpen post-secular society's awareness of the unexhausted force of the religious heritage of human beings.[111]

But in the same passage in which Habermas criticizes a "modernization threatening to spin out of control," he discusses his diagnosis of the "weakness of rational morality" that, according to Kant, is no longer able to appropriate the "images, preserved by religion, of the moral whole."[112] Therefore, Habermas argues, practical reason must learn to keep awake "an awareness of the violations of solidarity throughout the world" in a postmetaphysical way. Here the ambivalence of this new perspective becomes apparent, for, even if this awareness may have religious sources, as a moral awareness it must distance itself from these sources if it is to be valid in a pluralistic world and to free itself from distortions and exclusions that could stem from religious interpretations and appropriations. An autonomous morality is indispensable for such a process of secularization and, if this morality lacked motivating power of its own, it would not be capable of such autonomy.

These reflections show that there is no such thing as "the" Enlightenment position on questions of morality, religion, and law, but a variety of positions. Moreover, they show the changes in and distinctive features of Habermas's recent position. This is the position of a champion of the Enlightenment who defends an affirmative concept of modernity that rethinks the facets of the Enlightenment and arrives at a differentiated theory for which the word "post-secular" society stands. This should not distract us from the fact that it is an approach that continues the process of secularization but also seeks to provide clarity about this very process.

[111] Habermas, "An Awareness of What is Missing" (n. 80) 18. [112] ibid 18 ff.

6

One Court and Many Cultures

Jurisprudence in Conflict

1. The decisions of courts are inherently contested because they take a position on highly controversial issues—even when they manage to remain impartial as required by the goddess Justitia.[1] In making such decisions, constitutional courts find themselves in a special situation, because controversies over the basic understanding of the political community are refracted in the conflicts ruled upon in constitutional cases like in a prism. These disputes become more frequent and intense to the extent that a society is undergoing cultural change, which leads to conflicts in which the constitution—correctly interpreted—demands that familiar institutions be subjected to scrutiny or transformed. Then a peculiar dynamic of the constitutional state becomes apparent: its basic principles sometimes require that the existing constitution of social life be rethought from the ground up. Throughout its history, the German Federal Constitutional Court has been at the center of this dynamic, so that at times it is drawn into a maelstrom of decentering that exposes those involved to a severe test.

The problem of the continuity of the constitution, social change, and the necessity of institutional reform is especially apparent when issues of "multicultural" society are involved. One must be careful when using the "m" word in this context because, like so many others, its meaning becomes blurred in everyday ideological exchanges; on an objective definition, calling Germany "multicultural" is simply to assert that it has been a culturally and religiously pluralistic society for a long time, although this pluralism is increasing at an accelerated rate. The "formative power," as it is often put, of a culture shaped by Christianity already began to weaken in the 1960s, although this development was reinforced by the social changes brought about by immigration since the 1970s and, finally, by German reunification and the opening of European borders. This development is typical of many countries, and in Germany people tried to obscure this fact for a long time by claiming that Germany is not a country of immigration.

[1] I am indebted to Klaus Günther and Michael Stolleis for valuable comments; I am also grateful to the latter for urging me to make this contribution to a collection to mark the sixtieth anniversary of the German Federal Constitutional Court (*Herzkammern der Republik*, ed. Michael Stolleis) in 2011. In a more recent ruling on headscarf bans announced in March 2015, the Court corrected the judgment criticized here. However, the reactions to this ruling as well as new gray areas in its justification (see below, 116) show the continuing relevance of the following reflections.

Aside from its descriptive meaning, however, the concept of multiculturalism also raises a normative question: How should the basic institutions of the state and society respond to this cultural shift? What is meant by fair treatment of minorities who for many appear "foreign," even although in several urban areas they are in the meantime more the majority than a minority? The Court in the peaceful city of Karlsruhe finds itself in the eye of the storm when it comes to such questions and the corresponding conflicts. This is regrettable from a democratic perspective, because the voices of minorities should actually be more audible in the legislative process. But all too often they have to seek the assistance of the megaphone of constitutional law to make their voices heard. The concept of majorities and minorities is actually alien to the law; in the legal domain individuals fight for their rights, and when basic rights are pitted against legislatively enacted law, the guiding intention is in principle an anti-majoritarian one.

If we want to appreciate what this can mean, we must recall the conflict that stands out in the history of the Federal Constitutional Court for the vehemence of the opposition with which its ruling was met, even to the point that the Court was criticized for the first time as a threat to social stability, and in which resistance was frequently proclaimed and practiced—namely, the controversy surrounding the so-called "crucifix decision" which roiled the republic in the summer of 1995.

My main reason for invoking this decision is not the high value on the Richter scale of the associated social-political tremors, but because one can read off from it the structure of the conflicts that shape a multicultural society—and the corresponding challenges faced by the Court. The Court mastered these challenges, notwithstanding the high political risks involved, in the crucifix case, although it was less successful in this respect in another case that I also single out, the "headscarf ruling" of 2003. Many other cases could be cited, but the close affinity between these two cases makes them prime examples of what it means to interpret the law on the basis of clear principles in the midst of the resulting religious and cultural confusion. Connected with this is a set of controversial concepts that I will address: prominent among them are neutrality and toleration, but they also include "guiding culture" (*Leitkultur*) and "integration," to mention just a few. But the most important from my perspective (as a political philosopher) is the concept of justice, whose status within the law is not always easy to determine. For the conflicts in question turn on nothing less than the fair treatment of minorities and what form of coexistence in a liberal, democratic society is just(ified) toward all and is sufficiently reflexive to open its normative order up to critical examination. What is at stake, therefore, is the fundamental understanding of the state itself: Do we live in a political society in which the "house rules" of convention or the majority hold sway? Or do we live in a society that is so beholden to the principles of justice manifested in the constitutional rights that it respects minorities as equals, while at the same time allowing them to be different—"without fear," as Adorno would have said?[2]

[2] Theodor W. Adorno, *Minima Moralia: Reflections on a Damaged Life*, trans. E. F. N. Jephcott (Verso 2005) 103.

2. Let me begin with a brief review of the crucifix controversy. The legal issue involved was whether §13 I 3 of the School Regulations for Public Schools in Bavaria—"Every classroom is to be furnished with a cross"—is compatible with Article 4 § I of the Basic Law: "Freedom of faith and of conscience, and freedom to profess a religious or philosophical creed, shall be inviolable." The occasion was provided by a case brought by parents, who were followers of the anthroposophy of Rudolf Steiner, challenging the display of crucifixes (and later crosses) in the school of their three children in the Upper Palatinate. The problem involved in this case first becomes clear by juxtaposing the decision of the Constitutional Court with the views taken by the Bavarian authorities and by the administrative courts that initially dealt with the case. They make clear how important it is in such cases to identify discrimination against minorities already at the level of the language in which their claims are represented.

In dismissing the action, the Higher Administrative Court in Munich, for example, pointed out that the Bavarian Constitution not only cites "reverence for God" as one of the primary goals of education, but that it also states that schoolchildren in public schools are to be "taught and educated according to the principles of the Christian creeds." The "precept of tolerance" addressed to the state, it argued further, forbids the schools to interpret this principle in a missionary way; but Christian values, in the sense of general "cultural and educational values," may form part of the teaching of values.[3]

These remarks raise the question of what religious symbols such as the cross or crucifix on the walls of classrooms have to do with those cultural and educational values. On this question, the ruling clearly states that such symbols are "not an expression of allegiance to the faith of a particular religious confession," but are instead "an integral part of the general Western Christian tradition and the common property of the Christian, Western cultural sphere." And this generalization of the cross into a symbol of a worldview is followed by an instructive interpretation of the "precept of tolerance" with reference to dissident minorities. "According to the precept of tolerance that also applies to him, it is reasonable to expect" a non-Christian "to accept" such symbols, specifically "in the light of the respect owed to the beliefs of others."

This interpretation is as ingenious as it is contradictory. It is ingenious in that, against the background of a universalization of the cross into a symbol of the West, it applies the concept of toleration in such a way that now only those who want this symbol to be removed appear to be intolerant. This construction is contradictory, however, because when intolerance is described as disrespect for "beliefs of others," the cross (or crucifix) is nevertheless interpreted again as an expression of a particular religion or confession—unless, that is, one wants to say that rejecting the symbol amounts to rejecting the entire Western world and its values, which would be rather too much intolerance.

[3] In what follows, the judgment (Az. 7CE 91.1014) is quoted from the *Neue Zeitschrift für Verwaltungsrecht* 1991, 1099 ff.

Apart from this unsuccessful dialectical line of argumentation, there is another argument that appeals to the concept of freedom. Constitutional legal adjudication distinguishes for good reasons between negative and positive freedom of religion. The former is freedom from religious constraints, whereas the latter refers to the freedom to live according to one's beliefs and to be able to give them expression. Now it is interesting how the Higher Administrative Court applies this distinction to the present case. For, according to the Court, what is at stake here is a conflict between a negative claim of the plaintiffs and the positive right of Christian parents and children to express their creed—which in this case, the Court adds, is in line with "State law on school organization." In its submission to the proceedings, the German Bishops' Conference had stated somewhat more clearly that the negative freedom of minorities must not have "absolute primacy," since "no room would then be left over for the exercise of positive religious freedom" by a majority.[4] Once again, the precept of tolerance was invoked, and once again in such a way that the minority was admonished to respect the positive freedom of the majority, as also in the opinion submitted by the Bavarian State Government to the proceedings.

Here we are witnesses to a classic case of biased presentation of minority claims. Their concerns are formulated in negative terms, and not just as regards negative religious freedom, as if it were not also a matter of being able to profess freely one's faith as a minority. Moreover, the minority is represented as being hostile to religion and as undemocratic on the grounds that it wants to erect a barrier to the freedom of worship of Christians and is not willing to recognize the majority culture. Once again, strands of argument are knotted together that do not belong together, namely, the idea that this majority culture—and the cross—stands for the entire West and the idea that the cross represents the profession of faith of Christians. With this, the minority is disenfranchised in several respects: it is accused of placing itself outside the general cultural framework, of exhibiting an attitude that is hostile to religion and of indulging in an antimajoritarian "extremely exaggerated subjectivism," in the words of the Higher Administrative Court. In all these respects, as Erhard Denninger writes, the minority is declared to be the outsider and "abnormal," and thus "is forced into the peripheral gray area of legal inferiority."[5]

A society can count itself lucky if it has a constitution and courts capable of functioning as a corrective when lawmakers and public authorities fail to prevent such marginalization. A majority of the First Senate of the Federal Constitutional Court concluded that the provision in the Bavarian School Regulations for Elementary Schools requiring that crosses be affixed in classrooms is unconstitutional. It presents the reasons for this with absolute clarity, and they show that what it really comes down to here is the basic understanding of state institutions in a liberal and democratic republic.

[4] Reported in the account of the decision of the German Federal Constitutional Court published on May 16, 1995 (1 BvR 1087/91), quoted from BVerfGE 93, 1 ff. Quotations from the ruling are taken from the English translation https://law.utexas.edu/transnational/foreign-law-translations/german/case.php?id=615 (last accessed November 9, 2016).

[5] Erhard Denninger, "Der Einzelne und das allgemeine Gesetz," in *Kritische Justiz* 28 (2005): 30–49, 35.

According to the Court, there can be no question of a negative right of individuals not to be confronted with religious symbols in public; but neither can there be any question of a positive right to express one's religious convictions "with State support." Rather, the article on religious freedom entails the principle of state neutrality, and such a neutral state, the Court argues, cannot oblige any schoolchildren to learn "under the cross."

Following this line of argument, the Court has to take a position on what the symbol of the cross means. And here it states clearly, as no one can reasonably dispute, that the cross is not a general, trans-denominational symbol but a "symbol of faith as such"; more than that, it is also a symbol of the "missionary dissemination" of Christianity. There is no perspective, including that of Christianity, from which a "profanation" of this symbol would be plausible.

Now the principle of neutrality is not generally interpreted in a strict sense in German constitutional thought; rather, the special reference to the Christian churches is usually explained in terms of the "imprint" of Christianity on German society and on the German state. The crucifix judgment does not turn a blind eye to this either, although this again opens up a gray area. For when it is emphasized that even a state committed to neutrality toward religions and worldviews "cannot divest itself of the culturally conveyed, historically rooted values, convictions and attitudes on which the cohesion of society is based and the carrying out of its own tasks also depends," this brings an ambivalence into play to which I will return in the next section.

On the other hand, the Court emphasizes very clearly as a matter of principle that the conflict is not one between negative and positive freedom of religion, as the appellate courts claimed, for everyone has a right to positive freedom, minorities as well as majorities. However, negative freedom acquires special weight where by law certain religious symbols are installed in public institutions such as schools, thereby violating the precept of state neutrality.

At the time, the decision was reached with a majority of five to three, and the dissenting opinion of the minority objected that here a negative freedom as "a right to prevent religion" won out. Once again, minorities are reminded of their duty of tolerance. In line with this dissenting opinion, a public storm of indignation broke out, the likes of which the Federal Constitutional Court had never previously experienced.[6] In Michael Stolleis' words, it was difficult to avoid the impression that one was "witnessing the prelude to the decline of the West."[7] Then Chancellor Helmut Kohl called the ruling "incomprehensible" and underlined that the liberal social

[6] On the reactions, see Peter Pappert (ed.), *Den Nerv getroffen: Engagierte Stimmen zum Kruzifix-Urteil von Karlsruhe* (Bergmoser und Höller 1995); Heinrich Streithofen (ed.), *Das Kruzifixurteil: Deutschland vor einem neuen Kulturkampf* (Ullstein 1995); Alexander Hollerbach *et al.* (eds.), *Das Kreuz im Widerspruch* (Herder 1996). On the discussion in legal theory, see, in particular, Winfried Brugger and Stefan Huster (eds.), *Der Streit um das Kreuz in der Schule: Zur weltanschaulichen Neutralität des Staates* (Nomos 1998).

[7] Michael Stolleis, "Überkreuz: Anmerkungen zum Kruzifix-Beschluß (BVerfGE 93, 1-37) und seiner Rezeption," in *Kritische Vierteljahresschrift für Gesetzgebung und Rechtswissenschaft* 83 (2000): 376–87, at 378.

order is "based essentially on Christian values." The prime minister of Bavaria at the time, Edmund Stoiber, called the ruling a "judgment of intolerance" and claimed that it represented a "break with the constitutional tradition." He announced that he would "exhaust the legal possibilities" to ensure that the crosses would remain in place. Cardinal Meisner of Cologne called the ruling a "black day in the history of our people," and there were many declarations that any attempt to remove the crosses would be met with active resistance. The resulting ethical-political-historical conflict situation is made entirely clear by comparisons of the ruling with the (unsuccessful) attempt by the Nazis to have the crosses removed in 1941. The Bavarian school regulations were amended in accordance with the announcement of the prime minister so that the obligation to install crosses remains in place but now with a right to object; thus, they remained affixed in classrooms by law. This led to further legal disputes, in particular concerning whether atheistic beliefs could constitute good grounds for objecting, something the Bavarian Higher Administrative Court had doubted (on which point it was corrected by the Federal Administrative Court in 1999).

3. Not only the vehemence and prominence of these reactions, but also their content, should make us sit up and take notice, because this raises a fundamental question concerning the character of the German republic. No one disputes that the self-understanding of the German Federal Republic must be seen against the background of the Nazi regime and its collapse. But the lessons that people at the time thought should be drawn from this are controversial. One influential opinion held that there were important cultural factors that prepared the way for national socialism—more precisely, that relativism, positivism, or (at the extreme) nihilism concerning values had eroded the ethical substance of the Weimar Republic, so that a nationalist and racist ideology was able to fill the resulting vacuum. If a democratic and liberal republic was to succeed, therefore, its constitutional system had to be based on an objectively existing "value order" that was not subject to arbitrary change.

This interpretation of the "anti-totalitarian" foundation of the new republic entailed and entails for many that only a religiously grounded (read: Christian), yet inclusive "higher order" could provide ethical-political support and orientation. I cannot go into the genesis and the various facets of the founding doctrine of the republic in greater detail here. However, only in the light of this weighty justification narrative of the religious and ethical foundation of the constitutional system does the crucifix controversy become comprehensible, because many of those who defended the Bavarian practice saw themselves against this background as the true defenders of the liberal order and not merely as the mouthpieces of a dominant majority.

There is no better expression for this problem within German legal philosophy than the statement by Ernst-Wolfgang Böckenförde, often quoted since the 1960s, which he formulated in response to the question of what "supporting, homogeneity-guaranteeing force" the secular liberal state could rely upon. Böckenförde expresses his doubts concerning a moral or value system grounded in a purely "inner-worldly" fashion, and likewise about the recourse to the nation, and he draws his famous conclusion: "The liberal secularized state is nourished by presuppositions that it cannot itself guarantee."[8] And as one essential precondition of this kind, he cites the "inner impulses and bonding forces" that are "imparted by the religious faith of its citizens." The state becomes empty or totalitarian when it elevates itself to the source of morality or relies exclusively on the "eudemonistic expectations" of its citizens; rather, it must build on the fact that religion embraces the liberal state and makes the latter its cause.

Böckenförde is by no means to blame for all of the different readings to which this line of argument has been subjected.[9] It can be interpreted, on the one hand, as opposing the political instrumentalization of religion, but also, on the other, as arguing that a policy of neutrality, such as is advocated in the crucifix decision, undermines the very substance of a liberal republic that it purports to protect. This opens up a range of problems in the history of ideas extending far back beyond, but especially into, the Enlightenment era, in which opinions are divided over whether a binding and shared, universalistic conception of morality is possible that stabilizes law and the state without a theistic, or at least a deistic, foundation. Thinkers including Locke, Montesquieu, Rousseau, and even Voltaire were skeptical about this, whereas thinkers such as Bayle and Kant, by contrast, thought that there was no alternative to such a conception of morality if a liberal order was to be possible in a pluralistic world.[10]

With this we have arrived at the core of the problem under dispute in the crucifix controversy. What is at stake is the interpretation of the "value foundation" of a democratic republic and the question whether such a foundation can have sufficient normative substance "without God." Applied to the problem of the constitution, this means that it is doubtful to what extent the "objective order of values" [*objektive Wertordnung*] of the constitution (as this has been called since the 1958 *Lüth* ruling) can dispense with a transcendent anchor. Of course, the Court could not answer this question in its ruling and, notwithstanding its outspokenness concerning the legal issue, it remains ambivalent in this respect. For, as much as it defends the principles of liberty against their incorporation into a particular religious, ethical, and political tradition and symbolism, it is nevertheless prepared to trace "the state" back to "values, convictions and attitudes" that justify its cohesion and on which the performance of its tasks "depends," in the words of the ruling. And it adds that the "Christian faith and the Christian churches have in this connection, however one may today wish to assess their heritage, been of overwhelmingly decisive force." This—including the "however"—expresses the ambivalence that shines through this judgment concerning the question of the foundation on which a liberal and pluralistic society rests. If one's answer to this question is that this foundation consists

[8] Ernst-Wolfgang Böckenförde, "The Rise of the State as a Process of Secularisation," in Böckenförde, *State, Society, and Liberty: Studies in Political Theory and Constitutional Law* (Berg 1991) 46, 44–5.

[9] On this, see his own overview of the debate in Ernst-Wolfgang Böckenförde, *Der säkularisierte Staat: Sein Charakter, seine Rechtfertigung und seine Probleme im 21. Jahrhundert* (Carl Friedrich von Siemens Stiftung 2007).

[10] On this, see my comprehensive study *Toleration in Conflict: Past and Present*, trans. Ciaran Cronin (Cambridge University Press 2013). In ch. 12 of that book I offer a detailed discussion of the questions raised here. See also Rainer Forst, "Religion and Toleration from the Enlightenment to the Post-Secular Era: Bayle, Kant, and Habermas," ch. 5 in this volume.

of an "overlapping consensus" of the Christian confessions (to use an expression of John Rawls) and of all those who endorse this because from the perspective of their respective worldviews they see sources for supporting the state, then the liberal and democratic order lacks an independent normative basis. The result would be a constant struggle over how far the institutions of the state should distance themselves from their main religious sources.

This has important implications for the question of neutrality. Insofar as the neutrality of state institutions is regarded as an imperative of justice, only those grounds for its legitimate design will be acceptable that can be reciprocally and generally recognized by all citizens, and as a result do not favor any religious group, not even a majority. Contrary to what is often feared, such neutrality does not mean that it is hostile to religion, because atheism also counts on this conception as an evaluative stance that is not generalizable in a pluralistic society, and hence must not become dominant. But no religious evaluative stance may become dominant either. Therefore, the public sphere does not have to be kept "free from religion" as laicism proposes; but when it comes to fundamental questions of justice, no ethical-religious (or anti-religious) doctrine can take precedence. Here, only what can be justified to all is valid. The results do not have to be equidistant from all participating teachings or claims; what holds is not neutrality of effects, but neutrality of justification.[11] If a doctrine or confession is accorded a normative privilege within the state structure, by contrast, then neutrality is not possible in the full sense, but at best recognition of "others" who may indeed have a place in the structure but do not enjoy equal rights. In this context, the concept of "open and inclusive" neutrality often cited in legal judgments, which is supposed to grant religions "space to develop" and to foster them, all too often serves to disguise certain privileges of the Christian churches.

The difference between equal respect based on justice and privileging certain ethical and political values is shown by the political virtue of tolerance, which is the counterpart at the individual level of neutrality as the political virtue of the state. The differences can be read off from the use of the "precept of tolerance" by the aforementioned courts and they reflect two conceptions of toleration that have developed over the course of history and clash in such conflicts.[12] One classical conception I call the "permission conception." Here a dominant side, which claims political authority for itself, grants minorities certain permissions in the form of conditional and defined freedoms within the political and social domain; and the permission-granting side reserves the right to decide whether these freedoms are justified or should be curtailed. We encounter this conception of toleration in its paradigmatic, absolutist form in the famous toleration edicts and laws; in present-day societies, it returns in a democratic version in which majorities are now the permission-granting side. Although the power of the majority is constrained by constitutional basic rights, it is the majority that defines the meaning of the basic

[11] Rainer Forst, *Contexts of Justice*, trans. John M. M. Farrell (University of California Press 2002) 45–8.

[12] For a detailed account see Rainer Forst, *Toleration in Conflict* (n. 10), and "Religion and Toleration from the Enlightenment to the Post-Secular Era," ch. 5 in this volume.

rights. Thus, the plaintiffs were called upon by the judgments of the administrative courts and by many voices within the debate to respect the expressions of faith of the Christian majority and to tolerate the crosses or crucifixes, while the tolerance of the majority merely consisted in not proselytizing the minority. As a result, the relations of toleration are not reciprocal; minorities are not respected as equals, but are instead indulged, and they have to accept the dominance of others.

A justice-based understanding of toleration, by contrast—I call this the "respect conception"—would amount to structuring relations of toleration in such a way that, even if a majority had the power to legally enforce its ideas about crosses on walls, the construction of mosques or wearing religious headgear, it refrains from doing so because it recognizes that its view on the relevant issue is not generalizable in a pluralistic society, that is, in a society in which the most important state institutions are not the property of a particular group, even if it happens to be the largest. This has nothing to do with indifference or skepticism, as is sometimes feared. For, first, equal respect for others is itself a moral principle, and, second, the ethical and religious differences and rejections among the parties remain—only they recognize that these differences are not sufficient to mark a legal subordination and asymmetry.

Many more controversial concepts fall within the scope of the dispute between these notions of neutrality, fairness, and toleration, and of the constitution itself. Among them are the idea of a "guiding culture" shaped by Christianity and the much-touted "integration" into the same. In the crucifix decision, the Federal Constitutional Court interpreted the dynamic of a modern system of basic rights, which calls for a revision of established conceptions, quite rightly in the sense of fair neutrality and reciprocal tolerance. In so doing, it showed that the perspective of basic rights is one of justice and not of a specific system of values shaped by Christianity—without this perspective becoming anti-Christian as a result. In this sense it presupposes an understanding of justice on the part of citizens that accords fairness priority even when doing so means having to live with views that contradict their own ethical conceptions. This is how justice is administered in an advanced republic. However, this marks an important difference from a conventional constitutional understanding which presupposes that the constitution has a certain ethical-religious "substance" that the state cannot reproduce directly, although it can foster it, whether by financial or symbolic means.

4. The next such conflict was not long in coming. In many countries, heated debates have broken out over Islamic religious headwear extending to concealment of the entire body. These debates have been most intense in France and in Germany, again initially in connection with schools—in France with regard to schoolgirls, in Germany to teachers. This time, the ambivalence of the Constitutional Court alluded to above was even more apparent than in the crucifix decision.

In 2003, the Second Senate of the Federal Constitutional Court had to rule on a case involving a teacher candidate who was not willing to remove the headscarf, which she wore for religious reasons, in the classroom. The question to be decided was whether the decision of the school authorities in the state of Baden-Württemberg to refuse to accept her into the teaching service, even though she had already passed her final examination, violates Article 33(3) of the Basic Law, which states that access to public offices must be granted independently of religious affiliation. In addition, the complainant felt that her constitutional right to religious freedom had been violated. She also pointed out that colleagues who wore Christian or Jewish insignia were admitted to the teaching service, so that her exclusion from the service was contrary to the principle of equal treatment. Moreover, she pointed out that her headscarf had not given rise to any conflicts during her training period.

She was unsuccessful with this action right up to the Federal Administrative Court. In the justifications of the relevant court decisions, a strict requirement of neutrality for state institutions and the negative religious freedom of parents and pupils were cited as arguments, which in the crucifix controversy had been rejected as hostile to religion and one-sided. The essential difference that what was involved was not an officially mandated religious symbol, but one worn as a personal matter, was largely ignored. This amounted to justifying a violation of neutrality—namely, the exclusion of people of a particular faith from the public service—by unjustified appeal to this very neutrality.

It was argued that the headscarf is not only a religious but also a political symbol and, indeed, one of "cultural demarcation" (as also argued by the minister of education of Baden-Württemberg at the time, Annette Schavan). Occasionally, it was even denied that the headscarf is a religious symbol, since it is not compulsory. Moreover, it was claimed that the headscarf has an objective effect that schoolgirls would not be able to escape regardless of the teacher's intention. It was argued that this gives rise to "considerable pressure to conform,"[13] especially for Muslim schoolchildren, which violates the basic rights of pupils and parents to be protected from religious influences as well as the state's duty to be neutral.

These rulings can be seen as what they are explicitly trying to avoid, namely, expressions of cultural demarcation. They amount to a virtual occupational ban on people who lend their religious convictions a certain symbolic expression by politicizing and objectivizing this symbol, so that the different meanings that the practice of wearing a headscarf can have and what the individual intends by it become irrelevant. There is no doubt that the pressure on Muslim girls in particular to comply with certain patriarchal traditions must be taken seriously and criticized; but whether the value to be attached to this symbol in this context is so clear and whether this kind of exclusion can be a suitable means of integration or emancipation may be doubted.

What did the Federal Constitutional Court have to say about this? It did in fact decide that the decisions of the school authorities violated the basic rights of the plaintiff, which is hardly surprising considering the wording of Article 33. The justification offered demands attention, however, because the Court points out that the contested decisions interfere with the said basic rights "in the absence of sufficiently

[13] From the decision of the Stuttgart Supervisory School Authority, quoted in the ruling of the Federal Constitutional Court 2 BvR 1436/02, quoted from BVerfGE 108, 282 ff. A partial English translation of the latter decision (where possible quoted in what follows) is available https://law.utexas.edu/transnational/foreign-law-translations/german/case.php?id=613 (last accessed November 10, 2016).

specific statutory justification." This is also stated by the first guiding principle of the ruling.

As a result, the judgment is placed on a problematic twofold footing. On one hand, the justification involves a substantive discussion about basic rights and contradicts the argument of the authorities cited above; on the other hand, it opens the door for legislation that would only have to justify a prohibition in the right way. As for the former, the Court makes it clear that it is not the task of public authorities (or courts) to make rulings about religious duties, and it further makes it clear how controversial the interpretation of the practice of wearing headscarves is. It can be a symbol of cultural demarcation and the oppression of women, but it can also be a symbol of cultural self-assertion and the personal autonomy of women—and, of course, it is first and foremost a symbol of a profession of the Islamic faith. As for the effects of the symbol on schoolchildren, according to the Court there is no reliable empirical evidence that would justify regarding it as a threat to the educational mandate of the state. Also in the specific case the Court could not discern any "threat to the tranquility of the school."

However, the second point mentioned—namely, the lack of a "sufficiently specific statutory justification" for the decisions of the school authorities and the courts—jostles for position beside these constitutional corrections. In this regard, the Court argued, it remains open to the state legislator to offer a new specification "consistent with its constitutional role, [of] the extent to which religious clothing may be worn at school." This is uncontroversial from the perspective of democratic theory, especially the insistence that such decisions must not be taken at the executive level. The Court goes further, however, and leaves it open whether the legislator, in weighing up these considerations, opts to permit religious diversity in schools, and thus to practice mutual toleration,[14] or whether, in the face of growing social pluralism, "the state in its school policy adhere[s] to a very strict position of neutrality, even more restrained than heretofore," and "hence schoolchildren are to be protected in principle from religious references, including those conveyed by a teacher's external appearance." By granting the legislature a "prerogative of assessment," the Court creates the impression that these options are matters for political value judgements; and although the Court goes on to point out that, in the case of possible prohibitions, religions and denominations must be treated equally, it thereby waters down its previous emphasis on the protection of basic rights. For, even though it is correct that deciding what form the neutrality of state institutions should take is a matter for the legislator, it is no less correct that the framework of fundamental rights sets limits to this decision grounded in the respect for individual identities.

And so it is not surprising that, a couple of months later, the state of Baden-Württemberg enacted a reform of the State Education Act (§38.2) banning religious expressions that seem apt "to jeopardize or disturb the neutrality of the state toward schoolchildren and parents or the political, religious or ideological peace at school."

[14] As is argued by Ernst-Wolfgang Böckenförde, "'Kopftuchstreit' auf dem richtigen Weg?" in *Neue Juristische Wochenschrift* (2001): 723–8, 723 ff.

In particular, external behavior must be avoided "which can create the impression among pupils or parents that a teacher is taking a stance against human dignity, the equal rights of all human beings ..." At the same time it is highlighted with reference to the constitution that this prohibition does not apply to "the corresponding display of Christian and Western educational and cultural values or traditions." This law—which was emulated by other federal states such as Hesse—is an example of cultural demarcation and wholesale condemnation in conjunction with the blatant privileging of Christianity; it places the very equality of citizens of different faiths in question that it calls for at the normative level. Thus, in 2004, the said teacher candidate ultimately lost her case before the Federal Administrative Court, which referred to the new law.

But it is questionable whether the headscarf ruling handed down by the Federal Constitutional Court at the time allows these simple truths to be turned against such exclusionary laws. For this it would have to recollect the crucifix decision and that the Basic Law forbids state constitutions and legislatures from privileging a quasi-public religion, and thereby applying a double standard. Here, people are denied equal rights to choose their career because of their religious affiliation, quite apart from the symbolic dimension. The concern for girls in patriarchal families or traditions, be they Muslim or Christian, is a legitimate one; however, such prohibitions amount to wholesale discrimination against young women.

In a more recent judgment from 2015,[15] the Court duly corrected and refined its adjudication and accepted the complaint brought by two Muslim teachers who had been forbidden to wear headscarves or alternative headgear in the classroom under the terms of the Education Act of the state of North Rhine-Westphalia. In its ruling, the Court makes it clear that a teacher's wearing of a headscarf on religious grounds falls within the scope of the exercise of her basic rights and, unlike government-mandated crosses or crucifixes in classrooms, does not place the neutrality of the state in question. And in abstract terms, it went on, neither can this symbol be interpreted negatively nor can a danger of impairing the peace at school or the state's duty of neutrality be inferred from it. However, the judgment allows that, subject to proof of "a sufficiently specific danger to, or impairment of, the peace at school" (paragraph 113), it is possible to prohibit religious clothing at certain schools or even in certain "school districts" (paragraph 114). It is to be feared that this will serve as a gateway for further prohibitions. The exercise of a fundamental right should not be made dependent in this way on the arbitrariness and strength of social protests. That would invert the function of such fundamental rights.

5. If we are to maintain our footing amidst the storm of ideological arguments in these cases, it must be stressed that the essence of state neutrality resides in basing

[15] 1 BvR 471/10 and 1 BvR 1181/10 of January 27, 2015; quoted from the version published on the homepage of the Court, announced on March 13, 2015: https://www.bundesverfassungsgericht.de/SharedDocs/Entscheidungen/DE/2015/01/rs20150127_1bvr047110.html (last accessed November 10, 2016). A summary of the ruling in English can be found at https://www.bundesverfassungsgericht.de/SharedDocs/Pressemitteilungen/EN/2015/bvg15-014.html (last accessed November 10, 2016).

the corresponding institutions on principles that can be accepted by all as free and equal citizens, and thereby preventing unjustified exclusions and the establishment of privileges. This does not call for an antireligious or laicist system which banishes religion from the public domain. However, it does require that we take the term "equal rights" seriously and not reject neutrality and "negative" freedom as a sign of "exaggerated subjectivism" when it comes to defending crosses and crucifixes in classrooms, but emphasize them when it is a matter of keeping Islamic headscarves out of schools.

The central task of the Federal Constitutional Court is to implement the basic rights in such cases properly as bulwarks against discrimination. In doing so, it does not claim an undemocratic, antimajoritarian competence, but merely insists on the level of justification that should also be shown by legislative processes, assuming they were correctly conducted. Seen in this way, the Court acts in cases such as the crucifix decision as the custodian of a level of justification required in a democracy, whereas in the headscarf ruling it should have set clearer boundaries for the legislator as regards this level.

However, the amendment to the law in Baden-Württemberg shows once again what is actually at stake here—namely, as I stated, the self-understanding of the republic. This is the real controversy at whose center the Court finds itself and which pulls it one time in one direction and another time in another. It has often shown itself to be steadfast when highly controversial issues were to be decided, the crucifix controversy being the most contentious example (one could also mention registered partnerships for same-sex couples). But the position that advocates a different understanding of the constitution and its "imprint," and a different conception of the foundations of "social cohesion," has proved to be stubborn and can be explained in historical terms. Thus, the line of conflict is between those who defend the rule of law as a unity of principles for free and equal citizens and those who see in it the "house rules" of a political community which, although it puts up with "others," does not regard them as equals. The one side strives for a culture of justice and toleration that first allows minorities to be required to respect the principles (also toward their own minorities) that are applied fairly to them; the other side considers a "guiding culture" shaped by Christianity to be indispensable for the continued existence of the republic. It is to be hoped that, in this dispute, the Federal Constitutional Court will continue to help the law, and hence us all, to achieve clarity.

PART IV

JUSTICE, DEMOCRACY, AND LEGITIMACY

7

Justice after Marx

The German title of this chapter, "Gerechtigkeit nach Marx," has an ambivalent ring, for it can mean either "justice according to Marx" or "justice after Marx."[1] I prefer the latter title, because, although I want to address the question of whether Marx had a positive concept of justice (and, if so, which one),[2] my primary concern here will be how relevant Marx is for contemporary philosophical thinking about justice. In my view, we are indebted to Marx for essential insights into the correct understanding of social and political justice, quite apart from how he used the term "justice." At the same time, I want to point out some problems and ambivalences in his theory. My main thesis is that Marx can save us from adopting a one-sided and truncated view of justice, but that his thought also involves the danger of a reduced notion of justice. Thus, the reading I propose is a dialectical one.

1. The current landscape of theorizing about justice is complex and diverse; but it is helpful to divide it up into two continents which reflect two very different ways of posing the question of justice. One of these I characterize as reductive and misleading, the other as appropriate—and radical.[3]

Reflection on social or distributive justice is held "captive" by a powerful image that is beholden to a specific interpretation of the time-honored principle "To each his own" (*suum cuique*), where this is interpreted such that the main issue is what goods individuals receive or deserve—in other words, who "gets" what. The search for answers to this question leads either to comparisons between people's sets of goods, and thus to relative conclusions, or to the question of whether individuals have "enough" of the essential goods to lead a life fit for human beings, regardless of comparative considerations. These ways of thinking lead primarily to recipient-oriented views of justice centered on goods and their distribution which understand "distributive justice" exclusively as a matter of allocating goods.

[1] This text is based on a lecture delivered at the conference "Re-thinking Marx" at the Humboldt University in Berlin in May 2011. I am grateful to the participants in the conference for helpful questions and suggestions. The conference papers were published in a volume edited by Rahel Jaeggi and Daniel Loick, *Nach Marx: Philosophie, Kritik, Praxis* (Suhrkamp 2013).

[2] On this extensive debate see in particular Emil Angehrn and Georg Lohmann (eds.), *Ethik und Marx: Moralkritik und normative Grundlagen der Marxschen Theorie* (Hain bei Athenäum 1986); Allen E. Buchanan, *Marx and Justice: The Radical Critique of Liberalism* (Rowman & Littlefield 1982); Rodney G. Peffer, *Marxism, Morality, and Social Justice* (Princeton University Press 1990).

[3] On what follows (especially sections 1–3) see the more detailed reflections in Rainer Forst, *Justification and Critique: Towards a Critical Theory of Politics*, trans. Ciaran Cronin (Polity 2014) ch. 1.

However, this perspective obscures essential aspects of justice—in the first place, the question of how the goods to be distributed come into the world, hence questions of *production* and its just organization. Secondly, this approach neglects the *political* question of who determines the structures of production and distribution and in what ways—hence, the question of power—as if there could be a giant distribution machine that only needed to be programmed correctly.[4] But such a machine would mean that justice could no longer be regarded as an accomplishment of the subjects themselves; instead it would turn the latter into passive recipients. What this approach also disregards, apart from the social and political autonomy of persons, is, thirdly, that *justified claims* to goods do not simply "exist" but can only be ascertained discursively, which calls for procedures of justification that must in turn be defined in normative terms as a matter of justice.

Fourthly, the view of justice fixated on goods also leaves the question of *injustice* largely out of account. By concentrating on overcoming deficiencies of goods, it equates someone who—to put it in ideal-typical terms—is deprived of goods and resources as a result of a natural catastrophe with someone who suffers the same deprivation as a result of economic or political exploitation. Although assistance is morally required in both cases, as I understand the grammar of justice, it is required in the one case as an act of moral solidarity and in the other as an act of justice, depending on the nature of the involvement in relations of exploitation and injustice in either case.[5] Ignoring this difference can lead one—in a kind of dialectic of morality[6]—to regard what would actually be a requirement of justice as a generous act of "assistance."

These considerations show that it is necessary, also and especially when questions of distributive justice are involved, to recognize the *political* point of justice and to avoid a false picture focused exclusively on goods. On a second, more apt understanding, by contrast, justice must aim at *intersubjective relations and structures*, not at *subjective* or *putatively objective states* of the provision of goods. Only in this way, by taking into consideration the *first question of justice*—the question of the justifiability of social relations and, correspondingly, of the distribution of "justification power" in a political context—is a radical, critical conception of justice possible, one which gets to the root of relations of injustice.

2. Before I examine how Marx's thought relates to the difference between these two ways of thinking about justice, someone schooled in historical materialism might ask how the talk of a "correct" or "right" conception of justice can be justified. Isn't any conception of justice ultimately a reflection of a certain stage in the development of the relations and forces of production? And isn't the search for a moral or even

[4] The two points of criticism in question can be found in Iris Marion Young's critique of the "distributive paradigm" in *Justice and the Politics of Difference* (Princeton University Press 1990) ch. 1.

[5] Here we must distinguish a whole range of cases, in particular: direct participation in or (joint) causation of injustice; indirectly benefiting from injustice without actively contributing to relations of injustice; and the duty to put an end to unjust relations, even ones from which one does not benefit, if one has the means to overcome them.

[6] See Rainer Forst, *The Right to Justification: Elements of a Constructivist Theory of Justice*, trans. Jeffrey Flynn (Columbia University Press 2012) ch. 11.

a "natural" definition of justice completely in vain, as one could say with reference to Marx?[7]

As I see it, it is correct to point out the context-dependency of conceptions of justice and that they can have an ideological, distorting character that leads away from the real question of justice. But this does not mean that there is no such real question; nor does it mean that there is no core meaning of the concept of justice that is preserved across corresponding criticisms and contexts. When Marx criticizes bourgeois conceptions of justice, for example, is he also criticizing the *concept* of justice as such? Or is he not instead pointing out a contradiction between this concept and the concrete form it assumes? How else could he speak of the proletariat as a class within bourgeois society and, at the same time, as a non-class with a "universal character," as raising, not a specific claim, but a universal, general human claim—namely, the claim to overcome not a "particular injustice" but "injustice as such" (*das Unrecht schlechthin*) that weighs upon human history?[8]

The concept of justice as I understand it has a core meaning, although this must be understood in reflexive terms, so that it is not restricted to criticizing false notions of justice but is also self-critical and corresponds to the historical changes in concrete conceptions of justice. The core meaning of the concept becomes visible when one asks about the most important contrasting concept to justice—namely, that of arbitrariness,[9] whether it be arbitrary rule by individuals or by part of the community (for example, a class), or the acceptance of social contingencies that lead to asymmetrical social positions or relations of domination accepted passively as an unalterable fate. Rule is arbitrary when it is exercised over people without legitimate reason, and the main targets of social struggles against injustice are such forms of domination. The basic impulse that opposes injustice is not primarily that of wanting something, or more of something, but of no longer wanting to be dominated, harassed or overruled as someone who has a claim and *basic right to justification*. This claim contains the demand that no political or social relations should exist that cannot be justified adequately toward those involved. Herein resides the profoundly *political* essence of justice that tends to be concealed by the principle *suum cuique*; for the essential point of justice is who determines what is received by whom. On this conception, the demand for justice is an emancipatory one. To put it in reflexive terms, it rests on the claim to be respected as an autonomous subject and authority of justification—that is, to be respected in one's dignity as a being who can provide and demand justifications. The person who *lacks* certain goods should not be regarded as the primary victim of injustice, but instead the individual who does not *count* when it comes to producing and allocating goods.

3. Here it is helpful to take a brief look at contemporary philosophical discussions of justice, which shows that, when viewed against the background of the distinction

[7] Karl Marx, *Capital: A Critique of Political Economy*, Vol. 3, trans. David Fernbach (Penguin Books 1991) 460.

[8] Karl Marx, *Critique of Hegel's Philosophy of Right*, ed. and trans. Joseph O'Malley (Cambridge University Press 1977) 141 (translation amended).

[9] See also the definition in John Rawls, *A Theory of Justice*, rev. edn. (Harvard University Press 1999) 5.

between the two ways of thinking about justice, what are generally regarded as contradictory theories find themselves in the same boat. One example is the debate about equality. By this is meant at least two points of discussion: on the one hand, "Equality of what?"—of goods, resources, welfare, or capabilities[10]—and, on the other, "Why equality at all?" It is striking, however, that both advocates and opponents of equality proceed from the same understanding of justice, often expressed in a specific image—namely, that of the goddess Justitia as a mother who has a cake to divide up.[11] Then some egalitarians argue for the primacy of the equal distribution of goods, according to which arguments for legitimate unequal distributions—for instance, need, merit, or prior claims—must then be weighed as special reasons. Others apply an egalitarian calculation of welfare that serves as the goal of distribution.[12] Yet the question of how the cake came about and, and even more importantly, the question of who is entitled to play mother remain largely unthematized. However, these are the first questions of justice.

Mirror-image problems can be found on the side of the critics of equality. According to Harry Frankfurt, the value of equality cannot ever be the main concern of defenders of egalitarian conceptions of justice; for, if one asks them what is bad about inequality, they cite the negative consequences of conditions in a society of inequality—specifically, that some individuals lack important goods for leading a satisfactory life.[13] These arguments are taken up by "sufficientarian" positions which argue that "at least the especially important, elementary standards of justice are of a non-relational kind"[14] and justice is exclusively a matter of creating "conditions of life fit for human beings." Such positions generally refer to specific lists of such basic goods to provide as universal a concept of the necessary goods as possible.

But here it must be objected that not how much others have, but only whether I have "enough," could be the decisive issue of justice *only if* conditions of background justice prevail—that is, only if others have not previously taken advantage of me. However, this notion of justice cannot be founded on notions of sufficiency. Ultimately, the idea of "getting enough" does not capture the essence of justice at all, which is always a "relational" matter. Justice does not ask primarily about subjective or objective *states of affairs* (such as lack or abundance) but about justifiable *relations between human beings* and what they owe *one another* for what reasons. In particular, the demands of justice cannot be explained on the model of the moral duty

[10] See Gerald A. Cohen, "Equality of What? On Welfare, Goods, and Capabilities," in Martha Nussbaum und Amartya Sen (eds.), *The Quality of Life* (Oxford University Press 1993) 9–29.

[11] For example, in Ernst Tugendhat, *Vorlesungen über Ethik* (Suhrkamp 1993) 373–4; Wilfried Hinsch, *Gerechtfertigte Ungleichheiten* (de Gruyter 2002) 169–70; Stefan Gosepath, *Gleiche Gerechtigkeit: Grundlagen eines liberalen Egalitarismus* (Suhrkamp 2004) 250 ff. The cake example, although not yet featuring the mother, can be found in Isaiah Berlin, "Equality," in Isaiah Berlin, *Concepts and Categories*, ed. Henry Hardy (Penguin Books 1981) 84.

[12] This is especially true of "luck egalitarianism"; for a paradigmatic version, see Richard Arneson, "Luck Egalitarianism Interpreted and Defended," in *Philosophical Topics* 32 (2004): 1–20.

[13] Harry G. Frankfurt, "Equality as a Moral Ideal," in Harry G. Frankfurt, *The Importance of What we Care About* (Cambridge University Press 1988) 143–58, and "Equality and Respect," in Harry G. Frankfurt, *Necessity, Volition, and Love* (Cambridge University Press 1999) 146–54.

[14] Angelika Krebs, "Einleitung: Die neue Egalitarismuskritik im Überblick," in Angelika Krebs (ed.), *Gleichheit oder Gerechtigkeit: Texte der neuen Egalitarismuskritik* (Suhrkamp 2000) 17–18.

of assistance in certain situations of want or necessity. They come into play, rather, where what are at stake are relations in need of justification between human beings bound together in a social context in which goods are produced and distributed—or, as is usually the case, in a context of "negative cooperation," that is, of coercion or domination (whether exercised through legal, economic, or political means). There is a major difference between someone being *denied* certain goods and opportunities unfairly and without justification and someone *lacking* certain goods for whatever reason. To lose sight of the former relation is to miss or obscure the problem of justice as well as that of injustice. Duties of justice must not be reduced to moral duties to provide assistance out of solidarity. In a context of justice, all distributions of goods are in need of justification in principle, because these goods are part of a context of cooperation, and reasons for particular distributions must be found from within this context. Justice requires that those who are involved in a context of cooperation should be respected as equals, which means that they should be able to participate equally in the social and political *order of justification* in which *they themselves determine* the conditions under which goods are produced and divided up.

4. Let us now turn to the question already alluded to of the relation between Marx's theory and my distinction between two ways of understanding justice. I will address in turn the four above-mentioned points of criticism of one-sided, recipient-, and goods-oriented viewpoints.

(1) First, the question of production—which is, of course, *the* question in Marx. But is it also a question of justice? I think that it is undoubtedly a question of justice and that this also holds for Marx. "Exploitation" is clearly a moral concept that expresses the violation of personal autonomy and of the dignity of counting as an equal.[15] Exploitation involves the expropriation of people's labor, a form of theft and, at the extreme, of enslavement; more generally, it involves subjection to (often invisible) constraints of the capitalist system that benefit some and impoverish and degrade others. Only moral concepts such as that of exploitation can describe and criticize such relations. It is correct that Marx rejected "pure" moral criticism of society in the light of appealing ideals for a better world; instead he was interested in a scientific understanding of social developments and contradictions of capitalism. But that does not mean that Marx understood social science in a positivistic sense as devoid of normative contents and goals, and he used strong evaluative language to show this. There can be no doubt that capitalist society is unjust for Marx. But that does not tell us anything about whether overcoming this society and its constraints leads to a society that would be guided by an ideal of justice. I will come back to this question. However, I would like to point out that one can use a notion of justice for critical purposes and at the same time aim at a society that is in a certain sense "beyond" justice.[16]

[15] Thus Georg Lohmann, "Marxens Kapitalismuskritik als Kritik an menschenunwürdigen Verhältnissen," in Daniel Loick and Rahel Jaeggi (eds.), *Karl Marx—Perspektiven der Gesellschaftskritik* (de Gruyter 2013) 67–78.

[16] As Rawls argues in his interpretation of Marx in *Lectures on the History of Political Philosophy*, ed. Samuel Freeman (Harvard University Press 2007) 342 ff. and 370 ff.

Thus, in his "Critique of the Gotha Program," Marx famously raised fundamental questions about the program's goal of achieving a "fair distribution of the proceeds of labor."[17] According to Marx, the way of thinking informing the program is insufficiently wide-ranging and radical. It could be valid at most during a transitional period marked by the division of labor and the deficient principle of *suum cuique* in which differences in the unequal status of the workers would still be justified by differences in their levels of ability and productivity. In order to overcome this inequality, according to Marx, the social division of labor and the corresponding mode of production would have to disappear completely and be replaced by a form of social life in which work had become not merely a means of living but, in a transformed guise, itself an expression of life. Only under such conditions could the principle "From everyone according to his abilities, to everyone according to his needs" be realized, a principle that points beyond justice for Marx.

The distinction made above between two ways to think about justice is helpful for a correct understanding of Marx's critique of the program of the German Workers' Party. For, following his reflections on the different stages in the development of communist society, Marx criticizes the truncated social democratic view that focuses exclusively on the distribution of the "means of consumption" and marginalizes the real question, that of the organization and distribution of the means of production, which is, as I would say, the first question of justice:

> Quite apart from the analysis so far given, it was in general a mistake to make a fuss about so-called *distribution* and put the principal stress on it. Any distribution whatever of the means of consumption is only a consequence of the distribution of the conditions of production themselves.. . . . Vulgar socialism . . . has taken over from the bourgeois economists the consideration and treatment of distribution as independent of the mode of production and hence the presentation of socialism as turning principally on distribution. After the real relation has long been made clear, why retrogress again?[18]

The thrust of this critique can be understood in terms of the more comprehensive political picture of justice that I have outlined. Marx speaks in terms of collective control and sociopolitical autonomy and he aims at the fundamental question of a collective and no longer capitalist way of organizing the means of distribution. Overcoming capitalist injustice requires that criticism should concentrate on the central question of production, which must not be confused with the question of the distribution of the means of consumption. The primary issue is not that the oppressed classes should have some more goods and enjoy better material provision; what matters is that they should become autonomous subjects and actors in the process of production and no longer merely its objects.

(2) Which brings us to the central political question—the question of who has the power to decide the social structures of production and distribution. As I said, I regard this as *the* question of justice. Marx's position on this question is, however,

[17] Karl Marx, "Critique of the Gotha Program," in *The Marx-Engels Reader*, ed. Robert C. Tucker (W. W. Norton 1978) 525–42, at 528.

[18] ibid 531–2.

ambivalent. On the one hand, Marx would no doubt have been horrified by the idea of a pure distribution machine that would provide people with "sufficient" or "necessary" goods; instead, he called for the realization of extensive social and economic autonomy in an "association of free men."[19] On the other hand, it is questionable whether his perspective can really be called "political" in the aforementioned sense inspired by the notion of justice.

Marx's normative beliefs can be viewed in many different ways. There are major debates over whether his critique of exploitation rests on a basically Kantian conception of *moral* dignity that forbids people from using others as mere means, or whether his critique of alienation is based instead on a more Rousseauian *ethical* notion of the good individual and social life in unity with others and nature that liberates one's creative potentials as a species being (*Gattungswesen*).[20] There are good reasons for making this distinction. However, if we want to get to the heart of the normative problem in Marx, it seems indispensable to me to problematize this distinction and to connect the critiques of exploitation *and* of alienation in a way that enables us to develop a contrasting *non-ethical* understanding of the condition of alienation to be overcome.

A series of works suggest themselves for this purpose, but by far the most fascinating is the discussion of commodity fetishism in *Capital*. In this discussion, Marx is not primarily interested in a romantic notion of individuality and creativity that is negated by capitalism (even though this does play a certain role). On the contrary, what he stresses in particular is that in an estranged society social relations become relations between things and that these relations have a dominating or oppressive character that suppresses freedom, because (a) they benefit some, while others are exploited and (b) they are not transparent and therefore cannot be subjected to social control. Social relations assume the "fantastic form of a relation between things"[21] and the result is an artificial world of asymmetry and exploitation that is not intelligible to those who are part of it and is, in this sense, alien, even if it seems familiar. The emphasis here is not on interpersonal class rule but on a global and more anonymous form of domination—an artificial world of things that conceals the real relations between human beings in the process of production and shrouds it in an ideological veil of ignorance: "Their own movement within society has for them the form of a movement made by things, and these things, far from being under their control, in fact control them."[22] So, more than mutual instrumentalization and direct exploitation, it is the lack of transparency and control that Marx criticizes here; and the foundation of this critique is not a concept of the good life in an ethical sense but a notion of social autonomy as *collective autonomy*.

[19] Karl Marx, *Capital: A Critique of Political Economy*, Vol. 1, trans. Ben Fowkes (Penguin Books 1990) 171.

[20] On this see the concept of alienation as an "impeded appropriation of world and self" in Rahel Jaeggi, *Alienation*, trans. Fred Neuhouser and Alan E. Smith (Columbia University Press 2014) 151. Although Jaeggi develops her account primarily as an ethical problem, I see important parallels between her underlying concept of autonomy and the political concept of alienation proposed in what follows.

[21] Marx, *Capital*, Vol. I (n. 19) 165.

[22] ibid 167–8.

In the fetishism chapter, therefore, Marx contrasts his analysis of capitalist alienation with the "association of free men" in which the means of production are socialized, and hence under collective control, and social relations are, accordingly, "transparent,"[23] a word he often uses to describe the necessary kind of control: "The veil is not removed from the countenance of the social life-process, that is, the process of material production, until it becomes production by freely associated men, and stands under their conscious and planned control."[24]

If we look at earlier texts by Marx on the theme of alienation from this angle, then we can see that his concept of alienation was less an ethical one, connected with a conception of the personal good, and more a political one. In the section on alienated labor in the 1844 *Economic and Philosophical Manuscripts*, where Marx distinguishes the four aspects of alienation, the emphasis is on the transformation of the social process, which confronts the individual as an alien force, into something transparent that can be brought under control. The injustice to be overcome is not just one which produces palaces for the rich and deprivation and hovels (*Höhlen*) for the workers;[25] aside from the loss of the product of their labor, it also deprives workers completely of the ability and opportunity to determine in an autonomous way the basic structure to which they are subject. Their products, the activity of production itself, their potentials as free subjects, and, finally, other human beings all appear to them as part of an "alien power."[26] This shows that, in spite of the teleological ethical implications of the idea of species being, it is the loss of collective autonomy in particular that is the key feature of the condition of alienation—namely, that individuals cannot be social beings together with others in a self-determining collective. Throughout Marx's work, this political idea of overcoming alienation as an obscure power that dominates social relations is central:

> Freedom, in this sphere, can only consist in this, that socialized man, the associated producers, govern the human metabolism with nature in a rational way, bringing it under their collective control instead of being dominated by it as a blind power . . .[27]

But is Marx's idea of collective control and of the shared, fully transparent organization of the means of production really, as I just said, a "political" idea? It does indeed raise the question of who has central decision-making power over the structures of production and distribution, and thus avoids what I called a truncated understanding of justice. However, the guiding idea is more that of *social* than that of *political* autonomy, the difference being that social collective autonomy is no longer mediated by political institutions, which according to Marx would only be necessary in a society in which there are fundamental conflicts over questions of production and distribution. The vision of a *post-conflict society* is important for understanding the problem of a Marxian conception of justice. Marx thought he had discovered the truth about the contradictions inherent in capitalist society and about the crisis that

[23] ibid 172. [24] ibid 173.
[25] Karl Marx, "Economic and Philosophical Manuscripts," in Karl Marx, *Early Writings*, trans. Rodney Livingstone and Gregor Benton (Penguin Books 1975) 279–400, at 325.
[26] ibid 330. [27] Marx, *Capital*, Vol. 3 (n. 7) 959.

would eventually lead society beyond this historical malaise. He had a conception of injustice in capitalist societies and a view of a society beyond every half-hearted and petty form of justice—that is, a notion of a realm of complete human control and order. And, in between, historical materialism envisaged a series of events that would not be guided by normative ideals but would instead follow a necessary course of history and the laws of economics. Before this upheaval, political institutions are more part of the problem than of the solution; after it there would not be any need for them, because genuine universality and community would prevail in a "true realm of freedom"[28] beyond the realm of necessity. This is why the question of justice as the recovery a form of *political* autonomy over economic relations was not part of the Marxian program—before the great turn this is not possible, after it not necessary. Thus, his notion of overcoming alienation is essentially *apolitical*: a form of unmediated sociality based on trust in historical necessity and belief in iron economic laws. Here a deeply problematic form of determinism that marginalizes the question of political autonomy becomes apparent.

(3) This has many—and much discussed—implications on which I cannot elaborate further here. However, I would like to mention just one implication that concerns the third dimension of a non-truncated notion of justice—namely, the recognition that justifiable claims to political and social justice are not simply "there," as if they could be read off from a notion of the good or of historical truth. Rather, they have to be arrived at discursively in a legitimate way in and through social discussion and democratic discourse—although, from the perspective of discourse theory, this would not be possible unless a fundamental form of discursive justice had been realized, so that producing this is the first task of justice.[29] Its necessary social and political preconditions also consist in challenging (in the Marxian sense) "fetishized" or "mystified" notions that certain social and economic relations are unalterable and hence are "beyond justification." Recovering a political understanding of economic relations of production and distribution must have overriding importance for any conception of justice after Marx. This is one of the most important contemporary lessons to be drawn from his theory of alienation. At the same time, we need to recognize that Marx undermined this insight through the apolitical aspects of his thought.

(4) The fourth aspect of a comprehensive and radical conception of justice that goes to the root of the phenomenon is the analysis of injustice. This is important from a Marxian perspective, because everything depends on one being able to distinguish victims of exploitation from people who suffer for different reasons. If one focuses only on recipients, and hence only takes clusters of goods or basic needs into account, then the differences between the respective forms of suffering are disregarded. Still, we need to take a nuanced view of the injustices that pervade individual societies and the transnational domain as well; they cannot be reduced to one central contradiction. And as Herculean a task as this analysis may appear, the strict goddess

[28] ibid.
[29] On this see Forst, *The Right to Justification* (n. 6) and *Justification and Critique* (n. 3).

Justice does not brook any shortcuts, and she also demands the inclusion of a historical perspective. To generously offer "aid" to those who were and are part of a system of domination and exploitation is a twofold wrong.

5. Let me conclude with a brief summary of the argument. Thinking about justice after Marx means avoiding a truncated and distorted conception that focuses exclusively on the distribution of goods and neglects the essential question—the question of the structures of production and distribution and of who determines them in what ways. However, this must be conceived as a political question, as a question of social and political power. Normatively speaking, justice articulates the fundamental claim not to be dominated but instead to be an agent and equal authority of justification: that no one should be subjected to norms or social relations that cannot be justified in appropriate terms toward him or her. This is a parsimonious, yet at the same time productive, principle that provides the foundation for a theory of discursive justice. Moreover, it highlights the Kantian character of the approach, because it expresses the autonomy of those on whom a normative order of justice claims to be binding—namely, the autonomy and dignity of being a free and equal justificatory authority. This dignity is violated when individuals are regarded as mere objects of social relations or primarily as recipients of goods.

It is essential, therefore, that the construction of justice should be the autonomous work of those involved; thus, justice is a reflexive virtue that refers to its own discursive conditions and subjects positive norms to permanent criticism in the form of a critique of relations of justification. According to this view, the power of justification is the genuine power, the "mental" power in our heads that presents specific relations to us as natural and unalterable—or as the object of rational critique.[30] Thus, Marx's critique of alienated social forms and relations whose unjustifiable and asymmetrical real structure remains concealed from us by ideology has lost none of its topicality. Reconstructing it within the framework of a discourse theory of political and social justice remains an important task.

[30] See Rainer Forst, "Noumenal Power," ch. 2 in this volume.

8

Legitimacy, Democracy, and Justice

On the Reflexivity of Normative Orders

1. The question of the normativity of political orders is one of the oldest and most difficult questions in political theory.[1] Since the controversy between Socrates and Thrasymachus, which reverberates to the present day, there is disagreement over how ambitious answers to this question should be and how far removed they can or should be from political reality (assuming for the moment that we know how this "reality" should be understood) in order to avoid the twin extremes of utopianism and uncritical affirmation. When modern political theorists have sought to clarify the normativity of political orders between these two extreme positions they have appealed to three notions in particular—namely, legitimacy, democracy, and justice. It is commonly assumed that these three concepts are arranged in order of increasing normative content: the concept of legitimacy is thought to involve less extensive normative investments than that of democracy, whereas justice, by contrast, is not only regarded as the highest political good but also seems to be in rivalry with the concept of democracy and to go beyond legitimacy.

The relationship between these three basic concepts of political normativity that concerns me in what follows is not only of theoretical interest. For both within states and when it comes to the formation of transnational, international, and supranational normative orders, it is important to clarify the normative order between these notions. These evaluative questions are unavoidable for anyone who belongs to a political community, just as they are for anyone who takes a position on the reality of politics beyond the state. Here, research in international relations and in political theory overlap in such a way that they must enter into a dialog that calls for clarity concerning basic concepts.[2] In the following, I attempt to give a *reflexive* answer to

[1] This text is dedicated to my friend Rainer Schmalz-Bruns on his 60th birthday (and first appeared in the *Festschrift* devoted to his work entitled *Deliberative Kritik—Kritik der Deliberation*, edited by Oliver Flügel-Martinsen, Daniel Gaus, Tanja Hitzel-Cassagnes, and Franziska Martinsen (Springer 2014)). I would like to thank Christoph Möllers and Michael Zürn for intensive and productive discussion of an earlier version and Julian Culp, James Tully, Melissa Williams, Mattias Kumm, Enzo Rossi, and audiences at the University of Victoria, Wissenschaftszentrum Berlin, Frankfurt University, and the University of Warwick for valuable comments on later versions.

[2] Paradigmatic examples of such a dialog are Jürgen Habermas, *The Postnational Constellation*, trans. Max Pensky (Polity 2001); Michael Zürn, *Regieren jenseits des Nationalstaats* (Suhrkamp 1998); Fritz W. Scharpf, *Governing in Europe: Effective and Democratic?* (Oxford University Press 1999); Allen E. Buchanan, *Justice, Legitimacy, and Self-Determination: Moral Foundations for International Law* (Oxford University Press 2004); Allen E. Buchanan and Robert O. Keohane, "The Legitimacy of Global

the question of the relationship between the above-mentioned basic concepts, taking reflexivity as the ability to ascertain the ultimate justifying reasons for the claim to normative validity. This is not only a theoretical but also a practical virtue, since practices and institutions can exhibit reflexivity insofar as they adopt a critical stance on their justifiability.[3]

2. A political normative order claims *legitimacy*—in other words, it claims to be rightful, that is, justifiable in the right way. This claim is raised toward those who are subjected to this order and others who are supposed to recognize and respect the order from the outside. If the claim is redeemed, then binding power exists and arises—where by "exists and arises" I mean that this binding power always rests on an antecedent normativity and is not produced *ex nihilo* but, at the same time, it can transform these foundations (more or less radically) insofar as conceptions of legitimacy are changed.[4] We can distinguish, in accordance with the (simplified) formula of recognition from within versus recognition from without, between *internal* and *external* legitimacy, and the one does not automatically stand and fall with the other.[5] Through certain specified procedures, the internal legitimacy of an order—its worthiness of being recognized and its rightfulness (or justifiability)—generates further legitimate norms, rules, or laws. From the internal perspective, therefore, the legitimacy of the order *as a whole* must be distinguished from the legitimacy of *single* institutions or *individual* rules within it (call it "overall legitimacy" versus "individual legitimacy"); however, the latter presupposes the former. Overall legitimacy, by contrast, is preserved even when the latter on occasion fails, unless this failure points to structural deficits that place the legitimacy of the order as a whole in question.

It is often asked whether legitimacy is a *descriptive* or a *normative* concept. The straightforward answer is that the concept can be used in a descriptive or a normative way and it is important to keep these usages apart. One of the complexities of this debate is that legitimacy in its descriptive use refers to a normative state of affairs (rightfulness and acceptance, that is, the binding character of an order). So description may deal with substantive normative phenomena while remaining a description.

But even more confusing than the descriptive function is the normative function that the concept performs where the legitimacy of a normative order is affirmed or

Governance Institutions," in *Ethics and International Affairs* 20 (2006): 405–37; Jürgen Habermas, *The Crisis of the European Union*, trans. Ciaran Cronin (Polity 2012); Jean Cohen, *Globalization and Sovereignty: Rethinking Legality, Legitimacy, and Constitutionalism* (Cambridge University Press 2012).

[3] This is how I interpret the notion of reflexivity developed by Rainer Schmalz-Bruns, *Reflexive Demokratie: Die demokratische Transformation moderner Politik* (Nomos 1995); Rainer Schmalz-Bruns, "The Euro-Polity in Perspective: Some Normative Lessons from Deliberative Democracy," in Beata Kohler-Koch and Berthold Rittberger (eds.), *Debating the Democratic Legitimacy of the European Union* (Rowman & Littlefield, 2007) 281–303.

[4] "Validity" and "binding power" are the Weberian terms for this dimension of political normativity. See Max Weber, *Economy and Society*, 2 vols., trans. and ed. Guenther Roth and Claus Wittich (University of California Press 1978) vol. 1, §5, 31.

[5] On the complex relation between "internal political legitimacy" and "recognitional legitimacy" as two dimensions of legitimacy see Buchanan, *Justice, Legitimacy, and Self-Determination* (n. 2) chs. 5 and 6.

questioned (internally or externally). This seems to presuppose that the term in this usage is normative in nature, and thus that it expresses an evaluation that it contains of itself. But we must be careful here, because it is rather the case (this, at least, is what I claim) that, where legitimacy is used in this normative sense, and possibly even as a battle cry, the normative content stems from *different* concepts, such as God's will, stable order, legal certainty, freedom, democracy, equality, or justice. This usage may refer to primarily procedural or also to substantive norms or values (even if this distinction is often overworked, because every procedural version also contains substantive normative notions). Thus, I hold that legitimacy is a *normatively dependent* concept (similar to others, such as toleration[6] or solidarity): where it has a normative content, either in theory or in practice, it derives this content from another—if you will: deeper—"source." It does not follow that we cannot make a general connection between the concept of legitimacy and a "public interest orientation," as does Michael Zürn; but it does mean that interpretations of what fosters the public interest rest on other notions, and hence that legitimacy must be derived from further sources.[7] The concept of legitimacy is not sufficient of itself to contain or evaluate these principles or values.

Thus, we should follow the classical Weberian notion, however this must be qualified, that there are very different reasons or motivations for legitimacy depending on how the space of justifications is structured—understood in the broad sense of "noumenal power," in which even "faith" or "feeling" can generate recognition and binding power in the sense of the acceptance of an order, because they are connected with normative notions and beliefs.[8] Historical and local conceptions of legitimacy can be understood and differentiated in this way: the "legitimate" monarch and his "legitimate" successor, the "legitimate" harmonious order according to Confucian or Platonic ideas of the well-ordered polity, and so forth. In these cases, there is always a conceptual core that connects these ideas—*by legitimacy we mean in general the quality of a normative order that explains and justifies its general binding power for those subjected to it*—but this concept of legitimacy only becomes a specific conception through further normative sources that, like the narrative of the "good ruler," may be heterogeneous in nature. The concept of legitimacy is thus primarily descriptive in nature and its overlaying, more prominent function of normative criticism or defense depends on other resources. If this is not made clear, the concept acquires its normative power surreptitiously, as occurs whenever it remains unclear which source is being used to enrich a conception of legitimacy, so that the concept seems to be sufficient of itself to acquire a specific normative meaning.

[6] See Rainer Forst, *Toleration in Conflict: Past and Present*, trans. Ciaran Cronin (Cambridge University Press 2013) §3.

[7] As is argued by Michael Zürn, "Autorität und Legitimität in der postnationalen Konstellation," in Anna Geis, Frank Nullmeier, and Christopher Daase (eds.) *Der Aufstieg der Legitimitätspolitik: Rechtfertigung und Kritik politisch-ökonomischer Ordnungen, Leviathan* 40, Special Issue 27 (Nomos 2012) 47, who distinguishes between seven such sources based on empirical evidence.

[8] See Rainer Forst, "Noumenal Power," ch. 2 in this volume.

3. In modern societies, the idea of *democracy* is regarded as the most important normative resource for developing a conception of legitimacy.[9] Democracy can be understood in more or less demanding senses, especially when it comes to the political reflexivity of its institutions and the surrounding culture and to its material preconditions. At its core is the idea that those who are subjected to a normative order must be able to be the co-authors of this order (in its essential structures), specifically through real, critically testable procedures, and not just *in mente*. This includes representative procedures, insofar as they exhibit a corresponding degree of reflexivity that prevents institutions from becoming self-sufficient in ways that undermine the possibility of co-authorship. A purely "output-oriented" form of legitimacy, therefore, can hardly be called "democratic," even if it claims to achieve outcomes "for the people."[10] Democratic legitimacy, in whatever version of collective self-determination, is a specific variant of legitimacy that seems to rest solely on the binding power of the value of democracy.

Here, however, we must continue to inquire into the normative core of democracy. That democracy is a particular form of organization of *political* rule does not preclude, but instead presupposes, that its basic claim is *moral* in nature—namely, the claim not to be subjected to any norms to which one could not have agreed as a free and equal person, both from a normative perspective (with a view to reciprocally and generally rejectable reasons) and from an institutional perspective (concerning the existence of democratic, reciprocal, and general practices of justification). Thus, institutionalizations of democratic practices of justification always involve an inherent critical-reflexive dimension that questions these procedures and their results as regards their justifiability. This critical reflection is both *immanent* to democracy (corresponding to its idea) and *transcends* its concrete, practical manifestation. Therefore, democracy, properly understood, is necessarily a self-critical practice.[11]

The moral claim on which democracy rests as a justificatory practice is the right to justification, which, in the moral domain, asserts that nobody may be subjected to actions or norms that cannot be justified to him or her as an autonomous and equal justificatory authority. In the political context, it states that nobody may be subjected to a normative order of rules, norms, and institutions that cannot be justified to him or her as an equal, autonomous subject of justification, which implies the basic claim that a corresponding practice of justification should be established. The principle that those subjected to norms must be able to be their authors expresses a central moral idea, namely, the Kantian idea of autonomy, which, in the political domain becomes the idea of democracy as the expression of collective self-determination, keeping in mind the differences between morality and politics, which consist in particular in mastering social interest conflicts and in the mode of validity of political-legal norms. These differences sometimes lead thinkers to posit

[9] The most comprehensive treatment from the perspective of social theory and philosophy remains Jürgen Habermas, *Legitimation Crisis*, trans. Thomas McCarthy (Beacon Press 1975).

[10] Although this is argued by Scharpf, *Governing in Europe* (n. 2) 10 ff.

[11] On this see Forst, *The Right to Justification: Elements of a Constructivist Theory of Justice*, trans. Jeffrey Flynn (Columbia University Press 2012) ch. 7.

a negative claim—the avoidance of arbitrary rule, that is, domination—as central in the political domain.[12] But this should not obscure the fact that this negative claim has a positive counterpart, namely, the claim to be respected as a person with a right to justification, which implies that the political order must not only protect, but also express, the autonomy of individuals.

These reflections imply that the demand for democracy is not normatively independent. The idea of democracy does not express a stand-alone "value." It is based instead on the idea of autonomy, which is transferred to the political world and undergoes a transformation as a result; accordingly democracy has the meaning of avoiding political arbitrariness (i.e., domination). These aspects point to the conceptual core of *justice*, which is the real contrasting concept to arbitrary rule and political heteronomy. Democracy, properly understood, is thus the *political form of justice* expressed in the rule of democratically enacted law. Interpreted in terms of its normative core, democracy is not just a, but *the* practice of political and social justice.

Although the concept of democracy is less amorphous than that of legitimacy, it is normatively dependent on the concept of justice. Withholding democratic rights is a gross political injustice, and a democracy that does not seek to create justice in its procedures and results is not worthy of the name.[13] Given this normative ordering of the concepts in question, a democratically elected government that sets out to change the preconditions for a democratic order in order to secure its own power permanently can be criticized as illegitimate because it violates the imperative of justice to guarantee democratic practices of justification.

4. With this, the concept of justice takes center stage, which is no surprise since it is *the* basic normative concept with regard to political orders. In order to appreciate this, however, we must liberate ourselves from reductive or reified conceptions of justice that associate it in the Platonic sense with a fixed idea removed from democratic self-determination, or that are exclusively geared to results or goods and not only presuppose final patterns of distribution but also the figure of a central unquestioned distributive authority.[14] Theories of this type fail to recognize that the real question of justice is that of creating a *basic structure of justification* (in the sense of fundamental justice), such that the relevant political and social institutions can banish arbitrariness only if those subjected to norms can be co-authors of the norms within those institutions. The question of political and social justice is whether political and social

[12] As argued, for example, by Philip Pettit, *Republicanism* (Oxford University Press 1997) and Philip Pettit, *On the People's Terms* (Cambridge University Press 2012). I discuss the differences between our positions in Rainer Forst, "A Kantian Republican Conception of Justice as Nondomination," in Andreas Niederberger and Philipp Schink (eds.), *Republican Democracy* (Edinburgh University Press 2013) 154–68.

[13] On this see Simone Chambers, "Democracy and Critique: Comments on Rainer Forst's *Justification and Critique*," in *Philosophy and Social Criticism* 41/3 (2015): 213–17, and my reply in "A Critical Theory of Politics: Grounds, Method and Aims. Reply to Simone Chambers, Stephen White and Lea Ypi," in *Philosophy and Social Criticism* 41/3 (2015): 225–34.

[14] On this see Rainer Forst, *Justification and Critique: Towards a Critical Theory of Politics*, trans. Ciaran Cronin (Polity 2014) ch. 1, and Rainer Forst, "Transnational Justice and Non-Domination," ch. 10 in this volume.

relations are justifiable, and the answer to this question is the call for a basic structure of justification in which the question of justification becomes *practical*—not only as a question about the justifications that sustain relations of rule (including, of course, distributions), but in particular regarding whether there are justification structures that allow dominant justifications to be exposed to critical scrutiny. The rule of arbitrariness that justice is supposed to overcome is rule without adequate reasons and without adequate fora and procedures of justification. Domination must be diagnosed critically on both levels, that of existing (inadequate, possibly ideological) justifications and that of missing structures of justification.[15] To play the former off against the latter is an impermissible abbreviation.[16]

A (common) mistake is to respond that this is to confuse "legitimacy" with "justice." Legitimacy, so the objection goes, is responsible for producing and justifying political rule, justice for distributing scarce goods.[17] Based on what has been said thus far, it is correct that a necessary conceptual connection does not exist between legitimacy and justice, because the concept of legitimacy is descriptively flexible and normatively dependent. But not to regard the fundamental demand for democratic justification (where this is made) as a political requirement of justice would be implausible because what is at stake is overcoming or avoiding political arbitrariness (i.e., domination). It is also impossible that an undemocratic regime could give rise to social justice,[18] for justice cannot be produced by unjust means. Even the most well-meaning paternalistic system that bestowed favors on its citizens and was able to raise the standard of living significantly would still be an unjust system, politically *and* socially speaking (albeit one that obviously had brought about social improvements). The injustice of paternalism cannot be made good by improvements in material conditions. It is equally impossible for a state that seriously violates social justice to be legitimate (in the normatively ambitious, justice-based sense), because social injustice, insofar as it is structurally based, is a specific form of political repression.

5. It may seem arbitrary to regard the concept of legitimacy, but not the concept of justice, in this way as dependent and historically variable. What is the reason for this difference? Both concepts do indeed have a constant central meaning. In the case

[15] On this see Habermas, *Legitimation Crisis* (n. 9) 113: "A social theory critical of ideology can, therefore, identify the normative power built into the institutional system of a society only if it starts from the *model of the suppression of generalizable interests* and compares normative structures existing at a given time with the hypothetical state of a system of norms formed, *ceteris paribus*, discursively" (emphasis in original). Habermas goes on to speak of the " 'injustice' of the repression of generalization interests."

[16] Although this is argued by Jürgen Neyer, *The Justification of Europe: A Political Theory of Supranational Integration* (Oxford University Press 2012). For a critique, see Forst, "Justice, Democracy and the Right to Justification: Reflections on Jürgen Neyer's Normative Theory of the European Union," in Dimitry Kochenov, Gráinne de Búrca, and Andrew Williams (eds.), *Europe's Justice Deficit* (Hart Publishing 2014) 227–34.

[17] Thus Simon Caney, "Justice and the Basic Right to Justification," in Rainer Forst (ed.), *Justice, Democracy and the Right to Justification* (Bloomsbury 2014) 147–66, and on this Rainer Forst, "Justifying Justification: Reply to My Critics," in Forst (ed.), *Justice, Democracy and the Right to Justification* (ibid) 205–15.

[18] Although this is argued by Pettit, *On the People's Terms* (n. 12) 130.

of legitimacy, this relates to the binding power of an order, in the case of justice, to ensuring that arbitrariness is avoided in the same order and to creating a corresponding order of justification. Thus defined, the concept of legitimacy allows for greater variability than that of justice: binding power can be generated in many ways, ending arbitrariness cannot. Justice reflects critically on legitimacy, and hence represents a higher-level, normative reflection. Affirming or criticizing legitimacy from the participant perspective depends on other normative resources, but the same does not apply to justice: here the question cuts directly into practice because it radicalizes the question of justification *for us* as equal normative authorities. We have a different relation to the question of the binding power of an order than to the question of whether it is just. Justice ultimately obligates us for the sake of those who suffer injustice, whose moral claim does not leave us at liberty to answer the question of justice merely descriptively or arbitrarily. To put it metaphorically, there is a goddess of justice, but not of legitimacy. That is just another way of expressing the overriding binding force of justice. Viewed in normative terms, every notion of legitimacy must submit to it.

6. Various theories of legitimacy nevertheless assert that the concept of legitimacy has *intrinsic* binding force and normative content, one of which I will discuss here. According to Bernard Williams, legitimacy exists when the "first" political question of the creation of a stable social order is answered successfully. For this purpose he defines a *basic legitimation demand*, which states that a legitimate normative order must provide a justification to *every* person who is subjected to it (it "has to offer a justification of its power *to each subject*").[19] This does not have to be a justification that is equally acceptable to all or that treats everyone as an equal justificatory authority; but "something has to be said"[20] to those who are not treated as equals but toward whom legitimacy is nevertheless asserted. Thus far, this could still be compatible with a descriptive notion of legitimacy, depending on what it means to cite a ground of legitimacy toward subjects who as a result are still able to regard themselves as subjects and not as enemies of the state or as "radically disadvantaged."

At this point, however, Williams takes an important step in the direction of a more pronounced normative conception of legitimacy. He regards this as a moral conception, by which he means a morality "inherent"[21] in politics, although he does not explain this further; at any rate, the corresponding understanding of politics is as a result morally charged. Williams asserts that the exercise of power and domination do not provide any justifying reasons for rule over others but are in need of such reasons. Thus, he formulates the "*critical theory principle,* that the acceptance of a justification does not count if the acceptance itself is produced by the coercive power which is supposedly being justified."[22] This principle is highly plausible—but it invests the notion of legitimacy with a normative meaning derived from other sources, namely, a certain understanding of justice that springs from the right to

[19] Bernard Williams, *In the Beginning Was the Deed*, ed. Geoffrey Hawthorn (Princeton University Press 2005) 4.

[20] ibid 5. [21] ibid. [22] ibid 6.

justification. This is also the resource that drives this principle far beyond Williams's "basic demand for legitimacy," because it renders any justification for social asymmetries open to challenge in principle on the grounds that it is a product of relations of domination. Why should, based on Williams's principle, those who are subjected to an order demand only "a" reason for rule and not sufficient, reciprocal-general reasons to be generated in a domination-free discourse?

Here there is a point of contact, if not identity, between the conceptions of legitimacy of Williams and Jürgen Habermas, although the latter explicitly traces legitimacy back to a critical and reflexive discourse principle that connects democracy and justice by overcoming inadequate and ideological forms of justification.[23] As Habermas put it in an early formulation:

> How would the members of a social system, at a given stage in the development of productive forces, have collectively and bindingly interpreted their needs (and which norms would they have accepted as justified) if they could and would have decided on the organization of social intercourse through discursive will-formation with adequate knowledge of the limiting conditions and functional imperatives of their society?[24]

7. It is tempting at this point to proceed from the analysis of the quality of justification, which seems to reside in the concept of legitimacy, to a moral right to justification, and to argue that this represents the analytical reconstruction of a conceptual truth. I do not follow this path because, as I explained at the beginning, I doubt whether this is an implication of the concept of legitimacy as such. The question of legitimacy is, of course, a question of justification; but to answer it in a democratic, egalitarian, and reflexive way is a question of *justice* in political contexts. Only in this light is justification conceived as a comprehensive political practice of self-determination through justification procedures that generate democratic legitimacy. Then we call a normative order *legitimate* that exhibits, or credibly aims at, *fundamental justice* in the sense of a basic structure of justification, and we call those norms and laws legitimate that arise within this structure. They remain such even if they do not achieve a level of full justice that goes beyond fundamental justice. Laws that do not completely realize justice are illegitimate only when they violate fundamental justice.

8. In these brief reflections, I began with the concept of legitimacy and worked my way, by radicalizing the question of justification, to the more substantive normative concepts of democracy and, finally, of justice. These form a series in an order of justification practices that exhibits increasing reflexivity, which means, however, that there is a further basis of this order of the concepts, namely, *justifying reason*. As a form of practical reason, it contains the imperative that norms that claim to be equally binding for everyone must be justifiable to all as free and equal persons.[25] To this imperative correspond categorical duties of justification that, in the political domain, call for democracy as an indispensable practice of justice.

[23] See Habermas, *Legitimation Crisis* (n. 9) 112. [24] ibid 113.

[25] On this see Forst, "Critique of Justifying Reason: Explaining Practical Normativity," ch. 1 in this volume.

With this has our investigation detached itself completely from political reality, as Thrasymachus would claim, and drifted off into the abstract space of reasons? Yes and no. The political space of justifications is abstract and concrete at the same time: the critical question concerning better justifications for a normative order is a very concrete one that dissidents always raise; the contents and forms this demand for justification assumes vary, but their structure remains constant. The question of legitimacy is driven *by these actors*, not from a philosophical position, in the direction of democracy and justice. To engage in critical theory is to express the truth of these demands both abstractly and concretely. In this way, justifying reason can become a practical matter, although primarily in the mode of critique.

PART V

TRANSNATIONAL JUSTICE

9

Realisms in International Political Theory

1. Anyone who aspires to study politics in a scientific way should observe the imperative of realism. For what would be the use of a scientific analysis that was open to the reproach of being unrealistic?[1] But what exactly does "unrealistic" mean here: idealistic, utopian, quixotic, ideological? These concepts are very vague. A scientific treatment of politics requires a more specific vocabulary. According to a classical view, what sets political realism apart is the emphasis it places on the role of power and the power interests of individuals and collectives as opposed to on moral norms. "Moralism" would then be the contrasting concept to realism and would imply not only that one allows one's moral judgments to shape the scientific study but also, and especially, that one overestimates the power of morality and believes that politics conforms to morality or that it is even something like "applied ethics." However, as the realist knows, politics follows its own laws.

This problem of the opposition between a "world of interests" of power and a "world of norms" of morality has too many facets to be dealt with exhaustively here. I regard it as misleading, however, because neither interests nor power, neither morality nor norms, can be understood in this way. Such a conception of realism leads away from reality. The idealism that situates norms in a Platonic *Hinterwelt*, to use Nietzsche's polemical expression, is merely the undialectical mirror image of this conception. If we do not understand how norms and interests intermesh to generate and reproduce power, we are condemned to failure in political science.

2. There have been many attempts in recent times to challenge realism in political science. For example, there has been an extensive theoretical debate in international relations over the status of the justificatory dimension of norms that guide institutions and individual actions in ways informed by values. Here the studies by Harald Müller, Thomas Risse, and many others have forged important new paths for research.[2] Much

[1] Part of this chapter formed the basis of my plenary address at the 25th Congress of the German Political Science Association on "The Promise of Democracy" held in Tübingen in September 2012. I also presented it at a conference organized by Mathias Koenig-Archibugi and Lea Ypi held at the London School of Economics in 2014. To a large extent, I have retained the style of the lecture; references to further lines of argument have been added. I am especially grateful to Hubertus Buchstein, Katrin Flikschuh, and Dorothea Gädeke for helpful comments. The text originally appeared in *Social Research* 81/3 (2014): 667–82.

[2] See in general Peter Niesen und Benjamin Herborth (eds.), *Anarchie der kommunikativen Freiheit* (Suhrkamp 2007).

also depends in this context on not making an artificial separation between the concept of norms and the concept of interests. Norms are as much congealed reasons as they are expressions of clusters of interests, and interests in turn take shape around reasons of the most diverse kinds. An interest is not a raw datum. The important point is to understand systems of actions and institutions as orders of justification in such a way that the quality, complexity and potential inconsistency of the different justifications on which they are based become visible.[3]

But it is not just different forms of constructivism that have posed an important challenge to diverse "realisms"; in works such as those of Bill Scheuerman, for example, a revisionist interpretation of realism itself has emerged.[4] According to Scheuerman, "progressive realists" like Morgenthau and Niebuhr were not only moral cosmopolitans, but also argued for the establishment of strong supranational political and legal structures. Here, I do not want to take a stance of this thesis but only to note that realism is obviously a normative position that claims to rest on a Weberian ethics of responsibility. From an analysis of "reality" alone—even assuming such a thing were possible—no guidelines for action follow, not even for prudent "statesmen." I will return to the figure of the statesman as it features in realists like Morgenthau. After all, realism is often considered to be an instrument of prudent statecraft.

3. Whereas in major fields of research of political science, such as International Relations, we encounter a variety of critiques of the classical image of realism, in political philosophy, by contrast, there is a superabundance of literature by those claiming to be "realists." This reflects a general dissatisfaction with "ideal" theories of justice, such as those of John Rawls and Ronald Dworkin. Those who have Hegel's dictum about the empty and abstract "ought" ringing in their ears will be familiar with these tones. However, even these realisms are motivated by normative considerations. I will cite three examples.[5]

(1) Rawls himself initiated a realist turn. It is no accident that he developed the idea of a "realistic utopian" theory in *The Law of Peoples*, which deals with questions raised by the international system.[6] The theory in question is utopian insofar as it delineates a normatively justified world in which liberal and well-ordered peoples treat each other fairly; but it is realistic in rejecting the assumption that the relevant rules of fairness can stem from the self-understanding of liberal societies. This is an important theoretical orientation, because now liberal theory can no longer aim at a comprehensive program of justification; rather, it leads at best to the principles of the "foreign policy"[7] of liberal societies—here the idea of the "statesman" also sets

[3] On this see Rainer Forst and Klaus Günther, "Die Herausbildung normativer Ordnungen: Zur Idee eines interdisziplinären Forschungsprogramms," in Rainer Forst and Klaus Günther (eds.), *Die Herausbildung normativer Ordnungen: Interdisziplinäre Perspektiven* (Campus 2011) 11–30.

[4] William E. Scheuerman, *The Realist Case for Global Reform* (Polity 2011).

[5] Another approach would be that of Philip Pettit, which I discuss in "Transnational Justice and Non-Domination: A Discourse-Theoretical Approach," ch. 10 in this volume.

[6] John Rawls, *The Law of Peoples* (Harvard University Press 1999) 1–23.

[7] ibid 10.

the tone. Here realism means that we—in accordance with the "fact of pluralism" of different societies and cultures—have to reckon with *different perspectives* that we cannot fully comprehend. This is an important aspect of contemporary versions of normative realism—namely, the *idea of cultural difference.*

(2) In the recent work of Charles Beitz[8] and Joseph Raz,[9] to name just these two thinkers as representative of many others, we encounter another aspect of realistic political theory—namely, that of *immanence to practice.* If we want to understand the idea of human rights, according to Beitz, then we must not follow an abstract model; instead we should adopt a practical and functionalist approach that reconstructs the role played by human rights in an international normative order. This approach has also been adopted in recent debates on global justice, if one thinks, for example, of the idea of a "practice-based" theory formulated by Andrea Sangiovanni.[10]

(3) Finally, in contemporary philosophical discussion there is still a third source of realism in addition to the emphasis on cultural difference and on the autonomy of political and legal practices. It is nourished by impulses from a Nietzschean critique of morality and insists on the categorical difference between *morality and politics.* This is an old *topos* in political theory, if one thinks back to Thrasymachus, although also to such classical theories of power as that of Machiavelli. In recent political theory, it has led to demarcations that defend the autonomy of politics against (so to speak) colonizing claims of morality or justice. Examples that spring to mind are such original and different approaches as those of Hannah Arendt and Sheldon Wolin, but also those of Michael Walzer and Herfried Münkler. One might also think in this connection of Chantal Mouffe and other poststructuralists, and of a very different thinker such as Ingeborg Maus.

In the version we find in Bernard Williams, realist political theory asserts that the question of order is the first question of politics.[11] A political mode of social coexistence is one among beings who cannot agree on any shared system of morality or justice; the most that can be aspired to is a generally acceptable and legitimate order. According to Raymond Geuss, realist political philosophy should not be based on an assumption of idealized rational beings. Instead, it should proceed from historically situated and concrete "real motivations" within a game of interests and power that cannot be transcended in the direction of an "ideal theory."[12]

[8] Charles Beitz, *The Idea of Human Rights* (Oxford University Press 2009).

[9] Joseph Raz, "Human Rights without Foundations," in Samantha Besson and John Tasioulas (eds.), *The Philosophy of International Law* (Oxford University Press 2010) 321–38.

[10] Andrea Sangiovanni, "Justice and the Priority of Politics to Morality," in *The Journal of Political Philosophy* 16/2 (2008): 137–64. For a critique of this view, see Rainer Forst, "Transnational Justice and Democracy: Overcoming Three Dogmas of Political Theory," in Eva Erman and Sofia Näsström (eds.), *Political Equality in Transnational Democracy* (Palgrave Macmillan 2013) 41–59.

[11] Bernard Williams, "Realism and Moralism in Political Theory," in Bernard Williams, *In the Beginning was the Deed: Realism and Moralism in Political Argument* (Princeton University Press 2005) 1–17.

[12] Raymond Geuss, *Philosophy and Real Politics* (Princeton University Press 2008).

4. It is now time to explain—briefly—why I reject all of these realisms as unrealistic.

(1) *On Rawls*: Who would dispute, given the many well-founded criticisms of Western ethnocentrism as the continuation of colonialism with theoretical means, that the cultural idea of difference is of major importance? It is one of Rawls's merits to have pointed this out. But his theory loses track of reality the moment it makes "peoples" into normative entities which form sociocultural, almost personalized units that could agree on principles of international cooperation. In the process, it loses sight of what is primarily at stake in questions of transnational justice—namely, norms and institutions that respond to the problems rooted, in the first place, in the fact that peoples, societies, and states are not uniform but instead are plural entities, and in particular ones pervaded by conflict, domination, and oppression. Second, it must be noted that contemporary societies are parts of complex systems of control and cooperation marked by extremely asymmetric participation and profit structures.[13] A theory of transnational justice that is *realistic* must be responsive to these realities, which means in the first instance that it must reconstruct the reality of transnational and international ruling structures. In this context, a theory that envisages principles of international law for separate, culturally unified nations or peoples which regard each other as equals is extremely unrealistic.

Without having to accuse Rawls directly, one must bemoan another dead end into which the idea of cultural difference leads. I mean the idea that human rights could or should be justified in an overlapping consensus of cultures or peoples.[14] That is a strange idea, one which also passes reality by. Not only does it lead all too often merely to a minimal list of human rights that ignores the real social problems. More importantly, it is unclear what kind of "consensus" is supposed to exist when values or principles are shared but their arguments are not. Evidently, there can be no question of a justification of norms under such circumstances; at best, there would be a contingent and possibly fleeting or superficial overlap. But how would one actually establish the existence of such overlaps? Is it a matter of an empirical consensus and, if so, of an existing consensus or one that would first have to be produced—or, after all, of a counterfactual, fictitious consensus?

Finally, how plausible is it really to have an imaginary or real universal overlapping consensus decide which human rights are valid? Who would have hit upon the idea, for example, of grounding the *Droits de l'homme et du citoyen* in an overlapping consensus of the time—or the Universal Declaration of Human Rights in an overlapping consensus of the 1940s? And who would have the idea of telling the protesters in Tiananmen Square, or those protesting against the starvation wages of a multinational oil company in Nigeria, or those protesting against patriarchy and violence against women in India that they should keep in mind that their demands for justice

[13] See Rainer Forst, *The Right to Justification: Elements of a Constructivist Theory of Justice*, trans. Jeffrey Flynn (Columbia University Press 2012) ch. 12.

[14] Charles Taylor, "Conditions of an Unforced Consensus on Human Rights," in Joanne Bauer und Daniel Bell (eds.), *The East Asian Challenge for Human Rights* (Cambridge University Press 2009) 124–45; Stefan Gosepath, "Der Sinn der Menschenrechte nach 1945," in Gerhart Ernst and Stephan Sellmaier (eds.), *Universelle Menschenrechte und partikulare Moral* (Kohlhammer 2010) 17–32.

and human rights exceed the minimal intersection of an intercultural overlapping consensus that would be agreed between the "representatives of all world regions and all world cultures (even if 'only' state cultures)"?[15] Here there is a danger of exchanging diplomatic considerations for normative thinking, moreover in the wrong place. Again, we are being spooked by the shadow of the imaginary "statesman."

In this way, to use a typical Frankfurt-style formulation, purported realism becomes inverted into affirmation. The intention to proceed in a realistic way from the fact of sociocultural pluralism ends in speechlessness toward actual reality, the reality of social conflicts and struggles with strong moral claims—claims that are not raised or justified by "philosophy" or "the West" but by those involved and affected themselves who are rebelling against an existing normative order. These claims must be taken seriously from a normative perspective of the participants. If one overlooks this, even the critique of ethnocentrism that is rightly raised by different sides (not just by postcolonial theories) can become inverted into its opposite—into the idea that human rights are, for example, a purely Western idea and a possession of the West (or even of the Christian West). This would amount in practice to disenfranchising the protesters in non-Western societies who formulate demands for human rights in terms of idea current in these societies.[16]

(2) *On Beitz and Raz*: Normative justifications must always be immanent to practice in the sense that they arise out of practices and conflicts that need to be regulated or settled. Anyone who wants to justify norms of justice, therefore, should be aware of what constitutes a context of justice; and anyone who reflects on human rights should know what practice is associated with them—and, specifically, to which conflicts such norms primarily respond. If, like Beitz and Raz, one sees the essential function of human rights as being to urge states to observe basic norms governing the treatment of their members, and if one stresses further that noncompliance with these norms justifies intervention by the world community, then one easily finds oneself on a slippery slope. For one might then easily succumb to the overly hasty inference that an extensive interpretation and definition of human rights could open the floodgates to interventions (by interested parties, who moreover all too often invoke morality). The result is a reduced core list of human rights.

Such a position confuses different questions: the question of human rights and the legitimacy of states from the perspective of their citizens and, by contrast, the question of the external sovereignty of a state and of reasons for a legitimate external intervention. But, however intertwined these questions may be, they must first be answered separately. The scope and justification of human rights is one thing; the question of who can legitimately intervene, and when, is another. They are often short-circuited in practice, but this does not mean that theory must follow suit and curtail the notion of human rights.

When it comes to defining the function of human rights, they should be seen instead in their original political and social context, where they secure the basic

[15] As argued by Harald Müller, *Wie kann eine neue Weltordnung aussehen?* (Fischer 2008) 110.

[16] See also Rainer Forst, "The Point and Ground of Human Rights: A Kantian Constructivist View," in David Held and Pietro Maffettone (eds.), *Global Political Theory* (Polity 2016) 22–39.

status of free and equal persons who are not subject to legal, political, or social domination.[17] This status guarantees the standing of individuals as full members of a political community. In this way, a human right to democratic participation, such as is contained in the Universal Declaration of 1948, can be justified—a right placed in question by minimalist theories of human rights.[18]

International political theory is mistaken when it assumes the position of a global adjudicator who—to exaggerate somewhat—would understand human rights in the sense of minimal compromise formulas and would connect the validity of human rights too closely with the legitimacy of interventions. That would be to fail to accord adequate weight to the reality of the struggles for human rights in different states—not to take sufficiently seriously the perspective of those affected who have enough of being kept in leading strings by their government and do not want to be "liberated" or "patronized" by Western countries. If political science wants to be realistic, it must develop the perspective and logic of these struggles and claims.

(3) *On Williams and Geuss*: It is true that politics is not applied ethics, if that would mean ignoring political realities. Those who, like Peter Singer,[19] postulate individual duties to assist conceived in utilitarian terms as a response to systemically engendered world poverty neglect the structural injustice of asymmetrical transnational and international relations, which are the cause of persistent disadvantage and underdevelopment. And those who first construct a beautiful, unworldly "ideal" theory for themselves in such a way that it would have to be "implemented" by wise statesmen or insightful citizens overlook not only the contingency of the political world and its unpredictability, but also a fundamental principle—namely, that of *autonomy*. Politics is neither the space of the technical application of morality nor that of the prudent creation of order; rather, it is the space in which the question of the justification of a political order is posed in such a way that, on a radical understanding, it is at once a philosophical and a practical question. It is the question of those who are subjected to rule or domination and it is the question of the justification of such rule, which—in a reflexive turn—includes in the first place the demand to create a practice of political justification by those affected as justificatory equals. Politics is a matter of justifying forms of rule. This means that politics involves establishing *relations of justification* in which those who were subjected to rule can be the justification authorities of this rule.[20]

With this principle of justification, which calls for democratic justification of structures of rule, a principle enters the political world which, in my view, is as much moral as political, as much universal as historical, and as much rational as emotional.[21] It states that only those social or political relations can be called just

[17] Cf. Rainer Forst, "The Justification of Basic Rights: A Discourse-Theoretical Approach", in *Netherlands Journal of Legal Philosophy* 45/3 (2016): 7–28.

[18] For a critical treatment, see Rainer Forst, *Justification and Critique: Towards a Critical Theory of Politics*, trans. Ciaran Cronin (Polity 2014) ch. 2.

[19] Peter Singer, *One World: The Ethics of Globalization* (Yale University Press 2002).

[20] On this see Forst, *Justification and Critique* (n. 18).

[21] On this see my debate with Seyla Benhabib, "The Uses and Abuses of Kantian Rigorism: On Rainer Forst's Moral and Political Philosophy," in *Political Theory* 43/6 (2015): 777–92, in my reply "The Right

and sufficiently legitimate that can be justified by those who are subjected to them themselves.[22] This is the principle of autonomy, which calls for moral self-legislation in moral contexts and for political self-legislation in political contexts, where self-legislation assumes the form of discursive, intersubjective practices.

This is also confirmed by Williams more *nolens* than *volens*. He introduces the basic political "legitimation demand," which requires that political rule must always be able to justify itself toward those subjected to it. When he explains the criterion of "acceptability to each subject," he adds what he calls, alluding to Habermas, "the critical theory principle"—namely, "*that the acceptance of a justification does not count if the acceptance itself is produced by the coercive power which is supposedly being justified*."[23] At this point, Williams tries to explain in a somewhat convoluted manner that, although the basic principle of legitimacy, thus understood, is presumably a moral principle, it does not express a morality "prior to politics" but one "inherent in there being such a thing as politics."[24]

However, a moral argument cannot be converted into a conceptual argument. Here we are evidently dealing with a moral principle of politics—namely, that human beings, as individuals subjected to rule, have the *right* to demand a justification acceptable to them as free and equal persons. And since this principle is to be understood reflexively in the light of the principle of autonomy, the justifications should be understood as discursively generated—specifically, as being collectively and democratically generated—not as justifications that are "delivered" to their recipients. Then the first political right is the *right to justification*—namely, the right to be a democratic co-author of the norms that claim to be legitimate ruling principles.

5. The realists are right to warn, as Geuss does, that morality itself can degenerate into ideology. Hans Morgenthau, for example, warned against the "sin of pride" of declaring one's own values to be universally valid and enforcing them with the "blindness of crusading frenzy."[25] But realism can also turn into technocratic ideology when it places itself at the service of the wise "statesman" who upholds supposed "national interest,"[26] or when one confuses questions of justification with diplomatic questions or simply overlooks what is at stake in politics. Politics has the task of building, extending, and maintaining the institutions necessary for a just social order. Therefore, politics must always submit to the justification imperative inherent in it—namely, the imperative that only those who are subjected to rule have the authority to generate, through fair justification procedures, the legitimations which they can recognize as free and equal persons, and which they must recognize

to Justification: Moral and Political, Transcendental and Historical. Reply to Seyla Benhabib, Jeffrey Flynn and Matthias Fritsch," *Political Theory*, 43/6 (2015): 822–37.

22 See Rainer Forst, "Legitimacy, Democracy, and Justice: On the Reflexivity of Normative Orders," ch. 8 in this volume.

23 See Williams, "Realism and Moralism in Political Theory" (n. 11) 6 (emphasis added).

24 ibid 5.

25 Hans Morgenthau, *Peace Among Nations: The Struggle for Power and Peace* (McGraw-Hill 1993) 13.

26 ibid 5 and *passim*.

once they have been sufficiently tested. At this point, a discussion of the criteria for "good" justifications would be advisable, although I cannot provide one in the present context.[27]

The principle of justification is the normative foundation of a critical, realistic treatment of politics. It does not fit comfortably with the perspective of world rulers or global adjudicators but, instead, develops the participant perspective on political discourses and struggles—as a normative perspective that takes its orientation from the question of justification. This treatment takes up the language of emancipation as a critique of unjustifiable social relations, but in such a way that it subjects this critique itself to criticism. Not all critical claims are deemed to be valid in an uncritical manner but only those that are in conformity with the principle of justification. This is ultimately a principle of politics, of morality, but also of critique and, finally, of reason. Here, reason is necessarily a practical faculty, although also one that is able to subject practices to critical examination. And what could be more realistic than this faculty in virtue of which "reality" exists for us in the first place?

A critical, realistic form of constructivism builds on this. It adopts a perspective that is immanent to practice, although also one which is critical of practice. As a result, it is able to formulate what the demand for human rights, for example, or the call for justice and democracy expresses—in the first place, the demand no longer to be a legitimation nullity but, instead, to be recognized as a free and equal justificatory authority. Expressed in an older language, herein resides the *dignity* of human beings.[28]

6. For a realistic and at the same time normatively oriented political science, what is most abstract is also the most concrete. The justification requirement first generates the political dynamic that gives birth to orders, discursively opens them (prompting attempts at closure) and occasionally overturns them. We need to reconstruct their logic, which is not a pure logic of progress, in historical and sociological as well as philosophical terms.[29] Thus, critical realism has two essential components with regard to justice and democracy in transnational contexts.

The first is the *normative* component. This consists in the right to justification based on the principle of justification, which states that norms must always be justified in accordance with the criteria that are inherent in their claim to validity.[30] Here the question of rule always remains central, not as a free play of forces, but in the context of the struggle for adequate relations of justification. This is the first requirement of justice, understood as the rejection and avoidance of arbitrary—that is, unjustified—rule (i.e., domination) and as the establishment of democratic forms of political justice.

The second component is an *empirical* one. Since the question of justification always aims at actually existing relations of rule and domination, the question of

[27] See Forst, *The Right to Justification* (n. 13) chs. 4–8.
[28] See Forst, *Justification and Critique* (n. 18) ch. 4.
[29] This is what I tried to do with reference to the theme of toleration in Rainer Forst, *Toleration in Conflict: Past and Present*, trans. Ciaran Cronin (Cambridge University Press 2013).
[30] See Forst, *The Right to Justification* (n. 13) chs. 1 and 4.

justice and democracy in transnational contexts must begin by making an inventory of the precise contexts in which supranational and international rule or domination is exercised.

Therefore, the study does not begin in ideal space, but with an analysis of the complex interconnections between national, transnational, and international relations of rulership[31] and asks whether there exist corresponding adequate relations of justification—that is, those adequate to the level and quality of rule exercised. This is a practice-immanent approach but not a practice-positivist one which concentrates exclusively on international cooperation, for example, or on the "self-image" of political functional elites.[32] It does not start from the "point" of certain practices either, where this point is supposed to be extrapolated through interpretation, or from immanent political logics that could be deciphered by a clever theorist.[33] In accordance with the principle that every exercise of rule should be legitimized in relations of justification, a *critical theory of transnational, discursive justice* must begin by reconstructing the most important economic, legal, and political relations of rule or domination. In this context, national, regional, and transnational, as well as international and supranational contexts should be connected in the right way, both in an empirical analysis and in the corresponding conception of justification structures.[34] The theory that succeeded in doing this could be called a realist as much as a critical one.

[31] See e.g. Deborah D. Avant, Martha Finnemore, and Susan K. Sell (eds.) *Who Governs the Globe?* (Cambridge University Press 2010); Ulrich Beck and Angelika Poferl (eds.), *Große Armut, großer Reichtum: Zur Transnationalisierung sozialer Ungleichheit* (Suhrkamp 2010); Michael Zürn and Matthias Ecker-Ehrhardt (eds.), *Die Politisierung der Weltpolitik* (Suhrkamp 2013). Reference should also be made here to the important work of the Bremen Collaborative Research Centre "Transformations of the State" following Stephan Leibfried and Michael Zürn (eds.), *Transformationen des Staates* (Suhrkamp 2006). The Frankfurt University Cluster of Excellence "The Formation of Normative Orders" aspires to combine empirical and normative analysis of the formation of transnational orders; see the publications following Forst and Günther (eds.), *Die Herausbildung normativer Ordnungen* (n. 5). Indispensable for a systematic study of global political relations are the works of Dieter Senghaas, e.g. *Konfliktformationen im internationalen System* (Suhrkamp 1988) and *Weltordnung in einer zerklüfteten Welt* (Suhrkamp 2012).

[32] For a critique of practice positivism see Forst, "Transnational Justice and Democracy" (n. 10).

[33] As in Jürgen Neyer's idea of a "normative realism" in Jürgen Neyer, *The Justification of Europe: A Political Theory of Supranational Integration* (Oxford University Press 2012). For my criticism see Forst, "Justice, Democracy and the Right to Justification: Reflections on Jürgen Neyer's Normative Theory of the European Union," in Dimitry Kochenov, Gráinne de Búrca, and Andrew Williams (eds.), *Europe's Justice Deficit* (Hart Publishing 2014) 227–34.

[34] I discuss this in greater detail in Rainer Forst, "Transnational Justice and Non-Domination" (n. 5).

10

Transnational Justice and Non-Domination

A Discourse-Theoretical Approach

The title of this chapter could have also been "transnational injustice and domination," since we cannot make progress in thinking about justice beyond the state unless we develop a realistic and critical view of the many and complex relations of domination within, between, and beyond states that mark our current global predicament. But, in order to identify this predicament as one of "injustice," we need an appropriate conception of justice as non-domination.[1] So let me turn to this first. Then, in a second step, I will explain the difference between my Kantian, discourse-theoretical conception of non-domination and Philip Pettit's neo-republican conception of non-domination. In a third step, I will apply my conception of justice as non-domination to transnational contexts. In conclusion, I will explain the difference between my view and Pettit's notion of international justice.

1. Justice and Non-Domination

Let me begin with a brief reflection on the notion of injustice. In my view, injustice means more than that a person lacks certain important or even essential goods for a "decent" life. For if we were to focus only on deficiencies of goods, someone who is deprived of possibilities and resources as a result of a natural catastrophe would appear to be in the same situation as someone who experiences the same kind of deprivation as a result of economic or political exploitation. It is true that assistance is required in both cases. However, as I understand the grammar of justice, assistance is required as an act of moral solidarity in the first case, while in the second case it is required as an act of justice conditioned by the nature of one's involvement in relations of exploitation,

[1] Some sections of this chapter are based on my previously published essays "Transnational Justice and Democracy: Overcoming Three Dogmas of Political Theory," in *Political Equality in Transnational Democracy*, eds. Eva Erman and Sofia Näsström (Palgrave Macmillan 2013) 41–59, and "A Kantian Republican Conception of Justice as Non-domination," in *Republican Democracy*, eds. Andreas Niederberger and Philipp Schink (Edinburgh University Press 2013) 154–68. Permission to reproduce these sections is kindly acknowledged. I am grateful to Barbara Buckinx, Tim Waligore, and Dorothea Gädeke for their critical reading of an earlier version. The chapter originally appeared in *Domination and Global Political Justice: Conceptual, Historical, and Institutional Perspectives*, eds. Barbara Buckinx, Jonathan Trejo-Mathys, and Timothy Waligore (Routledge 2015) 88–110. It is dedicated to the memory of Jonathan Trejo-Mathys.

and hence of injustice,[2] and by the specific wrong in question. Thus, the reasons for assistance, as well as the content of what is required, are different in the two cases. Ignoring these differences can lead one to misrepresent what is in fact a requirement of justice as an act of generous "assistance" or "aid" to the poor or miserable, thereby possibly committing another wrong, namely, that of veiling the true nature of the injustice involved.[3] In order to do justice to those who suffer from injustice, one must grasp the relational or structural dimension of justice and liberate oneself from an understanding that is focused exclusively on quantities of goods. Justice must be directed to *intersubjective relations and social structures*, not to *subjective or supposedly objective states* of the provision of goods. Helping a person overcome misery, irrespective of what caused it, is a good thing, generally speaking. Yet overcoming forms of domination that lead to misery is a particular demand of justice.[4] The normative difference here is not one of urgency; rather, it is a matter of distinguishing different parts of our general normative framework for determining moral and political obligations.

What is it about the concept of justice that gives it this special place in our moral grammar? In my view, the concept of justice possesses a core meaning to which the essential contrasting concept is that of *arbitrariness*.[5] Arbitrariness can assume the form of unjustified rule by individuals or by one part of the community (e.g., a social class) over another, or the acceptance of social contingencies that lead to asymmetrical social positions or relations of domination as an unalterable fate, even though they are nothing of the sort. Arbitrary rule is the rule of some people over others without legitimate reason—what I call *domination*—and where struggles are conducted against injustice, they are directed against forms of domination of this kind.[6]

[2] Here a range of cases should be distinguished, in particular: directly participating in or contributing to injustice; indirectly participating in injustice by profiting from it but without actively contributing to relations of exploitation; finally, the "natural" duty to put an end to unjust relations, even if one does not profit from them but happens to be in a position to put an end to them. I cannot go into these distinctions further here.

[3] I discuss this as a "dialectics of morality" in Rainer Forst, *The Right to Justification: Elements of a Constructivist Theory of Justice*, trans. Jeffrey Flynn (Columbia University Press 2012) ch. 11. See also the following quotation from Immanuel Kant: "Having the resources to practice such beneficence as depends on the goods of fortune is, for the most part, a result of certain human beings being favored through the injustice of the government, which introduces an inequality of wealth that makes others need their beneficence. Under such circumstances, does a rich man's help to the needy, on which he so readily prides himself as something meritorious, really deserve to be called beneficence at all?" from Immanuel Kant, *Metaphysics of Morals*, in Immanuel Kant, *Practical Philosophy*, ed. and trans. Mary J. Gregor (Cambridge University Press 1996) 353–603, at 573, (6:454). Page references to English translations of Kant will be followed by the relevant volume and page numbers of the Prussian Academy of Sciences edition of Kant's works.

[4] For a contrasting view, see Stefan Gosepath, "Deprivation and Institutionally Based Duties to Aid," in Barbara Buckinx, Jonathan Trejo-Mathys, and Timothy Waligore (eds.), *Domination and Global Political Justice: Conceptual, Historical, and Institutional Perspectives* (Routledge 2015) 251–90.

[5] John Rawls also argues that the concept of justice is opposed to arbitrariness: "Those who hold different conceptions of justice can, then, still agree that institutions are just when no arbitrary distinctions are made between persons in the assigning of basic rights and duties and when the rules determine a proper balance between competing claims to the advantages of social life." See John Rawls, *A Theory of Justice*, revised edn. (Harvard University Press 1999) 5.

[6] For an historical account of struggles against injustice see Barrington Moore, *Injustice: The Social Bases of Obedience and Revolt* (Macmillan 1978).

The underlying impulse that opposes injustice is not primarily that of wanting something, or more of something, but that of no longer wanting to be dominated, harassed, or overruled in one's claim and *basic right to justification*. In contexts of justice, this claim involves the demand that no political or social relations should exist that cannot be adequately justified toward those subjected to them. Herein resides the profoundly *political* essence of justice that a purely goods or recipient-oriented view fails to grasp; for justice is a matter of *who determines who receives what* and not only or primarily of who should receive what. The demand for justice, as I conceive it, is an emancipatory one. Expressed in reflexive terms, it rests on the claim to be respected as an autonomous subject of justification; that is, to be respected in one's dignity as a being who can provide and demand justifications and who should have the status of a free and equal normative authority within a normative order of binding rules and institutions.[7]

The primary victim of injustice is not the person who *lacks* certain goods but instead the person who does not "count" in the production and allocation of goods. Justice requires that those who belong to a certain social structure and order should be respected as equals. This means that they should enjoy equal rights to participate in the social and political *order of justification* in which they are involved in determining the conditions under which goods are produced and distributed. They ought to enjoy a standing as justificatory equals within this order.

Justice, then, is the human virtue of opposing relations of arbitrary rule. "Arbitrariness" is the term for "groundless" rule, that is, for insufficiently justified rule that assumes the form of domination. The underlying assumption is that a just social order is one to which free and equal persons could give their assent—not just counterfactual assent, but assent based on institutionalized justification procedures. So, two aspects of political domination are relevant here: rule of some over others without justifiable reasons, and rule over others in a normative order which lacks sufficient institutional or social preconditions and possibilities of justification in the first place. The latter is the more severe form of domination.

The basic claim of justice is to have a social and political standing as a free and equal agent of justification. This is a *recursive* implication of the fact that political and social justice is a matter of norms of an institutional basic structure which claim to be reciprocally and generally valid. Thus a *supreme principle* holds within such a framework: the *principle of general and reciprocal justification*, which states that every putatively valid claim to goods, rights, or liberties must be justified and justifiable in a reciprocal and general manner, so that one side may not make claims that they deny to others and no side may simply assume that others accept its reasons. Instead all must justify their claims discursively—without excluding any affected parties. The criteria of reciprocity (of claims as well as reasons) and generality are reconstructed as criteria of the validity of justice norms, and then interpreted as criteria

[7] On this notion of dignity see Rainer Forst, *Justification and Critique: Towards a Critical Theory of Politics*, trans. Ciaran Cronin (Polity 2014) ch. 4.

of justifiable norms of justice and of the procedural quality of justice-generating discourses and discursive structures.

The normative grounding of such a conception of justice as non-domination does not rest on any values or norms other than the principle of justification itself as a principle of practical reason (which states that normative claims always have to be justified in accordance with their inherent criteria of validity).[8] Thus, the discourse-theoretical conception of justice is *autonomous* with respect to other values or comprehensive doctrines in Rawls's sense; but it also has a moral force of its own, since it rests on a reasonably non-rejectable claim to be respected as a normative agent or authority when it comes to the norms that claim validity over a person.[9] The principle of justification is thus a principle of practical reason in the Kantian sense, because it does not merely specify what it means to justify a claim to justice, but it also affirms that one has a duty of justice when one is part of a context of justification. Contexts of justice are distinctive kinds of moral contexts. A moral context is one in which others are affected by my actions in a relevant way, whereas a context of justice is one in which we are participants in an order of rule and/or domination[10]—in other words, one in which we are subjected to a social normative order. The grounding of the theory of justice as non-domination is therefore "thin" compared to theories that use substantive values of liberty or equality, or well-being or the good, because it only relies on the principle of justification or critique itself. However, it is also "thick," in that it interprets this principle as grounding a categorical and overriding right and duty of justification between those who are subjected to a normative order of rule and/or domination. And, to add a parenthetical remark on a complex issue, it is a grounding that is as much "immanent" to social practices of justification and critique as it is "transcendental" in reconstructing a principle that is inherent in and transcends all particular forms of practices of justification, thus opening up the possibility of testing their justificatory quality by radicalizing the criteria of reciprocity and generality. This transcending force is what is appealed to by those who say "no" to existing orders of justification and demand better ones.

Turning to social and political theory based on this conception of justice as non-domination, we arrive at an insight that is central for the problem of political and social justice, the insight, namely, that the first question of justice is the *question of power*. For justice is not only a matter of which goods should legitimately be allocated to whom, for which reasons, and in what amounts, but specifically of *how* these goods come into the world in the first place, of *who* decides on their allocation, and *how* this allocation is made. Theories of a predominantly allocative kind are "oblivious to power" insofar as they conceive of justice only from the "recipient side," without raising the political question of how the structures of production and allocation of goods are determined. The claim that the question of power is the first

[8] See Forst, *The Right to Justification* (n. 3) chs. 1–2.

[9] I explain the difference between Rawls's approach and mine in Forst, *The Right to Justification* (n. 3) ch. 4.

[10] I will return to the question of identifying such contexts at the transnational level in section 3 below.

question of justice means that the constitutive institutions of justice are those where the central justifications for a social basic structure must be provided and where the ground rules are laid down that determine social life from the bottom up. Everything depends, if you will, on the *relations of justification* within a society. Power, understood as the effective "justificatory power" of individuals, is the higher-level good of justice; it is the "discursive" power to demand and provide justifications and to repudiate false legitimations—whether in single instances or as systemic discursive complexes or whole languages of justification.[11] This amounts to an argument for a "political turn" in the debate concerning justice and for a *critical theory of justice* as a *critique of relations of justification*.

A comprehensive theory of political and social justice can be constructed on this basis, although I can only hint at this in the present context.[12] First, we must make a conceptual distinction between *fundamental* and *full* justice. While the task of fundamental justice is to construct a *basic structure of justification*, the task of full justice is to construct a *fully justified basic structure*. In order to realize the latter, the former is necessary—that is, a "putting into effect" of justification through constructive, discursive democratic procedures in which justificatory power is distributed as evenly as possible among the citizens. To put it in (only seemingly) paradoxical terms, this means that fundamental justice is a substantive starting point of procedural justice. Based on a moral and political right to justification, arguments are presented for a basic structure in which individual members have real opportunities to codetermine the institutions of this structure in a reciprocal and general manner. Fundamental justice guarantees all citizens an effective status as justificatory equals.[13]

2. Non-Domination: Neo-Republicanism versus Kantian Republicanism

The view I have presented is a Kantian one, and it provides the basis for what I call Kantian republicanism—although not "Kant's republicanism," since I go beyond Kant's position. For Kantian republicanism, a particular notion of autonomy in the moral and political realm is foundational. Its main point is to avoid a one-sided focus on the freedom of persons as "users" or "receivers" of legal freedom, or as protected in their legal status as persons with sufficient freedom of choice. After all, Kant insists on the freedom of persons also as lawgivers, as producers and guarantors of freedom—in short, as politically autonomous citizens. The *dignity* of a free person can never be understood merely in terms of the "enjoyment" of freedom or of certain liberties; it is always also a matter of the freedom of giving laws to oneself, the freedom of normative self-determination. This is a kind of freedom that comes

[11] I develop the notion of power relevant here in my "Noumenal Power," ch. 2 in this volume.

[12] For a more detailed treatment see Forst, *The Right to Justification* (n. 3) and Forst, *Justification and Critique* (n. 7).

[13] This involves a set of rights as well as institutional and social preconditions on which I cannot elaborate here. See Forst, *The Right to Justification* (n. 3) pt. 2.

in two modes—one moral and one political—but its *modus operandi* is the same, despite the difference between these modes. It is a practice of reciprocal and general justification—or, if you like, a practice of practical reason—in moral and political contexts. The laws that constitute this practice and the laws that are generated through it do not only protect freedom—they also express freedom.

I cannot go into the details of the Kantian view I have in mind here.[14] Suffice it to say that I translate the Kantian idea of the basic respect for the autonomy of persons into the language of a moral "right to justification." On a Kantian conception, a person has a categorically undeniable subjective claim to be respected as a normative authority who is free and is equal to all others. I call such a non-rejectable claim based on the principle of justification a moral right. Such a right is binding on every other moral person, and thus implies a categorical duty of justification. It is not a right to some good or a right based on some interest.[15] Rather, it is a right based on the status of the person as a reason-giving and reason-receiving being and an authority in the space of reasons. It is therefore the ground of all further claims to moral respect and to the validity of more specific moral norms that need to be justified in terms of reciprocally and generally non-rejectable reasons. I call this form of justification "moral constructivism." It is a discursive and recursive enterprise: it is discursive because justification necessarily involves a practice of exchanging reasons between free and equal persons, even if in a given case we can realize this (to the best of our abilities) only in the form of a counterfactual imagined discourse; and it is recursive since no content or value is given except that of the agents and criteria of construction through justification.[16]

In order to apply this to contexts of law and politics, we need to take a closer look at Kant's doctrine of right, which provides the principles that help us to understand the justifiable forms of freedom under law as well as the political justification of law that establishes the kind of freedom in question. Kant contrasts law as regards its content with all ethical doctrines of happiness and as regards its form with moral imperatives, because positive law refers only to external actions and not to inner motivation. The essential difference between legality and morality resides less in the content of the respective laws than in the "incentives": positive law is external coercive law and constrains freedom of choice, whereas moral laws determine the moral will.[17] Thus, the supreme principle of law specifies that restrictions on freedom are in need of general justification: "Right is therefore the sum of the conditions under which the choice of one can be united with the choice of another in accordance with a general law of freedom."[18] The foundation of this definition of law, according to which all forms of legal coercion are in need of reciprocal and general justification among free and equal persons, is a basic moral human right to *lawful* freedom prior

[14] But see Forst, *The Right to Justification* (n. 3) chs. 1–2.

[15] I elaborate this notion of a right in Rainer Forst, "The Justification of Basic Rights: A Discourse-Theoretical Approach," in *Netherlands Journal of Legal Philosophy* 45/3 (2016): 7–28.

[16] See Onora O'Neill, *Constructions of Reason: Explorations of Kant's Practical Philosophy* (Cambridge University Press 1990) ch. 1.

[17] See Kant, *Metaphysics of Morals* (n. 3) 383–4 (6:220).

[18] ibid 387 (6:230) (translation amended).

to any positive law: "*Freedom* (independence from being constrained by another's choice), insofar as it can coexist with the freedom of every other in accordance with a general law, is the only original right belonging to every man by virtue of his humanity."[19] Kant's "innate right" is the implication of the (to use my terminology) moral basic right to justification with respect to law, because it is the universal right of human beings to be respected as "ends in themselves."

According to the principle of right, only "general laws" can be laws of freedom, and they can be general only if they are in accordance with the "united will of the people."[20] The citizen can be politically autonomous—and here Kant takes up Rousseau's notion of autonomy—if he obeys only laws that he has given himself. He obeys no law other "than that to which he has given his consent"[21]—"for it is only to oneself that one can never do wrong."[22] As an active member of the polity, as a voting citizen, the person is a *citoyen*, not just a *bourgeois*: she[23] or he is simultaneously author and addressee of the law. Hence, generally and reciprocally binding law can be legitimate only if it can stand the test of being agreed upon in procedures of general and reciprocal justification. The mere "idea of reason, which, however, has its undoubted practical reality," states that "the touchstone of any public law's conformity with right" is its ability to command general agreement.[24] In short, just as the moral principle which makes it a duty to justify morally relevant actions and norms in a particular way becomes the foundation of the original right to freedom, in the same way it here becomes the foundation of the requirement to justify coercive laws in the medium of "public reason." Where there is no suitable opportunity to generate such discursively justified norms in democratic practice, the first duty of justice is to establish such institutions.

In Kantian republicanism, freedom in the state can be fully realized only if it is the freedom "of obeying no other law than that to which [the citizen] has given his consent."[25] This is the real meaning of legal independence or political-legal non-domination: you are only independent, or not dominated, if you are at once the subject *and* the author of the law. Otherwise your right to freedom—or your right to justification—is only half realized. You might *receive* freedom or some justification; but if you cannot be the *author* of the laws of freedom, you are not being offered real freedom. The laws securing freedom must be reciprocally and generally justifiable; but no one has the authority to fabricate these justifications for you, because you are an autonomous agent of justification.[26]

[19] ibid 393 (6:237) (translation amended).

[20] ibid 457 (6:313).

[21] ibid 457 (6:314).

[22] Immanuel Kant, "On the Common Saying: That May Be Correct in Theory, but It Is of No Use in Practice," in Immanuel Kant, *Practical Philosophy*, ed. and trans. Mary Gregor (Cambridge University Press 1996) 279–309, 295 (8:294 ff.).

[23] As I am phrasing it as a general point, I include both gender terms—which Kant did not.

[24] Kant, "Theory and Practice" (n. 22), 296–7 (8:297) (emphasis omitted).

[25] Kant, *Metaphysics of Morals* (n. 3) 457 (6:314).

[26] This is why I do not think that Kantian republicanism, especially in its discourse-theoretical version, is vulnerable to the criticism that it relies on a purely counterfactual notion of justifiability; for this critique see Philip Pettit, *On the People's Terms: A Republican Theory and Model of Democracy* (Cambridge University Press 2012) 147 ff.

I take this to be the essence of Kantian republicanism, which stresses independence as a basic moral principle of right for rational, end-setting beings who inhabit a shared social space.[27] It implies the right to have all other rights (and duties) justified in a strictly reciprocal and general way; thus the right to justification of independent agents grounds all other rights. It does so in a discursive and reflexive, rather than a deductive, way. In the mode of *moral* constructivism, this leads to a conception of moral rights; in the mode of *political* constructivism, it leads to a conception of human rights and to a conception of democratic political and social justice. Human rights include all of the rights that persons who respect each other as free and equal individuals cannot deny each other within a normative order of legal, political, and social life. The main point here is again a reflexive one: no one must be subjected to a normative order that cannot be adequately justified to him or her. This is the basic human right and the basic claim of justice.[28]

The Kantian republican conception I have sketched uses a discourse-theoretical notion of non-domination. Domination, to repeat, has two aspects: being subjected to a normative order that cannot be properly justified to you, and being subjected to a normative order in which no proper institutions and possibilities of justification are in place to begin with. The second is the more severe form of domination, because it denies the possibility of codetermining the normative order as a structural matter.

How does this relate to Philip Pettit's version of republicanism?[29] For Pettit, republicanism is essentially a theory of legitimate government grounded in a particular idea of freedom as "non-domination," understood as "the social status of being relatively proof against arbitrary interference by others, and of being able to enjoy a sense of security and standing among them."[30] In contrast to freedom as mere "non-interference," non-domination is bound up with being and seeing oneself as someone who is not at the mercy of the arbitrary will of others, even if these others happen to leave you alone for the most part. The republican notions of self-respect and freedom are directed against the *potential* of arbitrary interference.[31] The rule of law is thus important, as is a social status that protects persons "robustly" against social and political vulnerability to the possibility of arbitrary interference. Slavery is the counterpart of the notion of freedom used here, the slave being the extreme case of a dominated person. Even though Pettit correctly emphasizes that freedom

[27] In line with Arthur Ripstein, *Force and Freedom: Kant's Legal and Political Philosophy* (Harvard University Press 2009) 16 ff., 371.

[28] See Forst, *Justification and Critique* (n. 7) ch. 2 and Rainer Forst, "The Point and Ground of Human Rights: A Kantian Constructivist View," in David Held and Pietro Maffettone (eds.), *Global Political Theory* (Polity 2016) 22–39.

[29] I will have to be brief here. For a more extensive discussion see my essay "A Kantian Republican Conception of Justice as Non-domination" (n. 1).

[30] Philip Pettit, *Republicanism: A Theory of Freedom and Government* (Oxford University Press 1997) viii.

[31] ibid 5, 22 ff. In his recent work, Pettit prefers the term "uncontrolled" rather than "arbitrary" interference, yet with the aim of preserving the core meaning. See Pettit, *On the People's Terms* (n. 26) 58. Cf. Philip Pettit, "The Republican Law of Peoples: A Restatement," in Barbara Buckinx, Jonathan Trejo-Mathys, and Timothy Waligore (eds.), *Domination and Global Political Justice: Conceptual, Historical, and Institutional Perspectives* (Routledge 2015) 37–70.

as non-interference is distinct from freedom as non-domination, a negative conception of liberty lies at the heart of his view: the argument for non-domination ultimately serves to secure the realm of freedom of choice of persons against arbitrary interference.[32] This is why I refer to this view as *negative republicanism*: the republican infrastructure is primarily a sheltering mechanism for individual liberty understood in this way. In Pettit's republican theory, citizens are "law-checkers" interested in securing their freedom of choice, not "law-makers" as in a Rousseauian or Kantian scheme.[33]

So how distinct is my Kantian conception of republican justice as non-domination from Pettit's conception of republican freedom as non-domination? In answering this question, I would like to offer a (somewhat revisionary) reading of Pettit that brings him closer to the Kantian family. My reason for doing so is that, as I see it, the real force of freedom as non-domination derives from a notion of justice as justification that both grounds and defines this notion of freedom.[34] It grounds freedom as non-domination because in my interpretation the basic claim of republican citizens is not one of freedom in general, but one of freedom from *arbitrary*—that is, *unjust* and *unjustifiable*—interference or rule (that is, domination). The claim is based on one's standing as a free and equal agent of justification. It is a claim to a kind of liberty (and to liberties) defined by what oneself and others can justly and justifiably ask from one another in a basic social structure. As Pettit explains in a discussion of Quentin Skinner's view championing non-interference, justifiable rule is not seen by those subject to it as domination.[35] Only *arbitrary* rule is seen as domination, and that means *unjustifiable* rule over others that denies their standing as free and equal agents and normative authorities. Being denied such standing leads to the "grievance . . . of having to live at the mercy of another," which Pettit identifies as the main social and political evil.[36] If interference or rule by others is justifiable between equals, it is not seen as an infringement of freedom. The notion of *justice* which refers to the quality of the relations between free and equal participants in a basic structure of justification is thus central and *normatively prior* to that of freedom of choice. Justice as justification determines which freedoms are justified and what an arbitrary interference is in the first place.

This might seem to amount to reading a Kantian notion of freedom into Pettit's approach; but that is only a concern if one ignores the implications of Pettit's distinction between the non-arbitrary or "controlled" rule of law, which does not compromise freedom, and domination, which does. The rule of law is seen as "conditioning" freedom, and this is close to Kant's view.[37] Republican freedom is about the "full standing of a person among persons";[38] and as Pettit goes on to explain, explicitly referring to

[32] See especially Philip Pettit, "Keeping Republican Freedom Simple: On a Difference with Quentin Skinner," *Political Theory* 30/3 (2002): 339–56, at 340.

[33] Pettit, *On the People's Terms* (n. 26) 15.

[34] Thus, I take issue with the way Pettit distinguishes between justice and legitimacy in *On the People's Terms* (n. 26) chs. 2–3. For my own view see Rainer Forst, " Legitimacy, Democracy, and Justice: On the Reflexivity of Normative Orders," ch. 8 in this volume.

[35] See Pettit, "Keeping Republican Freedom Simple" (n. 32). [36] ibid 4 f.

[37] ibid 342. [38] ibid 350.

Kant: "The terrible evil brought about by domination, over and beyond the evil of restricting choice, and inducing a distinctive uncertainty is that it deprives a person of the ability to command attention and respect and so of his or her standing among persons."[39] Thus the main evil is that of not being regarded as "a voice worth hearing and an ear worth addressing"[40]—that is, in my terms, as a person with a right to justification. As Pettit formulates it: "To be a person is to be a voice that cannot properly be ignored, a voice which speaks to issues raised in common with others and which speaks with a certain authority: enough authority, certainly, for discord with that voice to give others reason to pause and think."[41] Every person is to be respected in this way as a justificatory authority, and this is the essential meaning of freedom as autonomy: to have a *categorical* right not to be subjected to norms that cannot be reciprocally justified.[42]

In my view, and on my preferred Kantian reading of Pettit, we have gone quite a way beyond a negative conception of freedom without also adopting a controversial positive conception of freedom. Thus, what matters in a republican account of non-domination is freedom as autonomy—that is, freedom *from* unjustifiable subjection or coercion and freedom *as* a self-determining agent of (moral, as well as political) justification. Only where practices of justification exist that prevent some from dominating others is freedom as non-domination guaranteed. Rather than focusing on the "robust" legal state of enjoying freedom of choice, we should instead focus on the relational freedom of being a codetermining agent of justification within the normative order that binds us.

3. Transnational Contexts of Justice

If we want to locate the Kantian, discourse-theoretical view of justice as non-domination in contexts beyond the state, we must use a broader definition of a context of justice than Kant's, which focuses on subjection to legal coercion within a state. We nevertheless have to hold on to the insight that justice, whether "political" or "social," presupposes in the first instance specific practices of justification—that is, a basic structure of justification—and that this political praxis of reciprocal and general justification is essentially what we mean by "democracy." Those who are subjected to general and binding norms should also be the authority who justifies these same norms—as active subjects of justification and not just *in mente* or in proxy or expert discourses. The goddess *Justitia* does not come into the world to dispense gifts; her task is instead to banish arbitrary rule, that is, domination. Democracy is the form of political order capable of accomplishing this in the right way. The task of democracy is to secure the political autonomy of those who are supposed to be both subjected to and authors of binding norms.

[39] ibid 351. [40] ibid 350. [41] See Pettit, *Republicanism* (n. 30) 91.

[42] Here I will not discuss whether that kind of basic moral-political status can be grounded in a consequentialist theory, which I doubt.

How can this conception be extended to transnational contexts? Thus far, I have stressed that the aim of justice is to create justified social relations and political structures, and to this effect it first calls, reflexively speaking, for the creation of a basic structure of justification. It follows that justice has its proper place wherever a threat of arbitrary rule exists, where a social context is disintegrating, or where it could degenerate into a context of domination. One might conclude from this that the existence of a specific social *context of cooperation* is a necessary presupposition of a context of justice.

A number of theories have drawn this conclusion. In the first place, we must mention that of John Rawls. Rawls locates social justice in the national sphere and views the international domain as one in which merely a minimal list of human rights is valid and otherwise only duties of assistance exist.[43] This is not so much a state-centered as a specifically cooperation-centered view. Interpreters often mistakenly underestimate how much weight Rawls attaches to the "most fundamental" idea of a "society as a fair system of social cooperation over time from one generation to the next," which he consistently situates at the center of his theory.[44] According to Rawls, only such a society provides the resources—in the twofold sense of material and normative resources—that a "well-ordered society" presupposes. Here alone are to be found the conditions of reciprocity and the economic, political, and moral cohesion that a just society requires.

Some theorists develop this idea in a communitarian direction so that "common sentiments"[45] or "shared understandings"[46] within a nation, understood as a political and cultural *community*, become a necessary presupposition for a complete context of justice. Others, by contrast, adopt an institutionalist perspective that emphasizes the *state* as the central context of justice. Thomas Nagel expresses the view that justice "is something we owe through our shared institutions only to those with whom we stand in a strong political relation. It is, in the standard terminology, an associative obligation."[47] The essential aspects of such a "strong political relation" are the existence of a collectively authorized source of law and the fact that the relation is not voluntary—that is, that the relation expresses the will of those involved as citizens and that this must also be so if they are not to be subjected to illegitimate coercion.[48] Positive normative authority and factual coercion must coexist in order to form a context of justice as a context of law.

Rawls's and Nagel's arguments carry considerable weight because a social context of justice is in fact a demanding one and presupposes certain relations among those involved. Nevertheless, these views are problematic because, when they argue that a particular social or legal institutional context of cooperation or legal force is

[43] Cf. John Rawls, *The Law of Peoples* (Harvard University Press 1999).

[44] Rawls, *Justice as Fairness: A Restatement* (Harvard University Press 2001) 5.

[45] David Miller, *National Responsibility and Global Justice* (Oxford University Press 2007).

[46] Michael Walzer, *Spheres of Justice* (Basic Books 1983).

[47] Thomas Nagel, "The Problem of Global Justice," *Philosophy & Public Affairs* 33/2 (2005): 113–47, at 121.

[48] Michael Blake emphasizes the aspect of coercion. See "Distributive Justice, State Coercion, and Autonomy," *Philosophy & Public Affairs* 30/3 (2001): 257–96.

a necessary precondition of justice, they employ a *conclusion* as a *premise*. For, as explained above, Justitia is a man-made deity who comes into the world to banish social arbitrariness, and this means that she has her (combative) place wherever arbitrary rule prevails (or represents a threat) among human beings. In such cases, she calls for specific institutions—for example, for the rule of law where previously a "state of nature" of arbitrariness existed—but then she cannot presuppose that these institutions are already in place. She presupposes that persons have the status of beings who have a right to justification and she calls for the creation of a basic structure of justification wherever arbitrary rule exists or is a threat; but her calling for this cannot be contingent on a basic structure already existing. Thus, the objection against Rawls, as certain globalist cosmopolitans assume, need not be that a "global basic structure" already in fact exists,[49] because the comparison between national contexts and a global basic structure is untenable when it comes to the "thickness" of the relevant social relations. And although one can point out, *contra* Nagel, that certain global institutions also exercise state-like legal coercion and claim authority for this,[50] there remains a striking difference from national law here as well. Instead, it is important to move beyond thinking in terms of the dichotomy between "state" and "world" and to assume a plurality of contexts of (in)justice that differ with regard to their relational quality, so that justice can be correctly located or "grounded" specifically, in a way informed by an appropriate social-scientific analysis of actually existing social relations.[51]

Viewed from a critical perspective, to assume that a context of justice exists only where norms of law and justice are already institutionalized in positive law, or only where positive, mutually beneficial forms and institutions of cooperation already exist,[52] would amount to a twofold "practice positivism." These two forms of positivism can be called "positive institutionalism" and "positive cooperationalism." Against this, it must be objected that a context of justice exists wherever relations of political *rule* and social *cooperation* exist *and* wherever forms of *domination* exist, whether or not they are legally institutionalized. The latter include various relations of *negative* cooperation, that is, forms of (legal, political, economic, or cultural) coercion and/or exploitation. This provides a point of entry for a critical and "realist" theory of justice, and such a theory presupposes an informed social-scientific analysis.[53] It recognizes a complex system of rule and of forms of domination at the national, international, and transnational levels. As a result, it sees the primary task

[49] Compare the original (and later differentiated) views of Charles Beitz, *Political Theory and International Relations* (Princeton: Princeton University Press 1979) part 3, and Thomas Pogge, *Realizing Rawls* (Cornell University Press 1989) ch. 6.

[50] Joshua Cohen and Charles Sabel, "Extra Rempublicam Nulla Justitia?" *Philosophy & Public Affairs* 34/2 (2006): 147–75.

[51] See my original argument for a critical theory of transnational justice, now in Forst, *The Right to Justification* (n. 2) ch. 12.

[52] Such a cooperation conception can be found in Andrea Sangiovanni, "Global Justice, Reciprocity, and the State," *Philosophy & Public Affairs* 35/1 (2007): 3–39.

[53] See, for instance, Andrew Hurrell, *On Global Order: Power, Values and the Constitution of International Society* (Oxford University Press 2007); Deborah D. Avant, Martha Finnemore, and Susan K. Sell (eds.), *Who Governs the Globe* (Cambridge University Press 2010).

of justice as being to create corresponding transnational and supranational structures of justification. Such structures must be capable of converting complex relations of domination into relations of reciprocal justification not marked by grave asymmetries of power, and they must open up space for discourses, and above all for critique, where the nature of existing conditions and appropriate responses are matters of dispute.[54] Justice, as it were, tracks arbitrariness in forms of domination and coercion wherever they occur. The assumption that this would first require an already existing, positive social or legal context of cooperation fails to appreciate the correct order of things: first and foremost, there is concrete injustice in the world, and justice calls for structures of justification and banishes human arbitrariness. Justice is a relational, as well as an institutional, virtue; it does not refer to all asymmetrical relations between human beings without discrimination, but it does refer to those which exhibit forms of rule or domination and social arbitrariness—whether in contexts involving only sparse legal regulation or in thicker institutional contexts, within and beyond the state.

The question of the extent to which a relational, discursive conception of justice can be described as "practice-dependent" must therefore be answered in a differentiated manner. "Practice-dependence" is the term used by Andrea Sangiovanni to describe approaches that, in contrast to "practice-independent" definitions of justice (such as those of luck egalitarianism or the universal provision of goods),[55] assume that the "content, scope and justification" of norms of justice depend on the concrete practices these norms are supposed to regulate. These practices thus enjoy normative priority and provide the context of interpretation for what justice requires.[56] Yet which practices these are and how they should be interpreted, it must be pointed out by way of criticism, is not revealed by the practices themselves, but is a prior requirement in need of justification: they could be legally regulated, democratic, or cooperative practices, for instance, but they could also be practices of domination or negative cooperation. Hence the identification and interpretation of the practices to be regulated in accordance with justice must occur in the light of principles of justice themselves, where these principles cannot follow from specific social practices alone but must be related to these practices in the right way. Otherwise there would be a danger of regress that could be broken off only in an arbitrary way through an abstract definition of which concrete practices are practices of justice.

Hence, a non-positivist approach that avoids a status quo bias which threatens to insulate existing contexts from external demands of justice (and often idealizes them

[54] I agree with Nancy Fraser on the importance of the latter condition; see Fraser, *Scales of Justice: Reimagining Political Space in a Globalizing World* (Columbia University Press 2009), especially chs. 2 and 4. Nevertheless I believe that a critical social-scientific analysis can adequately describe existing relations and structures and their need for justification, and thereby mark the entry point for discursive justification.

[55] Examples are Simon Caney, *Justice Beyond Borders: A Global Political Theory* (Oxford University Press 2005) and Stefan Gosepath, "The Global Scope of Justice," in Thomas Pogge (ed.), *Global Justice* (Blackwell, 2001) 145–68.

[56] Thus also Aaron James, "Constructing Justice for Existing Practice: Rawls and the Status Quo," *Philosophy & Public Affairs* 33/3 (2005): 281–316.

into contexts of cooperation or self-determination)[57] must distinguish between different notions of "practice." The higher-order principle of justification, which gives rise to the principle of reciprocal and general justification in contexts of social rule and domination, is itself a principle of practical reason which states that intersubjective validity claims must be justified in an appropriate way. This principle is thus practical in nature (because it is *immanent* to the practice of justification), yet it also *transcends* concrete practices. Only in this way can the necessary proximity to and distance from existing practices be generated by referring to the fundamental practice of justification.

Besides the basic notion of the practice of justification, various other notions of "practice" must be distinguished: practices of legal regulation, of political codification, and of economic and general social cooperation. Each of these can assume a *positive* or a *negative* form. Here it is a mistake to opt for a positive or a negative version of "practice-dependence," for both positive and negative practices give rise to duties of justification and justice. Contexts and practices of justice exist wherever there are—more or less institutionalized—forms of collective rule or domination that are in need of justification in accordance with the principle of reciprocal and general justification. This conception can be described as a *discursive and critical practice approach* that does not refer exclusively to already existing positive contexts of justification. It incorporates positive practices and their content just as it identifies negative practices—and to both it applies the principle of justification, which states that nobody may be subjected to norms or institutions that cannot be appropriately justified to him or her. Hence, the content and the scope of norms of justice are always defined with reference to relational social contexts, but not in a one-sided or selective manner.

A theory of transnational justice along these lines does not paint an idealized picture of a perfect global distribution as an "end state," nor does it start from a Rawlsian "original position" that includes all human beings. Instead, it pursues the existing forms of subjugation and exploitation, of structural asymmetries and arbitrary rule, in order to demand relations of justice, and hence of justifiability, wherever such forms of domination are to be found. This opens up a panorama of relations, structures, actors, and necessary institutions that at first sight appears highly confusing.

[57] On this, see also the critique of "justice positivism" in Darrel Moellendorf, *Global Inequality Matters* (Palgrave Macmillan, 2009) 36. Miriam Ronzoni tries to avoid a national status quo bias by criticizing international asymmetrical relations that arose in the context of positively established practices of economic exchange and of international commerce and no longer fulfill the internal purpose of these practices, as long as new global regulatory structures have not been erected; Ronzoni, "The Global Order: A Case of Background Injustice? A Practice-Dependent Account," *Philosophy & Public Affairs* 37/3 (2009): 229–56, It should be noted, however, that without a higher-order principle of discursive justice it would remain open how to resolve disputes over the meaning of certain exchange practices, for example, and whether justice is done to this meaning and how one should respond to it—if one thinks, for example, of conflicting libertarian and egalitarian interpretations of current practices. Also, the question of whether individual practices of this kind are even worth preserving would lack any basis. However, Ronzoni rejects a higher-order principle (244), so that the view remains fixated on positive practices, and thus the analysis of injustice remains confined to a conventionalist analysis and interpretation of these principles.

The appropriate response to this problem is a theory of *fundamental transnational justice*.[58] The basic structure of justification to which this theory refers aims to create structures of participation and legitimation that can assume and perform the tasks of opening and critique, culminating in the justification and adoption of binding transnational and international norms. The guiding principle is that of political autonomy and equality, although consistency also demands that this principle should hold within states, which often deny their citizens this autonomy, and as a principle that seeks to counterbalance the asymmetries between stronger and weaker states. The essential players in this process are in the first instance states, but reflexive forms of participation must be found that prevent these actors from continuing to dominate portions of their own population, other states, or parts of other states. Therefore, where existing supranational, international, and transnational organizations reproduce specific asymmetrical relations of rule, they can only provide the starting point for more participatory and reflexive political forms. The principle of fundamental transnational justice gives every political community the right to participate in cross-border, normative discourses on an equal footing, and affected parties below the state level simultaneously have the right to demand participation in such discourses if the latter would otherwise ignore or perpetuate specific relations of domination. This means that corresponding fora must be opened up to opposition parties from states,[59] although also to civil society actors as organized in the World Social Forum, for example.[60] In this way, transnational mechanisms of domination can also be uncovered and denounced through transnational critical alliances that constitute a politically relevant *demos* in virtue of being subjugated under specific structures of domination.[61] The political communities with corresponding means at their disposal have a duty to establish such a basic structure of justification. However, this does not give them the right to determine what form this structure should take. Rather, it is a fundamental demand of justice and of human rights[62] that relations of justification should be established in which the opportunities to generate and exercise justificatory power are fairly distributed.[63]

As a result, the first task of justice is to create structures of justification in which arbitrary rule is banished—structures in which those who are subjected to rule or domination, whether of an economic, political, or legal kind, can bring the "force toward the better argument" to bear against those who exercise such rule or domination. Democracy as a practice of justice acquires special importance in this context. In the first place, it must be liberated from the narrow choice between a "world

[58] On this see Forst, *The Right to Justification* (n. 2) chs. 10–12.

[59] On this see the corresponding proposal of Michael Zürn in the context of international institutions; Michael Zürn, *Regieren Jenseits des Nationalstaats* (Suhrkamp, 1998) 352.

[60] Corresponding modes of participation based on relevant social relations must be sought in this context, though I cannot discuss this further here.

[61] On this see the analysis of transnational politicization in Michael Zürn, "Vier Modelle einer globalen Ordnung in kosmopolitischer Absicht," *Politische Vierteljahresschrift* 52/1 (2011): 78–118, at 100–4.

[62] For a detailed account, see Rainer Forst, "The Justification of Human Rights and the Basic Right to Justification: A Reflexive Approach," *Ethics* 120/4 (2010): 711–40.

[63] On this see James Bohman, *Democracy across Borders: From Demos to Demoi* (MIT Press 2007). However, Bohman does not define his concept of the demos in the sense I propose.

state or world of states." It is best understood as a normative order in which those who are subject to rule or norms should also be the normative authority, and this in an active sense within a practice of justification. Thus the question of the relevant *demoi* is answered in terms of the existing structures of rule, and the answer to the question of co-determination and the requisite institutional form depends on the degree of subjection. Democratic rule is a discursively justified form of rule, which means a form in which structures of justification exist that are adequate to the scope of the rule exercised. This already extends the question of democratic rule conceptually beyond national borders according to the relations of rule in which a state is embedded—whether as ruler or ruled (or, in complex systems, both simultaneously to different extents). Here a principle of political proportionality holds according to which a structure of justification must be sufficiently open to participation and sufficiently effective to react to a given situation of subjection. However, this principle does not decide which model of order—ranging from a multilevel system to global federalism—follows. That must be decided with a view to the situation that is supposed to be transformed from an unregulated form of domination into a regulated form of justification or rule.[64]

Democracy, understood in processual terms, expresses the collective aspiration to subsume the exercise of rule under relations of effective justification and authorization of norms by those who are subjected to them. To assume that this requires a *demos* defined in terms of the state (or nation) would be to reify democracy. After all, the *demoi* that are constituted as states are already integrated into such diverse networks of international and transnational arbitrary rule (including non-state actors) that the "congruence condition"[65] of the authorization and exercise of rule is no longer satisfied. In a world scarred by colonialism and grave social asymmetries, there are *demoi* that, to simplify, are subjected to external power in different ways, nationally and transnationally, as well as internationally and supranationally, and there are demoi that profit from such subjugation—and there are hybrids of the two forms.[66] Justice and democracy are primarily recuperative and processual in nature and are not justified *ex nihilo*; they track the exercise of (arbitrary) power. *Demoi* generally take shape through prior social relations that stand in need of justification. Jürgen Habermas once coined the notion of "besiegement" for the exercise of communicative power: public discourses generate justifying reasons that the political

[64] Jürgen Habermas proposes a division of labor between a supranational world organization that would be authorized to deal with questions of international security and human rights within the framework of a global constitution, and a transnational "global domestic policy" that would presuppose negotiation systems in which questions of the global economy and the environment would feature centrally. See Jürgen Habermas, "Does the Constitutionalization of International Law Still Have a Chance?" in *The Divided West*, ed. and trans. Ciaran Cronin (Polity 2006) 115–93, at 136–37, and *The Crisis of the European Union: A Response*, trans. Ciaran Cronin (Polity 2012) 56ff. In the more recent version, Habermas emphasizes that institutions are needed to prevent such negotiation systems from reproducing existing asymmetries of power, and he proposes oversight by a "world parliament" (67ff.). That is one possible way to bring about more symmetrical relations of justification, but other possibilities for representing those affected or subjected are also conceivable.

[65] Zürn, *Regieren Jenseits des Nationalstaats* (n. 59) 17.

[66] See Thomas Pogge, *Politics as Usual* (Polity 2010); Iris Marion Young, *Responsibility for Justice* (Oxford University Press 2011).

system cannot ignore.[67] The concept of "justificatory power" that takes up these reflections, by contrast, is agnostic when it comes to the question of whether the mode of producing and exercising communicative power is an institutionalized one or not. What is essential, however, is that the force *toward* the better argument that challenges privileges and domination can be exerted in this way.

The recuperation of relations of rule and domination and their transformation into relations of justification is rightly called "democratization" when it succeeds in generating structures that successfully challenge arbitrary rule, for instance through effective "contestation."[68] This is so even if there is still a long way to go to their complete recuperation and containment. Whenever privileged actors are forced to surrender their prerogatives because these have lost their legitimation—after exposure to criticism within a system of justification and the formation of counter-power—this represents an increase in democracy. Democracy progresses—often only in modest steps—where non-legitimized rule, be it political, legal, or economic, is subjected to the justificatory authority of those affected. Democracy as a practice is always a matter of *democratization*, of expanding and equalizing justificatory power.

4. Two Kinds of Realism

In a number of recent texts, Philip Pettit has developed a republican conception of international justice.[69] At its core we find an ideal of "globalized sovereignty" that is animated by the idea of non-domination among states and that shares major assumptions with Rawls's account of a law of peoples. In the first place, it is based on respect for peoples as separate and autonomous political units (ideally forming representative states, the first part of the construction of international justice, as in Rawls) and it thus entails a rejection of political cosmopolitanism and of far-reaching arguments for global distributive justice. Pettit's approach takes the different forms of domination that exist or are possible at the international level into account, but believes that the dominating effects of a highly integrated, global, political, and legal structure would be greater than the dominating effects of an international system that leaves states and their different powers for the most part intact, although bound by an entrenched, internationally-recognized set of rights and obligations of states and human beings. Above all, Pettit is a political realist who does not believe that it is possible, given the fact of global cultural plurality, to move further beyond distinct political communities. Furthermore, he makes the normative argument that

[67] Jürgen Habermas, "Popular Sovereignty as Procedure," in Jürgen Habermas, *Between Facts and Norms*, trans. William Rehg (MIT Press 1996) 463–90, at 486–7. Habermas subsequently revised this conception in favor of a more institutionally mediated one. However, it is especially applicable at the transnational level.

[68] Philip Pettit, "Democracy, Electoral and Contestatory," in Ian Shapiro and Stephen Macedo (eds.), *Designing Democratic Institutions* (New York University Press 2000) 105–44.

[69] I refer to the most recent version of the conception to be found in Philip Pettit, *Just Freedom: A Moral Compass for a Complex World* (W.W. Norton & Company 2014) ch. 6. See also Pettit, "The Republican Law of Peoples: A Restatement" (n. 31).

citizens of a state have obligations toward one another that they do not have toward outsiders.[70]

I suggest that we call this form of realism "Realism 1." It places certain constraints on the normative horizon of thinking about global justice, restricting it to international justice as a law of sovereign peoples. I believe, however, that some of the conclusions that follow from these constraints are in tension with another kind of realism that is also implicit in Pettit's republicanism. This form, "Realism 2," is the source of many of the strengths of Pettit's view, as I understand it. Realism 2 details the actual and possible forces of social and political domination and tracks domination wherever it occurs or can realistically occur, that is, in asymmetries of power that lead to unjustifiable interferences with the liberty of subjects, persons, or states.[71] As one can see, these two forms of realism could pull in different directions. While the Realist 1 constructs a limited form of international republican justice as globalized sovereignty, the Realist 2 identifies domination in its many international, transnational, or supranational forms—just as he or she would do within a state—and demands "robust" structures of the rule of law, democratic legitimacy, or distributive justice to overcome and safeguard against political or social domination in contexts beyond the state. Obviously, much depends on an assessment of the existence or threats of domination at these levels beyond the state, and empirical considerations play a major role. Still, this assessment is guided by normative evaluations. For a non-domination republican, there are difficult questions here: is the proposed realistic (in the sense of Realism 1) account of international justice sufficient to secure non-domination given what we realistically (in the sense of Realism 2) know about domination beyond the state?

As Pettit's work shows, he is in many ways a Realist 2. He spells out the many dangers and forms of domination of states by other states in many dimensions of power—economic, political, military—as well as by international agencies and multinational corporations that "beggar the economy" of weaker states.[72] As a result, a system of entrenched protections is required, "entrenched in quite a deep manner," as Pettit adds.[73] The Realist 2 thus argues that there must be mutually justifiable "suitable rules" for the exploration of resources, for trade as well as climate policy, and for limiting the power of multinational corporations and banks.[74] Yet the Realist 1 then seems to counter that such rules and "universal standards" must be "negotiated in international forums."[75] However, here, the Realist 2, who knows about the reproduction of power asymmetries in such forms, asks about the justificatory standing of weaker states (as well as oppositional groups of states) in these negotiations—and I am not sure whether the notion of justice in negotiations proposed by the Realist 1 is sufficient to answer that question.

When it comes to the question of implementation, Pettit argues that the recognition of the proposed general liberties by some states will motivate others to

[70] Pettit, *Just Freedom* (n. 69) 158 ff.
[71] See also Rainer Forst, "Realisms in International Political Theory," ch. 9 in this volume.
[72] See Pettit, *Just Freedom* (n. 69) 162. [73] ibid 162. [74] ibid 164.
[75] ibid 164 ff.

follow suit, aspiring to be recognized and in good standing internationally—or trying to avoid pressure and criticism. Apart from such esteem-based motivations, pure self-interest will also help, since states would have good reason to want to be treated according to such norms. There will not be a robust system of sanctioning institutions such as exists in a state; rather, a system of institutions through cooperation will emerge. But here the Realist 2 wonders whether the Realist 1 would truly want to describe international institutions like the World Trade Organization or the International Monetary Fund as such cooperative schemes, and to what extent they reproduce structural asymmetries and forms of international domination. And if they do, would we not want to argue for a thorough reform that transforms them into institutions of justice?

In the section where Pettit discusses the relevance of interstate inequality, he stresses what he calls the "norm of norms," that is, that of discursive equality and justificatory generality and reciprocity (as I would phrase it). However, he does not conceive of a stronger form of democratic order that could impose such reciprocity (as the Realist 2 would prefer). Instead, he argues that it is a "lesson of history" that stronger states will only use "soft power" of persuasion and no other means to influence such rule-making and implementation. Again, the Realist 2 wonders just how realistic this is.

When it comes to dealing with impoverished states, Pettit argues for a policy of solidarity and aid in accordance with the principle "*pouvoir oblige*," although states are not allowed to force their citizens into "involuntary beneficence"[76] or "one-sided philanthropy." At this point the Realist 2 objects, because he sees a global system of economic interdependence with significant levels of power asymmetries, forced cooperation, and exploitation which create duties of justice, rather than duties of beneficence, on the side of the powerful and dominating agents. Much depends, of course, on how we describe global economic relations; but here the Realist 2 is of the opinion that the Realist 1 is *unrealistic* and gets the demands of justice wrong.

In sum, the critical Realist 2 does not argue against Pettit (or Nagel) that dominant states, multinational corporations, or international organizations have "the same" power over other states or peoples as a state has over its citizens,[77] so that there already exists a basic structure of domination that must be turned into the basic structure of non-domination of a world state. But the Realist 2 is convinced that there is *sufficient* domination at the international and translational levels that must be tracked, and that it must be overcome by establishing appropriately *robust* structures of justification that can curb such power asymmetries and realize basic forms of justice. This kind of realism strikes me as being more in tune with the basic republican idea of non-domination. But the theory of transnational justice that would result is different from the ideal of globalized sovereignty.

[76] ibid 175. [77] ibid 184.

Bibliography

Adorno, Theodor W. *Minima Moralia: Reflections on a Damaged Life*. Translated by E. F. N. Jephcott. Verso, 2005.

Adorno, Theodor W. *Negative Dialectics*. Translated by E. B. Ashton. Routledge, 1973.

Allen, Amy. *The End of Progress: Decolonizing the Normative Foundations of Critical Theory*. Columbia University Press, 2016.

Allen, Amy. *The Power of Feminist Theory: Domination, Resistance, Solidarity*. Westview, 1999.

Allen, Amy. "The Power of Justification." In Rainer Forst, *Justice, Democracy and the Right to Justification: Rainer Forst in Dialogue*, 65–86. Bloomsbury, 2014.

Allen, Amy, Rainer Forst, and Mark Haugaard. "Power and Reason, Justice and Domination: A Conversation." *Journal of Political Power* 7 (2014): 7–33.

Anderson, Benedict. *Imagined Communities: Reflections on the Origins and Spread of Nationalism*. Verso, 1991.

Angehrn, Emil and Georg Lohmann, eds. *Ethik und Marx: Moralkritik und normative Grundlagen der Marxschen Theorie*. Hain bei Athenäum, 1986.

Arendt, Hannah. *Crises of the Republic*. Harvest Books, 1972.

Arendt, Hannah. *On Violence*. Harcourt, Brace & World, 1970.

Arendt, Hannah. *The Human Condition*. University of Chicago Press, 1958.

Arendt, Hannah. "Truth and Politics." In Arendt, *Between Past and Future*, 223–59. Penguin Books, 1977.

Arneson, Richard. "Luck Egalitarianism Interpreted and Defended." *Philosophical Topics* 32 (2004): 1–20.

Augustine. *The City of God against the Pagans*. Edited and translated by R. W. Dyson. Cambridge University Press, 1998.

Avant, Deborah D., Martha Finnemore, and Susan K. Sell, eds. *Who Governs the Globe?* Cambridge University Press, 2010.

Bayle, Pierre. *An Historical and Critical Dictionary*. Selected and abridged in four volumes. Hunt and Clark, 1826. French: *Choix d'articles tirés du Dictionnaire historique et critique*. In Bayle, *Oeuvres diverses, vol. suppl.* Edited by E. Labrousse. 2 Volumes. Georg Olms, 1982. English translations of selections of abbreviated articles: *Historical and Critical Dictionary: Selections*. Edited and translated by Richard Popkin. Hackett, 1991.

Bayle, Pierre. *Commentaire philosophique sur ces paroles de Jesus-Christ "Contrain-les d'entrer"*. In *Oeuvres diverses* II. LaHaye, 1727. Reprint: Georg Olms, 1965. English translation of first two parts: *Pierre Bayle's Philosophical Commentary: A Modern Translation and Critical Interpretation*, ed. and trans. Amie Godman Tannenbaum. Peter Lang, 1987. English translation of complete text: *A Philosophical Commentary on These Words of the Gospel, Luke 14:23, "Compel Them to Come In, That My House May Be Full"*, ed. John Kilkullen and Chandran Kukathas. Liberty Fund, 2005.

Bayle, Pierre. *Historical and Critical Dictionary: Selections*. Edited and translated by Richard H. Popkin. Hackett, 1991. French: *Choix d'articles tirés du Dictionnaire historique et critique*. In *Oeuvres diverses, vol. suppl.*, ed. E. Labrousse, 2 vols., Georg Olms, 1982.

Bayle, Pierre. *Political Writings*. Edited and translated by Sally L. Jenkinson. Cambridge University Press, 2000.

Bayle, Pierre. *Various Thoughts on the Occasion of a Comet.* Translated by Robert C. Bartlett. SUNY Press, 2000.

Beck, Ulrich and Angelika Poferl, eds. *Große Armut, großer Reichtum: Zur Transnationalisierung sozialer Ungleichheit.* Suhrkamp, 2010.

Beckert, Jens. "The Social Order of Markets." *Theory and Society* 38/3 (2009): 245–69.

Beitz, Charles. *Political Theory and International Relations.* Princeton University Press, 1979.

Beitz, Charles. *The Idea of Human Rights.* Oxford University Press, 2009.

Benhabib, Seyla. *Situating the Self: Gender, Community, and Postmodernism in Contemporary Ethics.* Routledge, 1992.

Benhabib, Seyla. "The Uses and Abuses of Kantian Rigorism: On Rainer Forst's Moral and Political Philosophy." *Political Theory* 43/6 (2015): 777–92.

Benjamin, Walter. "Goethe's Elective Affinities." Translated by Stanley Corngold. In Benjamin, *Selected Writings, Volume 1: 1913–1926*, edited by Marcus Bullock and Michael W. Jennings, 297–360. Harvard University Press, 1996.

Benjamin, Walter. "Theses on the Philosophy of History." In Benjamin, *Illuminations*, edited by Hannah Arendt, translated by Harry Zohn, 253–64. Schocken, 1969.

Berlin, Isaiah. "Equality." In Berlin, *Concepts and Categories*, edited by Henry Hardy, 106–34. Penguin Books, 1981.

Blake, Michael. "Distributive Justice, State Coercion, and Autonomy." *Philosophy & Public Affairs* 30/3 (2001): 257–96.

Böckenförde, Ernst-Wolfgang. *Der säkularisierte Staat: Sein Charakter, seine Rechtfertigung und seine Probleme im 21. Jahrhundert.* Carl Friedrich von Siemens Stiftung, 2007.

Böckenförde, Ernst-Wolfgang. "'Kopftuchstreit' auf dem richtigen Weg?" *Neue Juristische Wochenschrift* 54/10 (2001): 723–8.

Böckenförde, Ernst-Wolfgang. "The Rise of the State as a Process of Secularisation." In Böckenförde, *State, Society, and Liberty: Studies in Political Theory and Constitutional Law*, 26 ff. Berg, 1991.

Bohman, James. *Democracy across Borders: From Demos to Demoi.* MIT Press, 2007.

Boltanski, Luc. *On Critique: A Sociology of Emancipation.* Translated by Gregory Elliott. Polity, 2011.

Boltanski, Luc and Ève Chiapello. *The New Spirit of Capitalism.* Translated by Gregory Elliott. Verso, 2005.

Boltanski, Luc and Laurent Thévenot. *On Justification: Economies of Worth.* Translated by Catherine Porter. Princeton University Press, 2006.

Bourdieu, Pierre. *Practical Reason: On The Theory of Action.* Translated by Randall Johnson. Stanford University Press, 1998.

Brandom, Robert. "Freedom and Constraint by Norms." *American Philosophical Quarterly* 16 (1979): 187–96.

Brandom, Robert. *Reason in Philosophy: Animating Ideas.* Harvard University Press, 2009.

Brown, Wendy and Rainer Forst. *The Power of Tolerance.* Columbia University Press, 2014.

Brugger, Winfried and Stefan Huster, eds. *Der Streit um das Kreuz in der Schule: Zur the state's neutrality Neutralität des Staates.* Nomos, 1998.

Brush, Craig B. *Montaigne and Bayle: Variations on the Theme of Skepticism.* Nijhoff, 1966.

Buchanan, Allen E. *Justice, Legitimacy, and Self-Determination: Moral Foundations for International Law.* Oxford University Press, 2004.

Buchanan, Allen E. *Marx and Justice: The Radical Critique of Liberalism.* Rowman & Littlefield, 1982.

Buchanan, Allen E. and Robert O. Keohane. "The Legitimacy of Global Governance Institutions." *Ethics and International Affairs* 20 (2006): 405–37.

Butler, Judith. *The Psychic Life of Power: Theories in Subjection*. Stanford University Press, 1997.
Caney, Simon. "Justice and the Basic Right to Justification." In Rainer Forst, *Justice, Democracy and the Right to Justification: Rainer Forst in Dialogue*, 147–66. Bloomsbury, 2014.
Caney, Simon. *Justice Beyond Borders: A Global Political Theory*. Oxford University Press, 2005.
Chakrabarty, Dipesh. *Provincializing Europe: Postcolonial Thought and Historical Difference.* Princeton University Press, 2007.
Chambers, Simone. "Democracy and Critique: Comments on Rainer Forst's Justification and Critique." *Philosophy and Social Criticism* 41/3 (2015): 213–17.
Cohen, Gerald A. "Equality of What? On Welfare, Goods, and Capabilities." In *The Quality of Life*, edited by Martha Nussbaum und Amartya Sen, 9–29. Oxford University Press, 1993.
Cohen, Gerald A. *Rescuing Justice and Equality.* Harvard University Press, 2008.
Cohen, Jean. *Globalization and Sovereignty: Rethinking Legality, Legitimacy, and Constitutionalism.* Cambridge University Press, 2012.
Cohen, Joshua and Charles Sahel. "Extra Rempublicam Nulla Justitia?" *Philosophy & Public Affairs* 34/2 (2006): 147–75.
Cooke, Maeve. *Re-Presenting the Good Society.* MIT Press, 2006.
Culp, Julian. *Global Justice and Development.* Palgrave Macmillan, 2014.
Dahl, Robert A. "The Concept of Power." *Behavioral Science* 2 (1957): 201–15.
Deitelhoff, Nicole. "Parallele Universen oder Verschmelzung der Horizonte?" *Zeitschrift für Internationale Beziehungen* 17/2 (2010): 279–92.
Denninger, Erhard. "Der Einzelne und das allgemeine Gesetz." *Kritische Justiz* 28 (2005): 30–49.
Detel, Wolfgang. *Foucault and Classical Antiquity: Power, Ethics and Knowledge.* Translated by David Wigg-Wolf. Cambridge University Press, 2005.
Diaz-Bone, Rainer (ed.). *Soziologie der Konventionen: Grundlagen einer pragmatischen Anthropologie.* Campus, 2011.
Dippel, Horst. *Die Amerikanische Revolution* 1763–87. Suhrkamp, 1985.
Dworkin, Ronald. *Justice for Hedgehogs.* Harvard University Press, 2011.
Erman, Eva. "The Boundary Problem and the Right to Justification." In Rainer Forst, *Justice, Democracy and the Right to Justification: Rainer Forst in Dialogue*, 127–46. Bloomsbury, 2014.
Fahrmeir, Andreas (ed.). *Rechtfertigungsnarrative: Zur Begründung normativer Ordnung durch Erzählungen.* Campus, 2013.
Fahrmeir, Andreas and Annette Imhausen, eds. *Die Vielfalt normativer Ordnungen.* Campus, 2013.
Feuerbach, Ludwig. *Pierre Bayle: Ein Beitrag zur Geschichte der Philosophie und Menschheit.* In Feuerbach, *Gesammelte Werke* 4, edited by Werner Schuffenhauer. Akademie Verlag, 1967.
Flikschuh, Katrin and Lea Ypi, eds. *Kant and Colonialism: Historical and Critical Perspectives.* Oxford University Press, 2014.
Flügel-Martinsen, Oliver, Daniel Gaus, Tanja Hitzel-Cassagnes, and Franziska Martinsen, eds. *Deliberative Kritik—Kritik der Deliberation: Festschrift für Rainer Schmalz-Bruns.* Springer, 2014.
Forst, Rainer. "A Critical Theory of Politics: Grounds, Method and Aims. Reply to Simone Chambers, Stephen White, and Lea Ypi." *Philosophy and Social Criticism* 41/3 (2015): 225–34.
Forst, Rainer, "A Kantian Republican Conception of Justice as Nondomination." In *Republican Democracy*, edited by Andreas Niederberger and Philipp Schink, 154–68. Edinburgh University Press, 2013.

Forst, Rainer. *Contexts of Justice: Political Philosophy beyond Liberalism and Communitarianism*. Translated by John M. M. Farrell. University of California Press, 2002.

Forst, Rainer. "Die Reise nach Phantasia": review essay on Peter Stemmer, *Normativität: Eine ontologische Untersuchung*. *Deutsche Zeitschrift für Philosophie* 58/1 (2010): 157–61.

Forst, Rainer. "Gerechtigkeit und Demokratie in transnationalen Kontexten: Eine realistische Betrachtung." In *Die Versprechen der Demokratie*, edited by Hubertus Buchstein, 125–39. Nomos, 2013.

Forst, Rainer. *Justice, Democracy and the Right to Justification: Rainer Forst in Dialogue*. Bloomsbury, 2014.

Forst, Rainer. "Justice, Democracy and the Right to Justification: Reflections on Jürgen Neyer's Normative Theory of the European Union." In *Europe's Justice Deficit*, edited by Dimitry Kochenov, Gráinne de Búrca, and Andrew Williams, 227–34. Hart Publishing, 2014.

Forst, Rainer. *Justification and Critique: Towards a Critical Theory of Politics*. Translated by Ciaran Cronin. Polity, 2014.

Forst, Rainer. "Justifying Justification: Reply to My Critics." In Forst, *Justice, Democracy and the Right to Justification: Rainer Forst in Dialogue*, 169–216. Bloomsbury, 2014.

Forst, Rainer. "Legitimität, Demokratie und Gerechtigkeit: Zur Reflexivität normativer Ordnungen." In *Deliberative Kritik—Kritik der Deliberation: Festschrift für Rainer Schmalz-Bruns*, edited by Daniel Cans, Oliver Flügel-Martinsen, Tanja Hitzel-Cassagnes, and Franziska Martinsen, 137–8. Nomos, 2014.

Forst, Rainer. "Lumières, religion et tolérance: Bayle, Kant et Habermas." Translated by Tristan Coignard and Maïwenn Roudaut. *Lumières* 19 (2012): 15–48.

Forst, Rainer. "Noumenal Alienation: Rousseau, Kant and Marx on the Dialectics of Self-Determination." *Kantian Review* (forthcoming).

Forst, Rainer. "The Justification of Basic Rights: A Discourse-Theoretical Approach." *Netherlands Journal of Legal Philosophy* 45/3 (2016): 7–28.

Forst, Rainer. "The Justification of Human Rights and the Basic Right to Justification: A Reflexive Approach." *Ethics* 120/4 (2010): 711–40.

Forst, Rainer. "The Justification of Progress and the Progress of Justification." In *Justification and Emancipation: The Political Philosophy of Rainer Forst*, edited by Amy Allen and Eduardo Mendieta. Penn State Press (forthcoming).

Forst, Rainer. "The Point and Ground of Human Rights: A Kantian Constructivist View." In *Global Political Theory*, edited by David Held and Pietro Maffettone, 22–39. Polity, 2016.

Forst, Rainer. *The Right to Justification: Elements of a Constructivist Theory of Justice*. Translated by Jeffrey Flynn. Columbia University Press, 2012.

Forst, Rainer. "The Right to Justification: Moral and Political, Transcendental and Historical. Reply to Seyla Benhabib, Jeffrey Flynn and Matthias Fritsch." *Political Theory* 43/6 (2015): 822–37.

Forst, Rainer. "Toleranz, Glaube und Vernunft: Bayle und Kant im Vergleich." In *Kant und die Zukunft der europäischen Aufklärung*, edited by Heiner Klemme, 183–209. de Gruyter, 2009.

Forst, Rainer. "Toleranz und Fortschritt." In *Sitzungsberichte der Wissenschaftlichen Gesellschaft an der Johann-Wolfgang-Goethe-Universität*, Vol. 52, No. 2. Franz Steiner, 2015.

Forst, Rainer. *Toleration in Conflict: Past and Present*. Translated by Ciaran Cronin. Cambridge University Press, 2013.

Forst, Rainer. "Transnational Justice and Democracy: Overcoming Three Dogmas of Political Theory." In *Political Equality in Transnational Democracy*, edited by Eva Erman and Sofia Näsström, 41–59. Palgrave Macmillan, 2013.

Forst, Rainer and Klaus Günther. "Die Herausbildung normativer Ordnungen: Zur Idee eines interdisziplinären Forschungsprogramms." In *Die Herausbildung normativer Ordnungen*, edited by Rainer Forst and Klaus Günther, 11–30. Campus, 2011.

Forst, Rainer and Schmalz-Bruns, eds. *Political Legitimacy and Democracy in Transnational Perspective*. Arena Report No. 2/11. Centre for European Studies University of Oslo, 2011.

Forst, Rainer, Amy Allen, and Mark Haugaard. "Power and Reason, Justice and Domination: A Conversation." *Journal of Political Power* 7 (2014): 7–33.

Foucault, Michel. *Analytik der Macht*. Suhrkamp, 2008 (German translation of selected writings on power drawn from Michel Foucault, *Dits et écrits 1954–1988*, 4 vols. Gallimard, 1999).

Foucault, Michel. *Power*, ed. James Faubion, trans. Robert Hurley. New Press, 2000.

Foucault, Michel. *The History of Sexuality*, vol. I. Translated by Robert Hurley. Vintage, 1978.

Foucault, Michel. "The Subject and Power." In Foucault, *Power: The Essential Works of Foucault*, 1954–1984, *Vol. 3*, edited by James Faubion, translated by Robert Hurley *et al.* The Free Press, 2001.

Foucault, Michel. "Truth and Power: Interview with Alessandro Fontana and Pasquale Pasquino." In Foucault, *Power/Knowledge: Selected Interviews and Other Writings 1972–1977*, edited by Colin Gordon, 109–33. Pantheon, 1980.

Foucault, Michel. "What is Enlightenment?" In *The Foucault Reader*, edited by Paul Rabinow, 32–50. Pantheon, 1984.

Frankfurt, Harry G. "Equality and Respect." In Frankfurt, *Necessity, Volition, and Love*, 146–54. Cambridge University Press, 1999.

Frankfurt, Harry G. "Equality as a Moral Ideal." In Frankfurt, *The Importance of What We Care About*, 134–58. Cambridge University Press, 1988.

Frankfurt, Harry G. *Necessity, Volition, and Love*. Cambridge University Press, 1999.

Fraser, Nancy. *Fortunes of Feminism: From State-Managed Capitalism to Neoliberal Crisis*. Verso, 2013.

Fraser, Nancy. *Scales of Justice: Reimagining Political Space in a Globalizing World*. Columbia University Press, 2009.

Fuchs, Lawrence H. *The American Kaleidoscope: Race, Ethnicity, and the Civic Culture*. Wesleyan University Press, 1990.

Geuss, Raymond. *Philosophy and Real Politics*. Princeton University Press, 2008.

Goethe, Johann Wolfgang. *Maxims and Reflections*. Translated by Elizabeth Stopp, edited by Peter Hutchinson. Penguin Books, 1998.

Goodin, Robert E. *Manipulatory Politics*. Yale University Press, 1980.

Gosepath, Stefan. "Deprivation and Institutionally Based Duties to Aid." In *Domination and Global Political Justice: Conceptual, Historical, and Institutional Perspectives*, edited by Barbara Buckinx, Jonathan Trejo-Mathys, and Timothy Waligore, 251–90. Routledge, 2015.

Gosepath, Stefan. "Der Sinn der Menschenrechte nach 1945." In *Universelle Menschenrechte und partikulare Moral*, edited by Gerhart Ernst and Stephan Sellmaier, 17–32. Kohlhammer, 2010.

Gosepath, Stefan. *Gleiche Gerechtigkeit: Grundlagen eines liberalen Egalitarismus*. Suhrkamp, 2004.

Gosepath, Stefan. "The Global Scope of Justice." In *Global Justice*, edited by Thomas Pogge, 145–68. Blackwell, 2001.

Habermas, Jürgen. "A Symposium on Faith and Knowledge." In Habermas, *Postmetaphysical Thinking II: Essays and Replies*, translated by Ciaran Cronin. Polity, 2017.

Habermas, Jürgen. "An Awareness of What is Missing." In Habermas, *An Awareness of What is Missing: Faith and Reason in a Post-Secular Age*, edited by Michael Reder and Josef Schmidt, translated by Ciaran Cronin, 15–23. Polity, 2010.

Habermas, Jürgen. *Between Facts and Norms: Contributions to a Discourse Theory of Law and Democracy*. Translated by William Rehg. MIT Press, 1996.

Habermas, Jürgen, *Between Naturalism and Religion: Philosophical Essays*, Translated by Ciaran Cronin. Polity, 2008.

Habermas, Jürgen. "Communicative Reason and the Detranscendentalized 'Use of Reason.'" In Habermas, *Between Naturalism and Religion: Philosophical Essays*, translated by Ciaran Cronin, 24–76. Polity, 2008.

Habermas, Jürgen. "Discourse Ethics: Notes on a Program of Philosophical Justification." In Habermas, *Moral Consciousness and Communicative Action*, translated by Christian Lenhardt and Shierry Weber Nicholsen, 43–115. MIT Press, 1990.

Habermas, Jürgen. "Does the Constitutionalization of International Law Still Have a Chance?" In Habermas, *The Divided West*, translated by Ciaran Cronin, 115–93. Polity, 2006.

Habermas, Jürgen. "Faith and Knowledge." In Habermas, *The Future of Human Nature*, translated by Hannah Beister, Max Pensky, and William Rehg, 101–15. Polity, 2003.

Habermas, Jürgen. *Legitimation Crisis*. Translated by Thomas McCarthy. Beacon Press, 1975.

Habermas, Jürgen. "Linguistification of the Sacred. In Place of a Preface." In Habermas, *Postmetaphysical Thinking II: Essays and Replies*, translated by Ciaran Cronin. Polity, 2017.

Habermas, Jürgen. *Philosophical-Political Profiles*. Translated by Frederick G. Lawrence. MIT Press, 1983.

Habermas, Jürgen. "Popular Sovereignty as Procedure." In Habermas, *Between Facts and Norms*, translated by William Rehg, 463–90. MIT Press, 1996.

Habermas, Jürgen. "Prepolitical Foundations of the Constitutional State?" In Habermas, *Between Naturalism and Religion*, translated by Ciaran Cronin, 101–13. Polity, 2008.

Habermas, Jürgen. "Rawls's Political Liberalism: Reply to the Resumption of a Discussion." In Habermas, *Postmetaphysical Thinking II: Essays and Replies*, translated by Ciaran Cronin. Polity, 2017.

Habermas, Jürgen. "Religion in the Public Sphere: Cognitive Presuppositions for the 'Public Use of Reason' by Religious and Secular Citizens." In Habermas, *Between Naturalism and Religion*, translated by Ciaran Cronin, 114–47. Polity, 2008.

Habermas, Jürgen. "Religious Tolerance as Pacemaker for Cultural Rights." In Habermas, *Between Naturalism and Religion: Philosophical Essays*, translated by Ciaran Cronin, 251–70. Polity, 2008.

Habermas, Jürgen. "Rightness versus Truth: On the Sense of Normative Validity in Moral Judgements and Norms." In Habermas, *Truth and Justification*, translated by Barbara Fultner, 237–76. MIT Press, 2003.

Habermas, Jürgen. "Some Further Clarifications of the Concept of Communicative Rationality." In *On the Pragmatics of Communication*, edited by Maeve Cooke, 307–42. MIT Press, 1998.

Habermas, Jürgen. "The Boundary between Faith and Knowledge." In Habermas, *Between Naturalism and Religion: Philosophical Essays*, translated by Ciaran Cronin, 209–47. Polity, 2008.

Habermas, Jürgen. *The Crisis of the European Union*. Translated by Ciaran Cronin. Polity, 2012.

Habermas, Jürgen. *The Future of Human Nature*. Translated by Hannah Beister, Max Pensky, and William Rehg. Polity, 2003.

Habermas, Jürgen. *The Inclusion of the Other: Studies in Political Theory.* Edited and translated by Ciaran Cronin and Pablo de Greiff. Polity, 1998.

Habermas, Jürgen. "The Lifeworld as a Space of Symbolically Embodied Reasons." In Habermas, *Postmetaphysical Thinking II: Essays and Replies*, translated by Ciaran Cronin. Polity, 2017.

Habermas, Jürgen. "The New Philosophical Interest in Religion. An Interview with Eduardo Mendieta." In Habermas, *Postmetaphysical Thinking II: Essays and Replies*, translated by Ciaran Cronin. Polity, 2017.

Habermas, Jürgen. *The Postnational Constellation.* Translated by Max Pensky. Polity, 2001.

Habermas, Jürgen. *The Theory of Communicative Action.* Translated by Thomas McCarthy. 2 Vols. Beacon Press, 1984, 1987.

Habermas, Jürgen. "Treffen Hegels Einwände gegen Kant auch auf die Diskursethik zu?" In Habermas, *Erläuterungen zur Diskursethik*, 9–30. Suhrkamp, 1991.

Habermas, Jürgen. "Was macht eine Lebensform rational?" In Habermas, *Erläuterungen zur Diskursethik*, 31–48. Suhrkamp, 1991.

Habermas, Jürgen. "What is Universal Pragmatics?" In *On the Pragmatics of Communication*, edited by Maeve Cooke, 21–104. MIT Press, 1998.

Hartmann, Martin. "Rechtfertigungsordnungen und Anerkennungsordnungen: Zum Vergleich zweier Theoriemodelle." *WestEnd. Neue Zeitschrift für Sozialforschung* 5/2 (2008): 104–19.

Hartz, Louis. *The Liberal Tradition in America.* Harvest, 1955.

Henrich, Dieter. "Der Begriff der sittlichen Einsicht und Kants Lehre vom Faktum der Vernunft." In *Kant: Zur Deutung seiner Theorie vom Erkennen und Handeln*, edited by Gerold Prauss, 223–54. Kiepenheuer & Witsch, 1973.

Herdtle, Claudia and Thomas Leeb, eds. *Toleranz: Texte zur Theorie und politischen Praxis.* Reclam, 1987.

Hinsch, Wilfried. *Gerechtfertigte Ungleichheiten.* de Gruyter, 2002.

Hollerbach, Alexander *et al.*, eds. *Das Kreuz im Widerspruch.* Herder, 1996.

Honneth, Axel. "Dissolutions of the Social: On the Social Theory of Luc Boltanski and Laurent Thévenot." *Constellations* 17/3 (2010): 376–89.

Honneth, Axel. *Freedom's Right: The Social Foundations of Democratic Life.* Translated by Joseph Ganahl. Columbia University Press, 2014.

Honneth, Axel. *Pathologies of Reason: On the Legacy of Critical Theory.* Translated by James Ingram. Columbia University Press, 2009.

Honneth, Axel. *The Critique of Power: Reflective Stages in a Critical Social Theory.* Translated by Kenneth Baynes. MIT Press, 1991.

Honneth, Axel and Hans Joas, eds. *Communicative Action: Essays on Jürgen Habermas's The Theory of Communicative Action.* MIT Press, 1991.

Horkheimer, Max. "Materialism and Morality." In Horkheimer, *Between Philosophy and Social Science: Selected Early Writings*, translated by G. Friedrich Hunter *et al.*, 15–48. MIT Press, 1995.

Horkheimer, Max. "Traditional and Critical Theory." In Horkheimer, *Critical Theory: Selected Essays*, translated by Matthew J. O'Connell, 188–243. Continuum, 2002.

Hurrell, Andrew. *On Global Order: Power, Values and the Constitution of International Society.* Oxford University Press, 2007.

Jaeggi, Rahel. *Alienation.* Translated by Fred Neuhouser and Alan E. Smith. Columbia University Press, 2014.

Jaeggi, Rahel. *Kritik von Lebensformen.* Suhrkamp, 2014.

Jaeggi, Rahel and Daniel Loick. *Nach Marx: Philosophie, Kritik, Praxis.* Suhrkamp, 2013.

James, Aaron. "Constructing Justice for Existing Practice: Rawls and the Status Quo." *Philosophy and Public Affairs* 33 (2005): 281–316.

Joas, Hans (ed.). *Vielfalt der Moderne—Ansichten der Moderne*. Fischer, 2012.

Kant, Immanuel. "An Answer to the Question: What is Enlightenment?" In Kant, *Practical Philosophy*, edited and translated by Mary Gregor, 11–22. Cambridge University Press, 1996.

Kant, Immanuel. *Critique of Practical Reason*. Edited and translated by Mary Gregor. Cambridge University Press, 1997.

Kant, Immanuel. *Critique of Pure Reason*. Edited and translated by Paul Guyer and Allen W. Wood. Cambridge University Press, 1998.

Kant, Immanuel. *Critique of the Power of Judgement*. Edited by Paul Guyer. Translated by Paul Guyer and E. Matthews. Cambridge University Press, 2000.

Kant, Immanuel. *Groundwork of the Metaphysics of Morals*. Edited and translated by Mary Gregor. Cambridge University Press, 1998.

Kant, Immanuel. "Idea for a Universal History with a Cosmopolitan Aim." Translated by Allen W. Wood. In Kant, *Anthropology, History and Education*, edited by Robert B. Louden, 107–20. Cambridge University Press, 2007.

Kant, Immanuel. *Kritik der reinen Vernunft*. First edition. In *Kants gesammelte Schriften* IV, edited by the Königlich-Preußische Akademie der Wissenschaften, Berlin 1903–11. de Gruyter, 1968.

Kant, Immanuel. "On the Common Saying: That May Be Correct in Theory, but It Is of No Use in Practice." In Kant, *Practical Philosophy*, edited and translated by Mary Gregor, 279–309. Cambridge University Press, 1996.

Kant, Immanuel. *Religion within the Bounds of Mere Reason*. Edited and translated by Allen W. Wood and Giorgio di Giovanni. Cambridge University Press, 1998.

Kant, Immanuel. "The Conflict of the Faculties." In Kant, *Religion and Rational Theology*, edited and translated by Allen W. Wood and Giorgio di Giovanni, 233–328. Cambridge University Press, 1996.

Kant, Immanuel. *The Metaphysics of Morals*. Edited and translated by Mary Gregor. Cambridge University Press, 1996.

Kant, Immanuel. "Toward Perpetual Peace: A Philosophical Project." In Kant, *Practical Philosophy*, edited and translated by Mary Gregor, 317–51. Cambridge University Press, 1996.

Kant, Immanuel. "What Does it Mean to Orient Oneself in Thinking?" In Kant, *Religion within the Bounds of Mere Reason*, edited and translated by Allen W. Wood and Giorgio di Giovanni, 1–14. Cambridge University Press, 1998.

Karst, Kenneth L. *Belonging to America: Equal Citizenship and the Constitution*. Yale University Press, 1989.

Korsgaard, Christine. *Self-Constitution: Agency, Identity, and Integrity*. Oxford University Press, 2009.

Koselleck, Reinhart. "'Space of Experience' and 'Horizon of Expectation': Two Historical Categories." In Koselleck, *Futures Past: On the Semantics of Historical Time*, translated by Keith Tribe, 267–88. MIT Press, 1985.

Krebs, Angelika. "Einleitung: Die neue Egalitarismuskritik im Überblick." In *Gleichheit oder Gerechtigkeit: Texte der neuen Egalitarismuskritik*, edited by Angelika Krebs, 7–37. Suhrkamp, 2000.

Kymlicka, Will. *Multicultural Citizenship: A Liberal Theory of Minority Rights*. Oxford University Press, 1995.

Laden, Anthony Simon. "The Practice of Equality." In Rainer Forst, *Justice, Democracy and the Right to Justification: Rainer Forst in Dialogue*, 103–26. Bloomsbury, 2014.
Larmore, Charles. *Vernunft und Subjektivität: Frankfurter Vorlesungen*. Suhrkamp, 2012.
Leibfried, Stephan and Michael Zürn, eds. *Transformationen des Staates*. Suhrkamp, 2006.
Lepenies, Philipp. *Art, Politics, and Development: How Linear Perspective Shaped Policies in the Western World*. Temple University Press, 2014.
Locke, John. *Two Treatises of Government*. Edited by Peter Laslett. Cambridge University Press, 1989.
Lohmann, Georg. "Marxens Kapitalismuskritik als Kritik an menschenunwürdigen Verhältnissen." In *Karl Marx—Perspektiven der Gesellschaftskritik*, edited by Daniel Loick and Rahel Jaeggi, 67–78. *Deutsche Zeitschrift für Philosophie*, Special Editions, Vol. 34. de Gruyter, 2013.
Lovett, Frank. *A General Theory of Domination and Justice*. Oxford University Press, 2010.
Lukes, Steven. *Power: A Radical View*. 2nd edn. Palgrave, 2005.
Machiavelli, Niccolò. *The Prince*. Edited and translated by Quentin Skinner and Russell Price. Cambridge University Press, 1988.
MacIntyre, Alasdair. *Whose Justice? Which Rationality?* University of Notre Dame Press, 1988.
Marx, Karl. *Capital: A Critique of Political Economy*. Vol. 1. Translated by Ben Fowkes. Penguin Books, 1990.
Marx, Karl. *Capital: A Critique of Political Economy*. Vol. 3. Translated by David Fernbach. Penguin Books, 1991.
Marx, Karl. *Critique of Hegel's Philosophy of Right* [1844]. Edited and translated by Joseph O'Malley. Cambridge University Press, 1977.
Marx, Karl. "Critique of the Gotha Program." In *The Marx-Engels Reader*, edited by Robert C. Tucker, 525–42. W. W. Norton, 1978.
Marx, Karl. "Economic and Philosophical Manuscripts." In Marx, *Early Writings*, translated by Rodney Livingstone and Gregor Benton, 279–400. Penguin Books, 1975.
Maus, Ingeborg. "Der Urzustand." In *John Rawls: Eine Theorie der Gerechtigkeit*, edited by Otfried Höffe, 65–88. Akademie, 2013.
McCarthy, Thomas. *Race, Empire, and the Idea of Human Development*. Cambridge University Press, 2009.
Mead, George Herbert. *Mind, Self, and Society: The Definitive Edition*. Edited by Charles W. Morris. Annotated by Daniel B. Huebner and Hans Joas. Chicago University Press, 2015 [1934].
Mill, John Stuart. *On Liberty*. Edited by Gertrude Himmelfarb. Penguin Books, 1974.
Miller, David. *National Responsibility and Global Justice*. Oxford University Press, 2007.
Moellendorf, Darrel. *Global Inequality Matters*. Palgrave, 2009.
Moore, Barrington. *Injustice: The Social Bases of Obedience and Revolt*. Macmillan, 1978.
Morgenthau, Hans J. *Peace among Nations: The Struggle for Power and Peace*. 6th Edition. Revised by Kenneth W. Thompson. McGraw-Hill, 1993.
Mousnier, Roland. *The Assassination of Henry IV*. Translated by Joan Spencer. Scribner, 1973.
Müller, Harald. *Wie kann eine neue Weltordnung aussehen?* Fischer, 2008.
Nagel, Thomas. *The Possibility of Altruism*. Princeton University Press, 1970.
Nagel, Thomas. "The Problem of Global Justice." *Philosophy and Public Affairs* 33/2 (2005): 113–47.
Nandy, Ashis. "Fortschritt." In *Vielfalt der Moderne—Ansichten der Moderne*, edited by Hans Joas, 53–66. Fischer, 2012.

Narayan, Uma. "Contesting Cultures: 'Westernization', Respect for Cultures and Third-World-Feminists." In Narayan, *Dislocating Cultures: Identities, Traditions, and Third World Feminism*, 1–40. Routledge, 1997.

Neyer, Jürgen. *The Justification of Europe: A Political Theory of Supranational Integration.* Oxford University Press, 2012.

Niesen, Peter (ed.). *Transnationale Gerechtigkeit und Demokratie.* Campus, 2012.

Niesen, Peter and Benjamin Herborth, eds. *Anarchie der kommunikativen Freiheit.* Suhrkamp, 2007.

Nye, Joseph S., Jr. *The Future of Power.* Public Affairs, 2011.

Olson, Kevin. "Complexities of Political Discourse: Class, Power and the Linguistic Turn." In Rainer Forst, *Justice, Democracy and the Right to Justification: Rainer Forst in Dialogue*, 87–102. Bloomsbury, 2014.

O'Neill, Onora. *Constructions of Reason: Explorations of Kant's Practical Philosophy.* Cambridge University Press, 1990.

Owen, David. "Criticism and Captivity: On Genealogy and Critical Theory." *European Journal of Philosophy* 10 (2002): 216–30.

Pappert, Peter (ed.). *Den Nerv getroffen: Engagierte Stimmen zum Kruzifix-Urteil von Karlsruhe.* Bergmoser und Höller, 1995.

Parsons, Talcott. "Power and the Social System." In *Power*, edited by Steven Lukes, 94–143. New York University Press, 1986.

Patton, Paul. "Foucault's Subject of Power." *Political Theory Newsletter* 6 (1994): 60–71.

Peffer, Rodney G. *Marxism, Morality, and Social Justice.* Princeton University Press, 1990.

Peters, Bernhard, "Deliberative Öffentlichkeit." In *Die Öffentlichkeit der Vernunft und die Vernunft der Öffentlichkeit: Festschrift für Jürgen Habermas*, edited by Lutz Wingert and Klaus Günther, 655–77. Suhrkamp, 2001.

Pettit, Philip. "Democracy, Electoral and Contestatory." In *Designing Democratic Institutions*, edited by Ian Shapiro and Stephen Macedo, 105–44. Nomos XLII. New York University Press, 2000.

Pettit, Philip. *Just Freedom: A Moral Compass for a Complex World.* W. W. Norton & Company, 2014.

Pettit, Philip. "Keeping Republican Freedom Simple: On a Difference with Quentin Skinner." *Political Theory* 30/3 (2002): 339–56.

Pettit, Philip. *On the People's Terms*, Cambridge University Press, 2012.

Pettit, Philip. *Republicanism.* Oxford University Press, 1997.

Pettit, Pettit, "The Republican Law of Peoples: A Restatement." In *Domination and Global Political Justice: Conceptual, Historical and Institutional Perspectives*, edited by Barbara Buckinx, Jonathan Trejo-Mathys, and Timothy Waligore, 37–70. Routledge, 2015.

Pico della Mirandola. *On the Dignity of Man.* Translated by Charles Glenn Wallis and Paul J. W. Miller. Hackett, 1998.

Pogge, Thomas. *Politics as Usual.* Polity, 2010.

Pogge, Thomas. *Realizing Rawls.* Cornell University Press, 1989

Popkin, Richard H. "Pierre Bayle's Place in 17th Century Skepticism." In *Pierre Bayle: Le philosophe de Rotterdam*, edited by Paul Dibon, 1–19. Vrin, 1959.

Prichard, H. A. "Does Moral Philosophy Rest on a Mistake?" In *Readings in Ethical Theory*, 2nd edn., edited by Wilfrid Sellars and John Hospers, 86–96. Prentice Hall, 1970.

Rawls, John. *A Theory of Justice*, revised edition. Harvard University Press, 1999.

Rawls, John. *Justice As Fairness: A Restatement.* Harvard University Press, 2001.

Rawls, John. *Lectures on the History of Political Philosophy.* Edited by Samuel Freeman. Harvard University Press, 2007.

Rawls, John. *Political Liberalism*. Columbia University Press, 1992.
Rawls, John. *The Law of Peoples*. Harvard University Press, 1999.
Raz, Joseph. "Human Rights Without Foundations." In *The Philosophy of International Law*, edited by Samantha Besson and John Tasioulas, 321–38. Oxford University Press, 2010.
Ripstein, Arthur. *Force and Freedom: Kant's Legal and Political Philosophy*. Harvard University Press, 2009.
Ronzoni, Miriam. "The Global Order: A Case of Background Injustice? A Practice-Dependent Account." *Philosophy & Public Affairs* 37/3 (2009): 229–56.
Rosa, Hartmut. *Weltbeziehungen im Zeitalter der Beschleunigung: Umrisse einer neuen Gesellschaftskritik*. Suhrkamp, 2012.
Rousseau, Jean-Jacques. *Discourse on the Sciences and Arts*. In Rousseau, *The Discourses and Other Early Writings*, edited and translated by Victor Gourevitch, 1–28. Cambridge University Press, 1997.
Saar, Martin. *Genealogie als Kritik: Geschichte und Theorie des Subjekts nach Nietzsche und Foucault*. Campus, 2007.
Sangiovanni, Andrea. "Global Justice, Reciprocity, and the State." *Philosophy & Public Affairs* 35/1 (2007): 3–39.
Sangiovanni, Andrea. "Justice and the Priority of Politics to Morality." *The Journal of Political Philosophy* 16/2(2008): 137–64.
Sangiovanni, Andrea. "Practice-Dependence Revisited: Confronting the Facts." Unpublished manuscript.
Sangiovanni, Andrea. "Scottish Constructivism and the Right to Justification." In Rainer Forst, *Justice, Democracy and the Right to Justification: Rainer Forst in Dialogue*, 29–64. Bloomsbury, 2014.
Scanlon, Thomas M. *Being Realistic about Reasons*. Oxford University Press, 2014.
Scanlon, Thomas M. *What we Owe to Each Other*. Harvard University Press, 1988.
Scharpf, Fritz W. *Governing in Europe: Effective and Democratic?* Oxford University Press, 1999.
Scheuerman, William E. *The Realist Case for Global Reform*. Polity, 2011.
Schmalz-Bruns, Rainer. "Deliberativer Supranationalismus." *Zeitschrift für Internationale Beziehungen* 6 (1999): 185–244.
Schmalz-Bruns, Rainer. *Reflexive Demokratie: Die demokratische Transformation moderner Politik*. Nomos, 1995.
Schmalz-Bruns, Rainer. "The Euro-Polity in Perspective. Some Normative Lessons from Deliberative Democracy." In *Debating the Democratic Legitimacy of the European Union*, edited by Beata Kohler-Koch and Berthold Rittberger, 281–303. Rowman & Littlefield, 2007.
Searle, John. *Making the Social World: The Structure of Human Civilization*. Oxford University Press, 2010.
Seel, Martin. "Narration und (De-)Legitimation: Der zweite Irak-Krieg im Kino." In *Rechtfertigungsnarrative: Zur Begründung normativer Ordnung durch Erzählung* (Normative Orders, Vol. 7), edited by Andreas Fahrmeir, 45–57. Campus, 2013.
Seel, Martin. *Versuch über die Form des Glücks: Studien zur Ethik*. Suhrkamp, 1995.
Sellars, Wilfrid. *Empiricism and the Philosophy of Mind*. Edited by Robert Brandom. Harvard University Press, 1997.
Sen, Amartya. *Development as Freedom*. New Edition. Oxford University Press, 2001.
Senghaas, Dieter. *Konfliktformationen im internationalen System*. Suhrkamp, 1988.

Senghaas, Dieter. *Weltordnung in einer zerklüfteten Welt: Hat Frieden Zukunft?* Suhrkamp, 2012.

Shapiro, Ian. *Democratic Justice.* Yale University Press, 1999.

Shapiro, Ian. *The Real World of Democratic Theory.* Princeton University Press, 2011.

Singer, Peter. *One World: The Ethics of Globalization.* Yale University Press, 2002.

Stemmer, Peter. *Normativität: Eine ontologische Untersuchung.* de Gruyter, 2008.

Stolleis, Michael (ed.). *Herzkammern der Republik: Die Deutschen und das Bundesverfassungsgericht.* C. H. Beck, 2011.

Stolleis, Michael. "Überkreuz: Anmerkungen zum Kruzifix-Beschluß (BVerfGE 93, 1–37) und seiner Rezeption." *Kritische Vierteljahresschrift für Gesetzgebung und Rechtswissenschaft* 83 (2000): 376–87.

Streithofen, Heinrich Basilius (ed.). *Das Kruzifixurteil: Deutschland vor einem neuen Kulturkampf.* Ullstein, 1995.

Taylor, Charles. "Conditions of an Unforced Consensus on Human Rights." In *The East Asian Challenge for Human Rights*, edited by Joanne Bauer und Daniel Bell, 124–45. Cambridge University Press, 2009.

Taylor, Charles. "The Politics of Recognition." In *Multiculturalism: Examining the Politics of Recognition*, edited by Amy Gutman, 25–73. Princeton University Press, 1992.

Tilly, Charles, *Why?* Princeton University Press, 2006.

Tugendhat, Ernst. *Traditional and Analytical Philosophy: Lectures on the Philosophy of Language.* Translated by P. A. Gorner. Cambridge University Press, 1982.

Tugendhat, Ernst. *Vorlesungen über Ethik.* Suhrkamp, 1993.

Tully, James. "On Law, Democracy and Imperialism." In Tully, *Public Philosophy in a New Key, Volume 2: Imperialism and Civic Freedom*, 127–65. Cambridge University Press, 2008.

Tully, James. *Public Philosophy in a New Key.* Vol. 1. Cambridge University Press, 2008.

Walzer, Michael. *Spheres of Justice: A Defense of Pluralism and Equality.* Basic Books, 1983.

Walzer, Michael. *What it Means to Be an American.* Marsilio, 1992.

Weber, Max. *Economy and Society.* 2 volumes. Edited and translated by Guenther Roth and Claus Wittich. University of California Press, 1978.

White, Stephen. "Does Critical Theory Need Strong Foundations?" *Philosophy & Social Criticism* 41/3 (2015): 207–11.

Wiener, Antje. *A Theory of Contestation.* Springer, 2014.

Willaschek, Marcus. "Bedingtes Vertrauen: Auf dem Weg zu einer pragmatistischen Transformation der Metaphysik." In *Die Gegenwart des Pragmatismus*, edited by Martin Hartmann, Jasper Liptow, and Marcus Willaschek, 97–120. Suhrkamp, 2013.

Williams, Bernard. *In the Beginning Was the Deed.* Edited by Geoffrey Hawthorn. Princeton University Press, 2005.

Williams, Bernard. "Realism and Moralism in Political Theory." In Williams, *In the Beginning was the Deed: Realism and Moralism in Political Argument*, 1–17. Princeton University Press, 2005.

Wingert, Lutz. *Gemeinsinn und Moral.* Suhrkamp, 1993.

Wittgenstein, Ludwig. *Philosophical Investigations.* Translated by G. E. M. Anscombe. Blackwell, 1978.

Young, Iris M. *Justice and the Politics of Difference.* Princeton University Press, 1990.

Young, Iris M. *Responsibility for Justice.* Oxford University Press, 2011.

Young, James P. *Reconsidering American Liberalism: The Troubled Odyssey of the Liberal Idea.* Westview, 1996.

Ypi, Lea. "Two Pictures of Nowhere." *Philosophy and Social Criticism* 41/3 (2015): 219–23.
Zaretsky, Eli. *Why America Needs a Left: A Historical Argument.* Polity, 2012.
Zürn, Michael. "Autorität und Legitimität in der postnationalen Konstellation." In *Der Aufstieg der Legitimitätspolitik: Rechtfertigung und Kritik politisch-ökonomischer Ordnungen*, edited by Anna Geis, Frank Nullmeier, and Christopher Daase, 41–62. *Leviathan* 40, Special Issue 27. Nomos, 2012.
Zürn, Michael. *Regieren jenseits des Nationalstaats.* Suhrkamp, 1998.
Zürn, Michael. "Vier Modelle einer globalen Ordnung in kosmopolitischer Absicht." *Politische Vierteljahresschrift* 52/1 (2011): 78–118.
Zürn, Michael and Matthias Ecker-Ehrhardt, eds. *Die Politisierung der Weltpolitik.* Suhrkamp, 2013.

Index